DATE DUE

FE 9 '06			

DEMCO 38-296

THE NEW
INFORMATION
REVOLUTION

A Reference Handbook

Other titles in ABC-CLIO's
CONTEMPORARY
WORLD ISSUES
Series

Books in the Contemporary World Issues series address vital issues in today's society such as terrorism, sexual harassment, homelessness, AIDS, gambling, animal rights, and air pollution. Written by professional writers, scholars, and nonacademic experts, these books are authoritative, clearly written, up-to-date, and objective. They provide a good starting point for research by high school and college students, scholars, and general readers, as well as by legislators, businesspeople, activists, and others.

Each book, carefully organized and easy to use, contains an overview of the subject; a detailed chronology; biographical sketches; facts and data and/or documents and other primary-source material; a directory of organizations and agencies; annotated lists of print and nonprint resources; a glossary; and an index.

Readers of books in the Contemporary World Issues series will find the information they need in order to better understand the social, political, environmental, and economic issues facing the world today.

THE NEW
INFORMATION
REVOLUTION

A Reference Handbook

Martin K. Gay

**CONTEMPORARY
WORLD ISSUES**

ABC-CLIO

Santa Barbara, California
Denver, Colorado
Oxford, England

Copyright © 1996 by Martin K. Gay

blication Data

The new information _____ a reference handbook / Martin K. Gay
      p.   cm.—(Contemporary world issues series)
    Includes bibliographical references and index.
    1. Information superhighway.   2. Information technology.
    3. Digital communications.   4. Information society.   I. Title.
    II. Series
    ZA3225.G39   1996   303.48′33—dc20   96-28832

ISBN 0-87436-847-2

02 01 00 99 98 97 96   10 9 8 7 6 5 4 3 2 1

ABC-CLIO, Inc.
130 Cremona Drive, P.O. Box 1911
Santa Barbara, California 93116-1911

This book is printed on acid-free paper ∞.
Manufactured in the United States of America

Contents

Preface

There is an attraction at Disneyland called Splash Mountain. It is an exciting roller coaster–like ride that makes twists-and-turns, ups-and-downs, and grand plunges into wet pools located at tricky spots in a marvelous re-creation of Uncle Remus's imaginary land. At a critical point on the wild journey, the log-shaped car slows to a crawl as it begins to make a steep climb up the highest mountain of the adventure. It finally crosses the summit, and the car immediately reacts to the intense pull of gravity, free-falling several feet and plummeting down the track to the cold water below. Right at the precise second when the passengers realize that their stomachs have been left somewhere above their heads, a video camera captures the panic-stricken expressions on their faces.

The hard-copy printout of that scene, purchased two minutes after disembarking from the log car, hangs over the computer screen that displays the electronic text for this book. It is the metaphor for the subject of this inquiry. Seconds before the sophisticated video technology was employed to capture that slice of time, the passengers were moving at a steady pace, secure in their seats and comfortable in their world.

Immediately after, the scene and the attitudes change dramatically: Wild-eyed and fearful of the consequences, the passengers are thrown into the void. They can only pray that the landing will be a safe one.

Insecurity about what is over the next hill colors many people's reactions to the world in which they now find themselves. Anthropologists and futurists say this is only natural. Analyses from most social scientists agree that we have entered the most intense period of substantive change that has ever affected the people of this planet. It began in the 1950s, gained momentum through the next 40 years, and now is hitting its stride. What is happening? Why are the "constants" shifting so much? What are the new rules for this time?

Alvin Toffler, the renowned futurist, posits answers to these questions in *The Third Wave* (1980). In this book he develops his theory of three distinct ages of human development. Others have divided history into similar segments before, but his use of the wave analogy proves to be an excellent device to explain the dynamics of change on a massive scale. More importantly, his analysis leads one to believe that the potential for this current shift is a positive one.

In very basic terms, the First Wave was that period when humans developed agricultural economies and agrarian societies, ending their primitive reliance on hunting and gathering skills. It began around 8000 B.C. and continued relatively unchanged until sometime in the eighteenth century. That was when the Second Wave, often considered the Industrial Era, began to overlap the First. A much shorter period, the Second Wave is still the historical experience that most adults today relate to when they talk about "their" world. It was the time that saw the United States gain dominance in world affairs because of its ability to produce more and better products than any other society on earth.

Americans, and citizens of most Western nations, are also products of the educational, commercial, and governmental institutions that were developed to facilitate efficient industrial output in the Second Wave. Their thinking and expectations are largely tethered to a past that is slowly sinking into the seas of change. Whether we call it the Techno-Revolution, the Global Village, or the Communication Age is of no consequence. No catchy moniker can describe this process accurately, and any attempt to name it is artificial. Be certain, however, that the new world has begun. It makes sense to try to understand our place in it. In Toffler's words,

Humanity faces a quantum leap forward. It faces the deepest social upheaval and creative restructuring of all time. Without clearly recognizing it, we are engaged in building a remarkable new civilization from the ground up. This is the meaning of the Third Wave (Toffler 1980).

No wonder we are feeling a little seasick. Most of us never asked for this upheaval, and many of us wish it would go away. However, major changes are already well established in the business sector, and they are starting to influence the way government operates. The remaining underpinnings of our once comfortable lives are eroding fast. Driven by emerging digital technologies, information has become the new currency of future wealth. Because the ability to "know" is being distributed among the many, political and cultural power is also beginning to decentralize. For some this is proof that the collapse of civilization is imminent; for others it marks the beginning of a true global consciousness.

At the very least, the potential of this age is fantastic. Some writer must have penned a similar thought about the new Industrial Era after witnessing Robert Fulton's steamboat power down Paris' Seine for the first time in 1803. Then, it was mechanization and the harnessing of energy that powered the possibilities. Today it is the intellect and imagination, packaged in the form of binary data, that are the building blocks in the new neighborhoods of this emerging space-time experience.

The Format

This book is designed to freeze a frame of the time continuum at the onset of what we will call the Communication Age. By the time you read this page, some of what is presented in the following chapters may be out-of-date. That is the nature of information today, and that is why a few writers have predicted the demise of traditional bound-paper publishing. Since we still have a foot in the Second Wave, however, let us press on using the medium that is most comfortable today.

The first chapter is an introduction to the subject of digital information and the communication structures that this technology has supported. It includes a brief look at the development of communicating devices so that the reader might be better equipped to place the new technologies in perspective. Then, using lay terminology whenever possible, it explains the tools of the digital realm. Without a grounding in the basics of binary capabilities, the realities and possibilities of information transfer and manipulation will seem like only so much magic. Similarly, the explanation of the Information Superhighway (also known as the National Information Infrastructure, the Matrix, the Web, the Net, cyberspace, etc.) might be construed as only another fantastic scenario in a science fiction novel.

A portion of the first chapter also reviews some of the services and products that are driving the development of the universal data connectivity structure, or the Net, as it will be called in these pages. Commerce is embracing the possibilities of the Communication Age that were developed by universities and the federal government. Business experiments and initial offerings on the expanding interactive computer networks are a good starting point for an overview of the way government, K–12 education, the media, and grassroots organizations are also modifying their operations and redefining their goals in response to the new tools. These tools were forged on the U.S. government's research and educational network that we now call the Internet, and a brief overview of that structure is included here as well.

The first chapter seeks to identify areas of concern that will need to be studied and debated by the citizens of this country and all nations for years to come. The application of the new technologies is driving the change, and it is difficult to understand how to even ask the questions if there is not some familiarity with the technical advances that have placed us at this threshold. Like the first Information Revolution of five and one-half centuries ago, when Gutenberg gave the world the printing press and moveable type, this current change *is* the technology. Information engineers, the new Gutenbergs, are just scratching the surface of the digital domain. Do not be surprised by what you are capable of achieving there in another year. The pace of the changes will only accelerate.

Chapter 2 is a chronology of important milestones in the development of communication systems, digital instrumentation (computers), interactive software implementation, and any events or inventions that were critical to the application of information technology. The key people behind some of the events and those who are helping to resolve the important issues that the technology has created are profiled in chapter 3. Chapter 4 is an extensive representation of charts and graphs, excerpts and reprints of selected texts, and interesting quotations that will help the reader define the issues of the Information Revolution. Organizations that have helped define communication technical standards or developed business applications, or that have risen in response to perceived threats to individual freedoms, are listed in chapter 5.

Chapters 6 and 7 include annotated bibliographic references for print and nonprint resources covering the general topics of computer-mediated communication and the future of digital communications. New publications about the Internet and the World Wide Web, especially those in the self-help category (how does one use the Internet, where does one go on the Web?), are arriving every week. A representative sample of some of the best sources is included in these chapters. The last chapter lists digitally available media that address the subject. CD-ROM and diskette material has not been included here because it often proves to be no more timely than the print resources listed in chapter 6. The focus is on the wealth of on-line sources where the best and most current information about this new world resides, and where activists are publishing the most important information on the issues. Most of it is freely available to those with access to the Internet. The final section is a glossary of some common terms used in digital information technology and the revolution that it is driving.

New Information Revolution

Introduction

Steven Spielberg sat at a computer terminal on the stage of an auditorium in Los Angeles recently to showcase a project that even the most ardent fans of his movies know little about. He had established the Starlight Foundation in 1982 to help seriously ill children, and this display for the press was to promote an initiative sponsored by that charitable organization. Connected to his computer in hospitals as far away as Boston was a network of children interacting in a virtual space called Starbright World. This fully rendered three-dimensional environment allowed the participants to "play" in real time with Spielberg and the others connected to the network in the guise of animated characters whose identities they had assumed.

As the play progressed, it became obvious that these children felt comfortable in the cyberland and that they were having fun. Spielberg and the creative engineers responsible for the software that enabled this play space expressed the hope that activity fostered in the virtual world would help to alleviate pain and perhaps aid the recovery of severely ill children. Plans are being finalized to expand the six-node pilot network into a multipoint Internetwork of many play areas where children of any nationality or with any handicap can visit to meet new friends and just be kids.

In 1982, when the Starlight Foundation was begun, a virtual space like Starbright World might have been only a dream in some imaginative programmer's mind. Today it stands as an example of the possibilities that are a result of the revolution in data technologies that are coming to all of us down the Information Superhighway.

The Information Revolution: Some Definitions

What is the Information Superhighway? Is it the Internet, that vast and expanding network of networks that links anyone with a computer and a modem to everyone else in the world who has similar hardware? Does it become clearer if we call it the National Information Infrastructure (NII), as the U.S. government has officially designated the phenomenon? For better or worse, the simplified highway analogy is how the popular culture, through the mass media, has chosen to describe the very technical capabilities that are changing our world. Perhaps the definition provided by Bonnie Bracey, the education representative on the president's National Information Infrastructure Advisory Council (NIIAC), will shed some light on the digital pathway to the future.

> It is more than the Internet. It is a series of components, including the collection of private and public high-speed interactive, narrow, and broadband networks, that exists today and will emerge tomorrow.
>
> It is the satellite, terrestrial, and wireless technologies that deliver content to homes, businesses, and other public and private institutions.
>
> It is the information and content that flow over the infrastructure, whether in the form of a database, the written word , a film, a piece of music, a sound recording, a picture, or computer software.
>
> It is the computers, televisions, telephones, radios, and other products that people will employ to access the infrastructure.
>
> It is the people who will provide, manage, and generate new information and those who will help others to do the same.

It is the individual Americans who will use and benefit from the Information Superhighway.

Information Superhighway is a term that encompasses all of these components and captures the visions of a nationwide, invisible, dynamic web of transmissions, mechanisms, information, appliances, content, and people (Bracey 1996).

Generally, experts agree with Bracey's interpretation of the meaning of Information Superhighway. For any of us to understand how this highway has been structured and why the revolution is possible, however, we will have to look closer at the term "information." Like so much else in this transitional period of history, the definition is evolving, becoming something that we no longer recognize.

In the Industrial Age, information *was* knowledge. For example, if you wanted to gain an understanding of a particular subject, you would do some research. Through interviews or reading, and the like, you would accumulate information; knowledge could be increased. That function of the definition is certainly still operative today. Need to know something? Ask, and you receive answers, data, and information.

During World War II, however, a substantial modification and enhancement of the term took place. *Information* "got redefined as something quantifiable that could be collected, moved, and processed," as John Verity of *Business Week* magazine explains it (Verity, 1994). The response to war led to the beginning of the new Information Revolution. Scientists created methods to transmit coded signals over noisy radio channels, and the designers of antiaircraft guns found ways for data to automatically position their new weapons.

In a real sense, the way humans interacted with information began to change. When information became something more than knowledge, it was translated into a commodity that could be used to operate a machine, guide a missile, and finally drive an entire economy. A new age was launched, and the currency of this age *is* information. Although they were spawned by government-supported research, in laboratories at universities and research centers, the new cybernetic technologies were nurtured by commercial interests that began to see the potential information had for creating additional sources of revenue. In the 1990s the transformation from the Industrial Age is almost complete. Businesses that want to stay competitive must make certain that "information" has a high priority in the organization of their company and in the end product that they distribute.

Companies that thrived in the past have had to adapt their products and services, modifying them with information-related enhancements. American Standard, the venerable bathroom fixture company, has marketed a "smart tub," for example. It can be programmed to fill with water at a specified temperature at a predetermined time, eliminating the need to direct one's butler to draw the bath.

Perhaps the most familiar application-of-information success story is that of Microsoft Corporation. Launched in 1975 by Paul Allen and Bill Gates, the company's initial product was a computer programming language called BASIC, which they sold to run one of the first low-cost computers. Their product was an information technology system that would create an environment in a machine to manipulate information. Two decades later, Bill Gates is one of the richest men on earth, and Microsoft has become the standard for a successful corporation making full use of the tools and possibilities of the information economy. All they do is make and market products that move data.

Digital: Information's Common Language

High-tech information-enhanced and information-manipulating devices are now integral parts of life. In fact, their acceptance and our increasing reliance upon them in society define how we will relate to our peers, the government, and the bulk of daily intercourse. Would we consider buying a stereo that did not include a compact disc player? Can you remember a supermarket where the cashier had to key in the prices by hand in the days before the scanner and universal price codes (UPCs)? Most of us would not attempt to write a paper without using a computer's word processor program and its spell-checker utility.

The compact disc player, the UPC scanner, and the computer are all information technology devices that work with a very distinct form of the raw material of data. These are all *digital* information reader-processors. Digital devices work with data that have been converted into binary language. Unlike the familiar decimal system, the binary system is based on only two digits—zero and one—which represent the commands for *off* or *on* to the electronic switches of a digital device. These basic units of information are known as the binary digits, or bits. Eight bits equal a byte, or 256 possible pieces of information. Each character of the alphabet, for example, is represented by a byte of data.

It is this binary encoding of information that makes the seemingly magical daily advances in technology possible. It is a digital world, and understanding the basics of "binary" is key to gaining some comfort level in this new age. While you may never need to know how to encode information, it is important to realize that this is the means by which others are affecting your life. Bits, those elemental pieces of binary data, are "the DNA of information" according to Nicholas Negroponte of the MIT Media Lab. In his book *Being Digital* (1995), Negroponte explains how bits are the building blocks of our time. Where people in ages past relied on the movement of atoms (things) to define their activities, he explains, the new reality is that we are establishing systems of digitally based interaction that move bits and bytes (information).

The advances of the Information Age were not possible until "information" itself was redefined, quantified, and turned into a new language. But what does one do with a new language? At first, we talked only to machines. Now we are beginning to see how to increase talk between human beings. That, after all, is the reason language came into being in the first place. Experts like Negroponte express the hope that this new language can lead to better understanding between all peoples and the beginnings of a true Communication Age.

Electronic Communication, Instantaneous Contact

Drum beats, smoke and light signals, semaphores, and flags are just a few of the ways humanity devised to communicate through space before electric power was harnessed. As imaginative as those methods were, however, it took an understanding of how electrons moved in a wire to reveal the true possibilities of real-time communication. The first device to utilize that energy was the telegraph, perfected in 1812 by Samuel F. B. Morse. Morse is credited with the creation of a code (dots and dashes) that came to be the language of telegraphy, and the establishment of this de facto standard put him in a position to link most of the major American urban centers by the 1840s. A few years later the first transatlantic cable was laid, and America and Europe have been linked ever since. Much of the rest of the world soon followed, and telegraph communications came to be a reliable mode of delivering news.

Alexander Graham Bell was working on an improvement to the telegraph that would allow multiple messages to be sent down the same line at the same time when he discovered a way to transmit the human voice instead. His famous first words, "Mr. Watson, come here; I want you," traveled across a short distance of wire in 1876. Thomas Edison and others made substantial improvements to the telephone by boosting the electrical current that carried the audio signal, and by the turn of the century many homes boasted their own personal communication tool. Like the telegraph wire, the telephone line found its way across the Atlantic Ocean in short order.

Analog and Digital: Two Ways To Measure Information

The mechanics underlying the operation of these two important communication breakthroughs is important to understand because it has considerable impact on today's communication environment. Both the telephone and the telegraph rely on changes in electrical current to facilitate communication. The difference is that the original telephone uses analog measurement for the encoding and subsequent decoding of "information," whereas the telegraph operates as a digital device.

The telegraph operator sends information by tapping out code on a key to represent any given alphanumeric character. The code for "S-O-S," as most schoolchildren learn, is three short taps of the key, followed by three long signals, followed by three more shorts. Activating the key turns electric current on and off in short or long bursts. The current travels down a wire, which is connected to the receiving station's key. Electromagnetic forces cause the receiving key to act in the exact manner as the key being tapped. The receiving attendant can see the key move and can hear three shorts, three longs, and three more shorts. The translation to "S-O-S" can then be made. The digital information in this case is not binary (based on two states), but based on three states: (1) off, (2) on short (dot), and (3) on long (dash).

It was different when Bell worked out the physics for analog measurement of speech so that he could "make a current of electricity vary in intensity precisely as the air varies in density during the production of sound" (Bell as quoted in Fabre 1963). He devised a way for words to be spoken into a horn, which caused a diaphragm to vibrate in response to the sound waves that were produced by the human body's voice box. Bell then converted the subtle variances into a continuously changing electrical wave pattern that was "analogous" to the sampled speech. At the receiving end, a decoding would occur to produce sound waves recognizable to the ear.

The importance of analog versus digital is apparent if one examines the infrastructure that exists today to facilitate the developing Information Highway. The only way that the promise of these networks can be achieved is through the deployment of digitally encoded data: voice, text, photos, video, sound, etc. Useful, broad-based access to services and products in a reasonable time will only happen through the manipulation and compression of data that digital sampling makes possible.

Will the data stream that connects us ride on high-frequency wireless waves through the air, like radio and television signals? Will it be bounced off low-flying satellites? Will it travel over cable or telephone wires? The answer is yes, probably all of these mechanisms will be utilized. At the end of the twentieth century, however, the method that shows the most immediate potential to become the Information Highway (I-Way) is the remarkably adaptable telephone system. Still relying for the most part on analog transmission, it can connect anyone with a computer and a modem to the Net.

Telecommunications: Merging Technologies and Goals

The ubiquitous presence of the telephone in nearly every business and household in the Western world makes it the immediate choice for the main carrier of the data flow. The "pipe" is everywhere already. Wireless systems are being tested, but there are real problems with interference in a crowded spectrum that have to be solved first. Coaxial video cable can actually pass along more data than the twisted-pair wiring of plain old telephone service (POTS), but this greater bandwidth is set up in most systems to go in one direction only. That is great for shopping networks and possibly for "video-on-demand" services, but it will take the deployment of new and relatively expensive digital processors to begin to realize the broadband potential of cable. The old cable infrastructure is available to only about 65 percent of U.S. residences in 1996.

The telephone line is interactive, virtually everyone has one, and the industry has already spent hundreds of millions of dollars to upgrade its existing infrastructure of copper-based wiring. That medium has served them well since the time of Bell and Edison as a carrier of analog electric signals that represent speech and sounds. The phone companies have even successfully implemented analog carrier waves that transport digital information along this same path. Modems were invented to take advantage of this by converting, or *modulating*, a computer's binary data into analog components that can then be shipped alongside normal telephone conversations. On the receiving end, the information is then converted back, or *demodulated*, into the computer's native binary language.

Unfortunately, there is a limit to the speed at which such converted data can be transmitted. The best lines with the fastest modems utilizing the latest compression schemes allow for a maximum transmission rate of about 30,000 bits per second. Integrated Services Digital Network (ISDN) technology, which uses the old lines but transmits in pure digital form, increases bandwidth to upwards of 128,000 bits per second. This is much faster, and users can see an obvious increase in interactive response. However, advocates for the type of synchronous two-way connectivity that will be needed for applications that are being talked about for the Information Highway claim that what's needed is a bandwidth 2,000 times greater. POTS cannot deliver this. Fiber-optic cable can.

Much of the work on the backbone of the fiber-optic telephone system has already been completed, allowing long-distance carriers to convert conversations into bits for routing, via computers, to points far and wide. This digital data is transmitted along the fiber-optic cable—a cable composed of extremely fine glass threads—in the form of pulses of light. One of these optical fibers is used to send data; another is used to receive. Because the voice information it carries has been converted into "packets" of binary data, each pair of fibers can carry 32,000 simultaneous conversations, without any "party-line" cross talk.

That sort of bandwidth creates a foundation for a superhighway connecting us to interactive gaming, banking, virtual sex, movies, radio, medicine, buying, selling, reading, publishing, campaigning, lobbying, registering, voting, learning, teaching, human potential, God, and the rest of the vision of cyberspace. It will take tremendous bandwidth to keep up with the demand for instantaneous, full-blown, three-dimensional graphical services when we all start connecting at the same time. But then, that is a long way down the digital road.

The local phone companies are just beginning to respond to the demand for increased data service by making ISDN available in most locales. There are also plans to bring fiber-optic cable to the curbside, if the phone companies can find a way to finance that. However, other information industries are not sitting by idly as telephony (the new term being used to reflect the emerging services of the old telephone systems) moves ahead to implement their new infrastructure. The cable companies especially have been bolstered by the signing of the Telecommunications Act of 1996 , which was designed to eliminate many of the barriers to competition among broadcast media, long-distance providers, local phone companies, cellular industry, cable, and the rest. This law is a revision of the 1934 telecommunications statutes, which were written when "digital" meant "having to do with the fingers and toes."

With the new regulations in place, the entire telecommunications landscape has begun to change. AT&T, MCI, and Sprint are positioning themselves to offer local phone services that were restricted to the Baby Bells and a few independent providers. Cable companies will be allowed to provide dial tone; phone companies will be able to send movies over their lines. The telecommunications landscape is already radically altered.

The business facts of life are this: No investment, no increase in services, no new implementation of infrastructure will proceed if bigger profits are not realized. Who will pay the projected $500 billion needed to connect every residence in the United States? The details are being worked out right now between the telecommunications giants, the White House, and congressional staffers, but the short answer is *the consumer*. Those who demand the service will pay the fee. Ten years ago, few experts would have thought that the American public was willing to pay for such an investment. That was before the Internet exploded.

The Internet: From Command and Control to the Information Highway

It was the 1960s, and the Cold War was at its height. Concern about a nuclear attack from the USSR led the Department of Defense (DOD) on a quest to implement a fail-safe communication mechanism that could facilitate emergency instructions and the command and control capabilities necessary to initiate a military response. The DOD's Advanced Research Products Agency (ARPA) was authorized to research and develop hardware and software that would meet that objective.

Communication between computers was already occurring in the government and within commercial networks that were sharing access time on the few huge and prohibitively expensive computers then in existence. The architecture of these first networks, developed by Massachusetts Institute of Technology (MIT) in 1963, was a first client-server model. The client, a terminal remotely connected through telephone lines, would access the data and programs running on the mainframe server. Should the server go down, a likely occurrence in the event of nuclear war, communications would cease abruptly. The ARPA effort was centered on creating a redundant system that had no hierarchical structure. If one section went down, the remainder of the network would continue to pass along information.

Researchers from all over the United States, including a brilliant graduate student from the University of California at Los Angeles (UCLA) named Vint Cerf (now a vice president at MCI), began working on a solution. Cerf's and others' efforts led to the creation of a binary networking language that established a new grammar, or software structure, called Internet protocol (IP). Also known as TCP/IP, or transmission control protocol, this system took advantage of technology that had been invented the year before. It divided binary files (text or any other digital data) into small packets that included an IP address destination in the header portion of its makeup. Packets so marked would then be sent along the network to a computer with that unique IP address. It did not matter which route a packet took or if packets from one file went down different paths. In the end, they would all meet at the appointed destination to be rebuilt into the complete original file. If a section of the network happened to be out, the packets would automatically find and reroute themselves along a complete path.

In 1969 the first Interface Message Processor (IMP) was installed at the UCLA and three other university sites. It was the antecedent of today's routers that direct-packeted data over the Net. This IP network was dubbed ARPAnet, and developers soon found new ways to utilize the connections. Since TCP/IP source code was made available to any programmer who wanted to build on its base structure, computer scientists moved quickly to implement new utilities. Remote log-in via Telnet happened first, then electronic mail and newsgroups were implemented. FTP, gopher, archie, veronica, and WAIS quickly followed as ARPAnet began to expand its reach. TCP/IP is an open architecture, meaning that new computers and whole new networks could link to ARPA's network as long as they spoke the IP language. Researchers in industry and university labs found these new tools to be a boon for collaboration because messages, graphs, pictures, and papers could be shared quickly and efficiently.

TCP/IP quickly became the accepted networking language for the emerging wide-area networks (WANs), and the number of sites that hosted this new "Internet" server software began to expand. At the end of 1969, five host machines were connected via telephone lines. In early 1971, 23 connections were made. This number was multiplied by ten a decade later, and in 1984, 1,024 ARPAnet servers were available for access by university students, faculty, and government researchers. Outside of these institutions, however, the Internet were hardly known. The utility was there—science data especially were more readily accessible—but the interface was not friendly, and few personal computers (PCs) were in use. That all began to change in quantum terms about 1987.

A year earlier, the National Science Foundation (NSF) established a high-speed (56 kbps, then T1 and finally T3) network backbone to enhance research communication for science. It also supported the development and implementation of technology enhancements to make connections easier and faster. Most traffic eventually migrated to this system, and ARPAnet was phased out in 1990 when some 313,000 hosts were on-line from all over the world. By now, the PC was beginning to be seen as a more common appliance in higher education, businesses, and homes.

The Marketplace: Driving Growth

Modems that could connect at 2,400 and 9,600 bps allowed the public to get a taste of the new on-line commercial services like

Prodigy, America Online, and CompuServe, which were beginning to implement graphical interfaces ala the Macintosh or Windows systems instead of the text-only commands. These services did not speak TCP/IP, and they provided no access to the Internet, but early adopters started to see what could happen when their new PCs were used as communication tools and not just as glorified typewriters. The demand was being created for access to the Internet, even though most people had never heard of it. Regardless, there was hardly any mechanism available to log on outside of the direct connections to NSFnet, which was continuing a rapid expansion. The number of hosts had reached over 1 million by 1992.

Four years earlier, Tim Berners-Lee of the European Laboratory for Particle Physics (CERN) in Switzerland had proposed implementing a new IP protocol that he was calling the World Wide Web (WWW or Web). His new software was designed to access the other common Internet services like gopher, FTP, etc., within a single client application. Soon after, the first Web "browsers" were implemented. These browsers were text-based, command-line applications that were designed to make Net "surfing" simpler and more intuitive. This new protocol was the first to take full advantage of *hyperlinks*, and it opened the possibilities of an unprecedented boom in the number of Internet users. In 1993 the National Center for Supercomputing Applications (NCSA) at the University of Illinois released the first graphic Web browser, which they called Mosaic.

In 1996 over 5 million hosts serve up information on the Internet. E-mail, newsgroups, etc., still account for much of the traffic on the Net, but the sharp upward curve in Web applications is nothing short of phenomenal. Estimates put the total number of Internauts (Internet users) at 30 million, a figure that has doubled in less than a year. Most of these people have gotten onto the Net because of the "killer app" of the 1990s: the World Wide Web. With new Internet service providers (ISPs) starting services every week, access to the Web is local, relatively inexpensive, fun, and empowering.

The Web is also where most of the activity in the development of Information Superhighway is happening. In two short years, the Web has changed expectations about interactive communication and has altered directions for entire industries. After years of steady growth, the commercial on-line services— America Online, CompuServe, and Prodigy—recently implemented gateways to the Net and provided their customers with

Web-browsing capabilities. They are investigating how to migrate to the TCP/IP structure, because that is where their clients demand to be. Less than three months after the controversial launch of the Microsoft Network that had been positioned as direct competition to the three major on-line services, founder Bill Gates abruptly announced that his network would be available to anyone with a Web browser instead.

IBM paid a premium for Lotus Corporation in 1995 to get its highly successful Notes application. That software had been the computer-mediated communication (CMC) standard of corporate collaboration for years. In the jargon of the day, Lotus Notes has been the mainstay of "enterprise computing." It did not "speak" the TCP/IP language, however, and analysts began to suggest that there was trouble ahead for the company. In January 1996 it reacted by slashing prices and introducing new Web access capabilities. It is not just Lotus and IBM and Microsoft that have found it necessary to make wholesale changes in their business plans, however. The entire software industry has reacted to the sweeping changes being made possible by the Net and the Web because the rules have changed.

Information Revolution: The Future Is Now

The digital ripples that began in the 1960s, when the U.S. government decided to establish the Internet, have become waves of change today. Information technology has had the greatest immediate effect on the way America and the other developed economies carry on commerce, but all our other institutions are being buffeted as well. From the way we spend leisure time in the home and access educational materials to the way we participate in politics or express an opinion, and even to the manner in which we interact with medical professionals, our lives are evolving and involving the new information systems. The change is rapidly inundating everything we do, and it is causing us to redefine some of the basic tenets of our culture.

Difficult issues are forcing their way to the table to be debated in corporate boardrooms, government hearings, local school board meetings, and our family dining rooms. The technology opens up possibilities that were the stuff of science fiction a decade ago. The pace of implementation is so rapid that today science fiction writers can hardly keep up. It is not surprising that much of what was stable, much of what was standard

operating procedure of the Industrial Age, is evaporating before
our eyes. New ways of doing and being have to be invented.

The infrastructure is at the top of the list. The technology
that allows data to move down the Information Highway was
subsidized and unregulated:

> Who should be responsible for the deployment of the new
> broadband "pipe" that experts say will be needed in the
> short term?

> Should there be an Internet government or regulatory
> facility that is responsible for traffic flow and content?

> What type of fee structure will be implemented when ser-
> vices such as voice communication or video conferencing
> become common Internet activities?

Freedom of speech is a critical question:

> How does the architecture of the new digital media matrix
> impact the individual's ability to express opinions and
> publish information? Is the system designed to deliver
> high resolution video in one direction but only receive
> "buy" commands and credit card numbers in the other?

> Will only the large corporations that have made the
> millions of dollars in infrastructure investment be able to
> determine the content of what gets transmitted there?

> Should the content of Internet communications be held
> to a stricter standard of decency, security, and homogene-
> ity than other segments of the society?

> What laws should be held to apply in the new region of
> cyberspace? If material is accessed from a computer con-
> nected to the Net in Germany when you log on in Denver,
> who has jurisdiction over the content?

> Is an Internet Service Provider liable for defamatory
> remarks published by one of its customers?

Copyright laws are being redefined as the nature of intellectual property evolves:

> How do artists and writers protect their work from theft
> and redistribution in a medium that was designed to facili-
> tate cooperative work and the repositioning of data?

How do publishing houses change to meet the needs of clients who will increasingly expect books to come in digital formats? How are rights assigned?

Since digital media is so readily manipulated, at what point in the process does a computer-generated image become the work of a person editing the file?

What types of digital signatures will be incorporated into creative works to prove ownership, date of execution, etc.?

Privacy concerns are also at the top of many lists:

What will supermarkets do with the information they collect about your shopping habits when you help them by scanning in your own merchandise and then link your name and vital financial statistics to the data with an electronic debit card?

Are your transactions over the Net really secure, or will thieves find it simple to decode your credit card numbers?

Do the new electronic cash schemes, including so-called smart cards that hold a microchip equivalent of U.S. currency, also incorporate mechanisms that will track your every move in the marketplace? Will that data be linked to IRS computers?

Will we want to give the FBI or the NSA the authority to "listen in" on phone conversations or e-mail exchanges in order to keep the nation safe from internal or external threats to security?

As more of your personal history becomes digitized, what safeguards need to be developed to keep the data private?

Equity of access to information and services is just as sticky:

Will the information have-nots be left out of the debate and the processes that will define the Communication Age?

Can a means be found to bring connectivity to the traditionally underserved segments of our population?

Can electronic voting ever be instituted if 100 percent access is not guaranteed?

Who will pay the huge bill that universal service requirements will place on telecommunications providers?

Does a minimum bandwidth to each residence requirement make sense?

What about schools? Will we be willing to pay more to
make certain our children have the tools and the knowledge to help us grow the digital domain? Is information
technology the answer to education reform?

We are only at the beginning of this great change. There are
many more questions than answers. The remainder of this chapter looks at a few of these important questions and some of the
solutions that have been proffered to shape the manner of our
interactions for years to come.

The National Information Infrastructure: Defining and Regulating the Information Superhighway

The data highway metaphor was born when then-Senator Al
Gore wrote an article for the January 1991 *Futurist*. "What we
need," he said, "is a nationwide network of 'information superhighways,' linking scientists, business people, educators, and
students by fiber-optic cable" (Gore 1991). He had actually addressed the issue as far back as 1979, when he was one of the
first in government to see that "exformation," his term for too
much information, and the digital technologies that were being
deployed by government researchers and businesses to manipulate it were already having a profound effect on the lives of
citizens.

Gore led the effort that resulted in the passage of the High
Performance Computing Act of 1991, which funded National
Science Foundation (NSF) research on the Internet to improve
speed and reliability. The act also approved the establishment of
the National Research and Education Network (NREN), which
was designed to improve digital information access for the areas
of K–12 education, libraries, health care, and manufacturing.

President Clinton allowed Gore to take the lead in this area
when they took over the White House in 1993, and the administration quickly provided the public with some high-visibility
demonstrations of digital communication. Clinton was the first
president to have an e-mail address and to send an e-mail message. The vice president took part in a CompuServe chat forum,

becoming the first vice president to answer questions in a real-time on-line environment. Volunteers designed and mounted the White House's home page on the Web, providing the first general access to on-line government information.

At the urging of the members of the Computer Systems Policy Project (CSPP), whose members were CEOs of 13 U.S. computer companies, the administration lobbied for legislation that would extend the NREN beyond its original design and into offices and homes across the United States. They called this new vision the National Information Infrastructure. The federal government has followed through in the succeeding years by making much of the information it archives available via the Net. Data from the Patent Office and the Smithsonian, congressional legislation, Supreme Court decisions, Securities and Exchange Commission filings, and the census bureau are readily accessible to anyone with a modem-equipped computer. The Postal Service has also initiated interactive programs in response to the new way Americans are doing business. Many states, governors' offices, and their associated legislatures and agencies have followed the federal lead.

Politics: Legislating the "Knowledge Age"

Republicans in Congress were in substantial agreement with many of the broad concepts outlined by the Clinton administration in its vision for the NII. The consensus was that some movement had to be made to take advantage of the changes new technologies were making possible or America would not remain in a superior competitive position on world markets and the country's security might actually be compromised. Government should get out in front of the issue, they agreed. They also knew that the cost to implement the physical infrastructure of fiber optics, low-orbit satellites, or cable hybrid systems necessary to make the dream a reality could not be borne by government.

Speaker of the House Newt Gingrich is an especially vocal promoter of new information technologies. His own initiative, called Thomas, makes all pending federal legislation and all congressional speeches available via the Internet. The Speaker counts Alvin Toffler and George Gilder among his friends and advisors. These futurists advocate a laissez-faire position for government as the business community works within a context of capitalist competition to implement the NII.

Much of the American electorate had no idea about or interest in the complicated technical issues that were brought to the table when Congress agreed to consider language for the telecommunications reform legislation in 1993. The House, Senate, and administration proposed legislation that would enhance competition in media and information service industries and provide some guarantee of universal service to the American public. Few disagreed that something had to be done to update the archaic statutes that controlled radio, television, cable, and telephone service in the United States. The media are converging, and from a technical standpoint the laws that banned one industry, or one segment of the industry, from impinging on the territory of another were counter to healthy competition.

Technology pundits, futurists, Democrats, and Republicans agreed that reform is critical if we are to see the strategic partnerships and economies of scale that it will take to build the broadband highway. The new regulatory era has already spawned numerous mergers and strategic partnerships. Disney has joined with ABC, AT&T is buying part of Hughes DirecTV, the cable companies are searching for suitors. All of the giants are looking for a new position and ways to leverage more resources for a retooling that will build the infrastructure and, in Marshall McLuhan's terms, "control the content."

The National Information Infrastructure Advisory Council: Dealing with the Defining Issues

The Commerce Department is the lead agency for the presidential administration's effort to create the new model of government service and support in the digital realm. Secretary Ron Brown was given jurisdiction over the inquiry regarding legislation, business-government partnerships, standards, and initiatives that might be needed to realize the NII. Several committees were established to advise the president on the basic issues emerging around the subject, with none more important than the National Information Infrastructure Advisory Council. This volunteer 37-member group was composed of representatives from media outlets, entertainment, information services, K–12 and higher education, computer companies, and software developers. They held meetings throughout the country between 1993 and 1996 to get feedback from experts and the public in the areas of universal access and services, privacy and security, intellectual property, education for lifelong learning, and electronic commerce. Their final report was delivered to President Clinton early in 1996.

Under the leadership of Delano Lewis, CEO of National Public Radio, and Edward R. McCracken, CEO of Silicon Graphics, the council wrestled with the most difficult issues as they sought to construct a model of the information future. The inquiry was substantially free of political posturing, and the participants took the charge seriously. As member John Sculley, former CEO of Apple Computer noted, their final vision of the NII had as much to do with the development of community and democracy as it did with the facilitation of virtual commerce.

Private versus Public Interest

It is a fact, however, that many billions of dollars are in the pot at the end of the information rainbow. That is why corporations lobbied so heavily for regulatory reform, say critics of the Telecommunications Act. They contend that business got most of what it wanted and is now in the driver's seat. While others assert that the infrastructure and the new information services will best be deployed by profit-making entities, organizations like the Benton Foundation are fearful that individual rights like equal access, privacy, and freedom to speak and to publish might be severely limited.

A case in point is the issue of spectrum allocation for the deployment of the new high-definition television (HDTV) standard. Between 1987 and 1992 the Federal Communications Commission (FCC) held meetings to determine how broadcasters might convert from standard (analog) television signals to HDTV (digital) transmission. As a result of these hearings, the FCC set aside a huge chunk of extra broadcast spectrum for each current TV licensee. It doubled the amount of spectrum currently allocated to broadcasters so that they could use it to convert to the digital system.

What the FCC and most experts could not predict at the time was how fast digital encoding and compression technology would advance. New technology makes it possible to transmit many more voice, video, and data messages using much less spectrum than was originally anticipated. Broadcasters now see that it is possible to provide many other services with the extra spectrum, and their industry representatives are petitioning the government to change the parameters of the proposed agreement to allow them to provide additional services like paging and data transmission.

That policy was nearly approved in the Telecommunications Act of 1996, but in the last few days of the debate former Senate Majority Leader Bob Dole raised the issue of a multibillion dollar giveaway to television broadcasters. It was becoming clear that the industry could generate substantial funds from the use of the spectrum. Why, Dole asked, should the American public not benefit by auctioning the airwaves to the highest bidder? The provision was removed from the pending legislation, and it became part of the standards definition process undertaken by the FCC after the bill was signed into law.

During the public comment period in the spring and summer of 1996, the Benton Foundation submitted input regarding this issue on behalf of other nonprofits and public interest groups. This included options designed to force concessions from the industry. Among those ideas:

1. Give broadcasters additional spectrum to convert to digital and to broadcast multiple channels simultaneously. Once the conversion is completed, require the broadcaster to lease a number of channels to other unaffiliated program and service providers.
2. Impose special public interest obligations, like giving one hour of time every day for use by candidates for two months prior to a federal election. Reserving capacity for low-cost public or nonprofit use (i.e., public access channels) is another possibility.
3. Provide a smaller allocation to broadcasters for HDTV deployment, since it is possible to provide HDTV using much less bandwidth than was expected, and auction off the remaining spectrum.
4. Allocate the new spectrum to parties other than existing broadcast licensees by comparative hearing. This would diversify the field of service providers and provide a mechanism to review public interest objectives of the applicants.

The distribution of spectrum is one area where the government will continue to provide a service that facilitates the growth of the NII. Even the most vocal free-market advocates accept that some sort of regulatory entity must be involved in the growing process if the system, which simply is not systematized at this point, is to be developed quickly and efficiently. One area where government regulation has created a great deal of controversy is in the role it has decided to play as an arbiter of content.

Cyperporn: Law and Order Comes to the Net

Pornography on the Net and obscene digital images and text that depicted everything from bestiality to child sex was the introduction many people received to cyberspace and digital communication. On 3 July 1995, *Time* magazine exploited this issue with a cover depicting an astonished child's face illuminated by the glow of a computer screen. Under the little boy's chin was written the reason for his horror: "CYBERPORN. Exclusive: A new study shows how pervasive and wild it really is. Can we protect our kids—and free speech?"

The cover article reported on an 18-month study sanctioned by Carnegie Mellon University, which revealed that sexually explicit material was readily available, in quantities much larger than had been imagined, to anyone with access to the Net. The methodology of the study, which was authored by Marty Rimm, was subsequently debunked by many critics familiar with the situation. Rimm, for example, had actually attempted for a time to profit from marketing a "how-to" book that told about selling pornography on-line. However, the issue had already found its way into the national debate in the form of the Exon Amendment to the telecommunications bill.

Dubbed the Communications Decency Act (CDA) by its author, Senator J. James Exon of Nebraska, this portion of the larger telecom bill provides penalties for the transmission of material that can be deemed indecent over computer networks. While the intent of the legislation is to protect children from accessing what most people would consider prurient material, many legal experts have taken exception to the vague definition of *indecent*. They assert that the provision is unconstitutional, violating the First Amendment as well as recent privacy rulings.

The CDA sent a chill through the Net community when the Telecommunications Act was signed on 8 February 1996. One of the axioms of veteran Net users seems to be "information wants to be free," and they view any attempt to legally limit access as an abridgment of their rights. It would be difficult to find anyone willing to take a stand that advocates providing pornographic material to people under the age of 18, but the issue is much larger than that. They point to the ready accessibility of "filtering" software that can be configured by parents or school authorities to deny access to questionable material on the Net. Their answer to the problem takes the responsibility for protecting children out of the realm of government and puts it back in the traditional child-rearing domain. Filtering products currently on the market include CYBERsitter, CYBER PATROL, InterGO, the Internet Filter for Windows, NetNanny, Net Shepherd, Safe Surf, and TattleTale.

In reaction to the CDA, the Citizens Internet Empowerment Coalition (CIEC)—which includes some 40 organizations representing over 30,000 individual Internet users, libraries, book publishers, newspaper publishers, editors, advertisers, commercial on-line service providers, Internet service providers, nonprofit groups, and civil liberties advocates—filed a lawsuit as soon as the telecom bill was signed. The suit sought a preliminary injunction of the Communications Decency Act, which was granted pending the resolution of court proceedings on the issue.

The trial, which was held in the spring of 1996, heard testimony supporting the government contention that the law was necessary and not overly restrictive. On the other side, the CIEC presented experts who showed the effectiveness of filtering software and suggested the implementation of a rating system for Internet sites.

Regulations: Whose Should Apply?

Meanwhile, appeals over the basis of the definition of obscenity and community standards are under way in a case that has already proven to have far-reaching consequences. That was the 1994 prosecution of Robert and Carleen Thomas of Milpitas, California. A jury in a Memphis, Tennessee, federal court convicted the couple of providing obscene material on their adult-oriented electronic bulletin board service (BBS). A Memphis postal inspector, working with a federal attorney, joined the BBS to download images that were considered obscene in his community. Although neither the Milpitas nor the California state authorities found enough cause to prosecute the couple under their local community standards guidelines, digital communication had redefined the concept of *local*.

Civil liberties advocates have criticized the conviction and the subsequent denial of the first appeal on the grounds that the Thomases did not attempt to distribute pornography in the more conservative community of Memphis. Such an action would have made them liable for prosecution under current understanding of the 1973 Supreme Court ruling *(Miller v. California)* that defined obscenity under the community standards test. The technology, they contend, is more at fault than the system operators. The automated software blindly answers commands from modem calls that can originate anywhere in the world. There is no way that such a service could effectively deny access to users from communities where the standards are higher or simply different. Since technology is changing the landscape and redefining "community," argues Mike Godwin, staff counsel for the Electronic Frontier Foundation, the courts should revisit *Miller v. California.*

A related incident occurred on the international stage late in 1995, when the German state of Bavaria threatened to bring legal sanctions against the European division of CompuServe for allowing subscribers from that region access to over 200 newsgroups that they claimed were of an inappropriate sexual or violent nature. Some of these on-line forums were created to meet gay and lesbian needs, as well as to discuss AIDS and other sexually transmitted diseases. When CompuServe reacted by temporarily ending access to the targeted groups for *all* of their subscribers, a hew and cry went up from one end of the Net to the other.

CompuServe was forced to respect the wishes of the Bavarian government or face lengthy prosecution and possible fines. Their only solution was to cut out the groups until their programmers were able to write a program that would circumvent access for the Bavarian subscribers only. Within three weeks the company had worked out the problem by implementing new software, but not before a boycott of CompuServe was mounted across the Net. It is not known how many subscribers canceled their accounts because of the company's response to the Bavarian government's threat.

That number is probably comparable to the total that quit using America Online, the most popular commercial on-line service, when it implemented filtering software that wiped out any postings to their forums that included words the company deemed inappropriate for a family-oriented user base. One of those words was "breast." When frequent contributors to forums on breast cancer, breast feeding, and the like found their on-line gatherings decimated by the new policy, there were a lot of unhappy subscribers.

Monitoring content, censoring information, and setting "acceptable" standards for others has been a controversial activity in an open society. Regardless of the media and the level of technology employed to distribute or access information, the federal government historically has treaded softly in this area. John Perry Barlow of the Electronic Frontier Foundation (EFF) has noted that the members of Congress who passed the CDA attempted "to place more restrictive constraints on the conversation in cyberspace than presently exist in the Senate cafeteria." They have done this, he argues, having virtually no experience with the technology or knowledge of the on-line community.

Cyberhate: Freedom of Speech Is the Issue

In 1993 the Department of Commerce's National Telecommunications and Information Administration (NTIA) did make an attempt to learn more about the technicalities of on-line communication when they began to study a phenomenon about which they were receiving a rising number of complaints: the use of Internet newsgroups, mail lists, on-line services, Web pages, and electronic bulletin boards for the purpose of publishing literature that advocated "acts of violence and intimidation motivated by prejudice based on race, religion, sexual orientation, or ethnicity." A 1985 study of electronic bulletin boards by the Anti-Defamation League of the B'nai B'rith indicated that there were many such systems operated as information exchange and distribution centers by such groups as the Aryan Nations (Idaho, Texas, and North Carolina) and the neo-Nazis (West Virginia). Today it is relatively easy to find World Wide Web pages that are maintained by skinheads, the Ku Klux Klan, anti-Semites, and the like. The NTIA wanted to gather information about how "cyberhate" related to hate crime statutes at the federal and state level and to see what others thought should or could be done to counter these messages.

Many civil liberties organizations, following the lead of the EFF's response to the NTIA on this issue, have advocated that the government pass no further legislation that might restrict a citizen's right to free speech. They contend that there are currently enough laws on the books that address slander, libel, and "fighting words" concerns. They also point to the fact that measured counterresponses that cite facts and historical evidence can be the best weapon against hate mongering. Shari Steele, writing for the EFF, noted what happened in 1991 when the Prodigy on-line service saw a heated discussion in one of their interactive forums. A Holocaust revisionist had posted a message claiming that very few Jews were actually murdered by the Nazis, and this provocative posting prompted immediate rebuttals from many of the services' subscribers. In the end, Steele claims, the revisionists were shown to be racists because of the free exchange of messages. However, Prodigy changed its policy to limit postings that were deemed "grossly repugnant to community standards" in the future.

Avi-Jacob Hyman, a Canadian Jew whose relatives died in Nazi death camps, teaches about computer-mediated communication issues. He has warned that people like Ernst Zundel (reputedly the largest print publisher of Holocaust denial material) and other individuals who question the authenticity of the Holocaust are attempting to gain direct access to the Internet. While he supports the efforts of the EFF and others to ensure civil liberties and freedoms in cyberspace, he disagrees with the EFF assertion that there now exists a representative community of users on the Net who will be willing or able to rebut the language of hate. He points to the fact that there are many more males than females, many more young than old, and many more wealthy than poor on the Internet at present. In the age category especially, he asserts, there are simply not enough "survivors" on-line to relate their personal stories and to publish their truths about the genocide. He advocates more proactive Net-based publishing on the part of Jewish groups so that the Net community can report hate mongers when they cross the line of current law.

On-Line Activism, Democratic Ideals, and Digital Lobbies

Much media coverage of the emerging power and changes that have occurred because of the increasing use of the Internet have centered on provocative issues like pornography, pedophilia, and the accessibility of bomb-making instructions. Such coverage is natural given the culture's apparently insatiable appetite for stories and sound bites about sleaze, sex, and the bizarre. In that same vein, television news reported on the way militia groups in the United States have used the electronic networking capabilities of fax machines, desktop publishing, videos, and connected computers to stay "well regulated," as the Second Amendment has provided. In a modern world, these citizen armies have used modern tools to remain prepared. Whether they are preparing for an assault from foreign invasion or an attack from their own government is a question that many are asking today, but their use of computer-aided communication is an example of one of the ways grassroots activism is thriving.

More typical of the groups using the Net as a key communication and dissemination vehicle are organizations and groups of individuals who have been longtime Internet users. Their causes typically revolve around the issues that they perceive to be a threat to the communal nature of the cyberworld in which they spend many of their productive hours. As an example, immediately after the Telecommunications Act of 1996 was signed into law, Shabbir J. Safdar and Steven Cherry, who began Voter Telecommunication Watch (VTW), organized a widespread protest of the Communications Decency Act. As President Clinton lifted his pen from the legal document, thousands of Web pages went black for 48 hours in a mass demonstration of dissatisfaction with the CDA portion of the law. When the Web pages returned to normal configuration, many included a graphic of a blue ribbon as a symbol of continuing protest against what was viewed as on-line censorship.

Protest against the CDA may have galvanized the largest number of Net users to join in an organized action on-line, but it certainly wasn't the first time that users became politically involved. Veteran Internet users have built relationships and interacted in variations of civic life for years via their keyboards and computers. As Howard Rheingold has noted in his work *The Virtual Community*, millions of citizens engage each other in an electronic agora discussing politics and government in an unfettered fashion that is rare in the real world. Some have suggested that it is the best way to attend to civic duties in the postindustrial society because the interactions take on the quality of a barn raising: Individuals come together to help others with little thought of receiving compensation.

When they function well, these electronic communities can give rise to very optimistic expectations about the future, as in Marshall McLuhan's vision. "It has reconstituted dialogue on a global scale. Its message is Total Change.... Ours is a brand-new world of allatonceness. 'Time' has ceased, 'space' has vanished. We now live in a global village...a simultaneous happening" (McLuhan 1967).

It is because of these positive humanizing experiences that many veterans of the Net would like to close the door to access for the masses and do all they can to keep the government from regulating their environment. Some critiques have noted that far from being inclusive, an elitist culture has developed among the veteran Netizens, and they liken it to the nascent democracy of ancient Athens, where only the privileged could participate in the civic life. Surveys show that the typical Web user is a well-educated white male, earns a substantially higher-than-average income, and is slightly over the age of 30. This demographic has changed somewhat over time, with women and minorities beginning to make up a greater percentage of the on-line population. However, the environment is not yet a place that resembles the real society when measured against any yardstick. Nevertheless, the door has been opened, and the newcomers *(newbies)* now outnumber the old-timers. The newbies are being integrated into the many cultures that already exist on the Net, and they are helping to define the new ones.

Netizens, those heavy users of the Internet, Usenet, Bitnet, Fidonet, and the other wide-area networks, have invested a great deal of time and energy into building relationships, businesses, and collaborative communities. There are over 8,000 Usenet newsgroups, for example, that have evolved unique codes of conduct and group-specific cultural values. Listserve technology has allowed for the establishment of untold numbers of electronic mail lists that keep subscribers up-to-date on specific areas of interest and provide forums for free interaction of ideas. Internet relay chat (IRC), multiuser dimensions (MUDs or MOOs), and lately, Web-based habitats like Spielberg's Starbright World for sick kids have been used to interact in real time. Even given the limitation of the bandwidth now available on the Internet, virtual 3-D environments are beginning to appear that allow users to manipulate "avatars" within highly imaginative cyberworlds.

In most cases, the rules within which the on-line users interact have been created from the consensus of the subculture at work there. The same technology that created a delivery system based on *no* central authority also spawned a human counterpart that flourished in the anarchy. In the absence of government, a remarkable ethos of cooperation and civility developed there. An overriding principle is, if you can help a fellow with a problem, you do it just because it is the right thing to do.

But could the Net remain substantially the domain of privileged white men because of the cost of the technology and level of technical skill that is required to interact fully in the digital world? That is a question many advocates for the poor and minorities have asked. Richard Civille of the Center for Civic Networking (CCN) is one of those people concerned that the "information have-nots" will be at a tremendous disadvantage as the "information haves" get the best jobs and wield the greatest power because of their access to critical data. The Telecommunications Act does include a provision to provide some sort of universal access for citizens of the United States, but that model has yet to be defined. Some have suggested the same sort of subsidizing that characterized the distribution of telephone service to the rural United States might be appropriate, but others point to the fact that access now means more than wires and hardware. It means that users will have to be trained to use the equipment. A 1995 Rand report recommends that the minimum level of guaranteed service for each household should be access to an e-mail account.

Richard Civille, along with other interested parties, has filed a response to the FCC in regard to their call for suggestions on how to implement universal access. Civille and others suggest providing incentives in tax credits and via the market to lower the cost of computers for low-income families and businesses. They believe that children and those looking for work should be given e-mail accounts. Civille also sees the need for community networks to provide important information that has an impact on local issues and to provide computer literacy training through schools or libraries.

Experts, like those who met at the Exploratory Aspen Workshop to discuss the implications of on-line community-building, have expressed concern that there may be a backlash from those who have not had an opportunity to gain advantage from the Information Revolution. They have recommended action that parallels Civille's suggestions, but they also call for urgent proactive policy that will mitigate possible negative reactions to a perceived cybernetic colonialism on the part of developing peoples worldwide

The companies that will be required to provide services under the FCC rules are anxious to see a return on their investment. They are generally pleased with the outcome of the legislation, which some accounts report they spent $40 million to influence. The long-distance market alone is worth $70 billion per year. This is a high-stakes game.

Education: Collaborative Learning To Reform the Process

The Telecommunications Act provision for universal service specifically targets schools and libraries as institutions that should be provided discounted pricing for access to telecommunications services. A federal-state advisory board will be recommending what level of service should be appropriate and how providers will be expected to subsidize educational access. Many telecom companies have decided to proactively create programs to wire schools, train teachers in the use of Internet protocols, and/or supply limited (one to two years) free dial-in access to Net services. There seems to be a consensus among educators, business, and the government that classrooms must have the infrastructure in place.

President Clinton even used his State of the Union address in January 1996 to publicize the need to bring the tools of the Communication Age into the schoolroom. "Every classroom in America must be connected to the Information Superhighway with computers, good software, and well-trained teachers. We are working with the telecommunications industry, educators, and parents to connect 20 percent of the classrooms in California by this spring, and every classroom and library in America by the year 2000."

A consortium of government organizations, hundreds of businesses, and thousands of volunteers led by the U.S. Tech Corps—an industry-sponsored, nonprofit organization established to match technology-literate trainers with teachers and students—came together on 9 March 1996 in California for NetDay96. On that Saturday, hundreds of the state's classrooms and libraries were connected to the Net. This initiative follows the lead of numerous school districts around the country that have passed bonds and levies, held fund-raisers, partnered with sponsors, or found other imaginative means to create networks within their buildings and get hooked to the Net. The overwhelming sentiment within the national education community is that students without access to computer-mediated communication tools and information that is available on the Internet or on-line services will be at a tremendous disadvantage in the burgeoning international information economy.

No one today expects the federal government to pay the high cost of wiring all of the nation's public schools and libraries. Much of the foundation that was laid for the concept of the National Information Infrastructure was built on the assumption that the risk would be borne by commercial interests. The Department of Education's estimate of the cost to accomplish such a feat is about $10 billion. A study completed in 1995 for the National Information Infrastructure Advisory Council estimated the cost for the kind of system proposed by the president, with one connected computer per five students, to be nearly $47 billion. Those estimates only consider the infrastructure.

What of the upgrades to hardware and software that rapidly changing technology continues to demand? Are teachers going to learn to use the new tools on their own time? How will the digital tools be integrated into the existing structure? Who will maintain the infrastructure once it is installed? These are just a few of the problems that the application of information technologies bring to the fore.

Arthur C. Clarke, author of *2001* and other visionary works, supplies another caveat: Accumulating information is not the same as gaining knowledge, knowledge is not equal to wisdom, and wisdom is not foresight. If the public education system is to serve its clients well, the technology that makes the information available must be integrated into a new method of teaching.

School Restructuring: Paradigm Shift to a Knowledge-Based Model

Certainly education is one of the institutions of our society in a state of tremendous flux. The issues involved in the many efforts that are taking place to make school more relevant, to redefine its task, and to reestablish it as a center of community life are the subject of other books. However, it is important to investigate just how information technology might help to accomplish what its proponents, among them Secretary Richard Riley of the U.S. Department of Education, believe is possible: the complete restructuring of a system that was put in place at the beginning of the Industrial Age.

Many educational reformers argue that the goal of the public schools was to train people to be successful workers for the factories that were being built in the urban centers of the mid-nineteenth century. Students were rewarded for punctuality, neatness, cooperation, standardized output, and respect for authority. The school day was divided into manageable sections, desks were arranged in straight rows, and teachers were the ultimate keepers of knowledge and the unquestioned authorities in their spaces. Consciously designed or not, such a system could produce a factory worker willing to come to work on time every day, stand along an assembly line, and produce a widget that did not vary from the first to the ten-millionth until the day of retirement.

Mike Bookey, of Digital Network Associates, a firm that consults on communication infrastructure for corporations and schools, has said that in many cases today's schools are set up to teach to the same goals, ignoring the fact that well-paid manufacturing jobs are not in the students' futures. The Second Wave is receding, and new skills are already in demand. Information-based economies require information-literate workers. Business leaders know that. *Fortune* magazine reports that businesses spent $2 billion training their people in the use of technology. Ninety percent of schoolteachers report that they are 100 percent self-taught in this area.

Corporations have discovered that it is in their best interest to help schools restructure their systems, in large measure to obtain better-qualified employees. It now costs companies so much to train high school and college graduates in the basics of reading, writing, math, creating, collaborating, and completing tasks that investing in public education looks like good strategic planning for the future bottom line.

Businesses donate money and personnel to wire schools, do in-service training for teachers, mentor students, and involve themselves in experiments in community-based pedagogy. A surprising number of these so-called information technology (IT) test beds are operational today, because no one has *the* answer about how to make information technology the driver of educational reform. Apple Computer, Microsoft, Compaq, and U S West are a few of the corporations that have concentrated on bringing IT to education. The U.S. Department of Education and the National Science Foundation have sought to leverage taxpayer monies with corporate and foundation donations so that worthwhile projects can be tested.

ELTEC: An Experiment in On-Line Learning

The National Science Foundation recently funded a project in Washington State that will have ramifications for educators around the country as they look for models that take advantage of computer-mediated communication as a way to increase knowledge. Enhanced Learning through Electronic Communities (ELTEC) has brought together partners from business, higher education, K–12 schools, state educational offices, federal agencies, and nongovernmental organizations to design a program that improves problem-solving skills for students by giving them the opportunity to study a local environmental issue.

The project involves five separate geographic communities that will test current and developing communication tools as facilitators for knowledge-building. They have plans to use e-mail, the World Wide Web, desktop videoconferencing facilities, and some new software that actually helps students understand the different levels of thinking that go on when collaborative inquiry takes place. The goal is to incorporate the digital tools as seamlessly as possible, and to actually create one of the first broad-based cyberschools in the country.

The ELTEC project, like many other reform experiments happening in America, places a great deal of emphasis on the reestablishment of community-based goals for educating not only K–12 students but any member of the locality who wants to take part. As Katherine Baril, director of a pilot Washington State University Extension Community Learning Center, says, "The goals and the decisions have been decentralized through the use of digital communication tools and good old common sense. This is the new face of education that speaks to both the health of the community and the business sector as well."

The Information Economy: New Bottom-Line Expectations

In many ways the legacy of TCP/IP, the system without a head, is the anarchy of the Internet and the new wide-open spaces of Web-based entrepreneurism. Much of what has been offered in these beginning stages of cybermalls and Net shops has caused some consumers to pause. Who knows if a business established last week in a world made of ones and zeroes will be there tomorrow when you have a complaint? How do you follow up when your browser gives you the error message, "that server is not accepting connections at this time"? Are they out of business or is the server just too busy? Get-rich-quick players are undoubtedly taking advantage of the low costs and quick development time required to get a commercial page up on the Web. Like everywhere else in the capitalist world, let the buyer beware.

However, evidence is everywhere of the positive side of this new economy and the changes the technology is making possible. Much of this is based on the redefining of goals within large corporations to provide better products and services for the customer and to provide them in an efficient manner. Bill Gates is one of the best examples to look at when analyzing any aspect of information entrepreneurship. He positioned his company to dominate the new PC market with his operating system software after Apple Computer's Steve Jobs had already established a base there. He did not look in the rearview mirror as he led Microsoft over the hill into the digital future.

Gates is the man people love to hate because the supremacy of his company in the information economy gives him remarkable influence in defining our future. He is not bashful about his role, either. Strategic alliances, partnerships, mergers, and innovative start-ups have put his touch on content (entertainment, education, business applications) and the infrastructure (networks, set-top boxes, and satellites) of the developing digital Information Highway. One of his least-known projects, for example, is Corbis, which is located at http://www.corbis.com/ on the Web. This enterprise was founded in 1989 to purchase the electronic rights to great works of graphic art from collections all over the world. The company scans the images and then makes them available to publishers and others for a fee or to students for personal use free of charge. Gates himself has deployed flat screen panels in his house in Seattle that rotate high-resolution displays of some of these works.

Although Gates is an entrepreneurial master, the strategy he employs and the business environment he has helped to create have given others hope that their dreams can yield monetary returns. If you ever want to find out who might be out there today emulating Gates, you'd most likely start your Net-based search with Yahoo. This service is a prime example of what is possible today in pure on-line business.

Located at http://www.yahoo.com, this very popular Web search service receives 4 million inquiries a day from people trying to navigate the Internet maze. Jerry Yang and David Filo, the founders of Yahoo, were graduate students at Stanford in 1994 when they took note of the proliferation of Web sites beginning to appear on-line. They decided to archive the addresses, or universal resource locators (URLs), of useful places because no other service at the time provided that information. They figured, at best, this could be a useful hobby. A year later the computer at Stanford where they had loaded their data was in danger of meltdown from constant access. Another wunderkind, Marc Andreessen of Netscape, stepped in to offer them computers and contacts in the venture capital world. Now Yang and Filo oversee a growing enterprise that has agreements with some of the most powerful service providers on the Net, and the company went public in April 1996.

On-line business experts like Michael Strangelove believe that while it may take a couple turns of the technology cycle before we see another person with the combination of skills and timing that made the CEO of Microsoft, there are many niches in the new economy waiting to be exploited. The rewards will go to those who understand the possibilities of the new media and who have the skills to take advantage of the decentralized production and distribution that Net-based business affords.

Decentralization has been the result of three factors, according to Joseph Boyett of the consulting firm of Boyett and Associates: (1) workers no longer have loyalty to a single firm for which they will expect to work for an entire career, (2) much of what gets accomplished now is the result of self-led teams that set their own goals, and (3) there has been a steady increase of 20 percent per year in the number of workers who use telecommuting to accomplish their work tasks.

Boyett and others believe that these trends will lead to significant changes in the worker, the organization, and the economy as a whole. Workers will need to have enhanced technical skills and be able to apply them in ever-changing circumstances. They will work on any number of projects as independent contractors, so they will have to learn how to be their own agents. Their work will pervade more of their time. They will do much of it in the home, and there is a likelihood that retirement will never be considered.

Companies will be organized very differently when they have smaller, agile workforces that will spend little or no time at a central location. This will mean that business will have to define a core vision that both the permanent and the constantly changing contingent workers can assimilate and follow. Success will be measured by the businesses' ability to bring a project team together, in virtual or real space, that has the correct mix of people with skills to do the job at hand.

The economy that grows from this new relationship between the organization and the information workers it employs will be increasingly global in nature as the real barriers to distribution become a factor of bandwidth on a digital network, not shipping schedules and customs inspectors. Some believe that this will lead to radical changes in the traditional nation-state as people come to identify more with their on-line business counterparts than with their geographic neighbors.

It is interesting to see how a typical worker today has adjusted to the changes in opportunity that the new business realities are bringing. Alan Zerobnick is a shoemaker. Dedicated as he is to his honorable and ancient craft, he also has one foot firmly planted in the information economy. In 1985 he began to investigate a way to improve the measuring of feet so that he could give people a better fit.

The University of North Carolina (UNC) had just been awarded $7 million by the federal government to develop a three-dimensional digitizer that would be capable of scanning a foot to create the perfect shoe for military and NASA applications. Zerobnick followed the progress of the research, but he was disappointed to learn that after five years the money was all gone and nothing was developed. The UNC team concluded that the digitizer probably could not be produced.

Zerobnick did not believe that. He was not especially computer literate, but he did have experience in applying technology to practical situations. Using his credit card and more perseverance than most people possess, he spent eight months in 1991 buying equipment off the shelf and writing software that would make his vision a reality. In 1996 he expects to open his first prototype retail manufacturing center for Digitoe, his company. There, a customer will step into Zerobnick's 3-D scanner and have his or her feet digitized. That binary data will then be used to make a shoe "fast," or foot model, on the premises via robotic assembly. Then any style of shoe, custom made on computerized equipment, can be manufactured to the precise model of the foot of the customer, who walks out with the shoes and the fast ready for the next time a perfect fit is needed.

Zerobnick foresees Digitoe regional satellites in strategic locales. Customers could be scanned at these sites and their data could then be passed along via the Internet or a dedicated network to a manufacturing center for assembly of the final product. He is not certain how he will use the Web in his scheme, but he does see it as a viable catalog and ordering alternative once customers have their feet on file.

Millennium Shift: Hold on to Your Hat

So much has not been defined about the new age we have entered that most of us have the tendency to want to look the other way, keep an eye on the past, and wax nostalgic about the good old days. "Family values" is the battle cry of both political parties. "Back to the basics" still drives a lot of educational reform. Laissez-faire economics has certainly made a comeback. All of these conservative responses are natural reactions to the uncertainties that have become manifest in this time of great change. It might do us all well to understand this and have some compassion for each other as we traverse the cusp of the millennium. In all likelihood, the pace of change will accelerate and the anxiety level will rise.

Very few among us have embraced the new technologies. Fewer still understand how the new digital world really works, but that is not keeping engineers and scientists and creative designers from pushing the envelope more each day. People who want to feel more comfortable about all of this today are going to have to make the effort to learn about the capabilities of information technologies. They will likely have to incorporate new behaviors into their daily routines if they want to move to the next level and take advantage of cyberspaces.

Paul Saffo directs the Institute of the Future. He asserts that the only victims in this emerging world will be those who opt out of trying to make sense of digital technology. They are the ones who say "my job won't change, and the way I relate to other people won't change."

"Those are the people who are going to be big losers in this revolution," Saffo says. All it takes to succeed, he adds, is some common sense and the ability to stay open to change that will not end.

References

Bracey, Bonnie. *Why Should Administrators* . . . e-mail message, 10 April 1996, sent to the mail list nii-teach@wais.com.

Elmer-Dewitt, Philip. "Cyberporn." *Time* 146 (3 July 1995): 38.

Fabre, Maurice. *A History of Communications.* New York: Hawthorn Books, 1963.

Gore, Al. "Information Superhighways: The Next Information Revolution." *The Futurist* 28 (January/February 1991): 21–23.

McLuhan, M., and Quentin Fiore. *The Medium Is the Massage.* New York: Random House, 1967.

Negroponte, Nicholas. *Being Digital.* New York: Alfred A. Knopf, 1995.

Rheingold, Howard. *The Virtual Community: Homesteading on the Electronic Frontier.* New York: HarperPerennial, 1993.

Toffler, Alvin. *The Third Wave.* New York: William Morrow, 1980.

Verity, John F. "Introduction." *Business Week Special 1994 Bonus Issue: The Information Revolution* (18 May 1994): 10–14.

Chronology 2

This chapter presents selected milestones in the development of information and communication technologies from three and one-half millennia before Christ up to 1996. The intent is to provide a context in which you will be able to analyze the evolving issues that are beginning to have an impact on the deployment and the direction of technology.

3500 B.C.   Sumerians are using a type of pictographic writing.

3100 B.C.   Egyptians first communicate with hieroglyphs that develop from the Sumerians' graphical language.

2500 B.C.   Papyrus is invented as a writing material. This primitive paper is made from the stems of reeds, and it is an acceptable medium for the new cursive hieratic script used for religious tracts.

1800 B.C.   Palestinians begin to use the first alphabet. It will eventually be discovered and improved by the Phoenicians and then the Greeks in the tenth century B.C.

1500 B.C.	The *Book of the Dead* is written. This is considered to be the first "book" written on papyrus.
540 B.C.	The first public library is founded in Athens by Pisistratus.
200 B.C.	The Chinese perfect a method of creating a fine grade of paper out of silk.
150 B.C.	A process is perfected to turn animal skins into a very smooth two-sided surface for writing. Named parchment after Pergamum, the city in Asia Minor where it is invented, the medium enables the reproduction of manuscripts that are considered to be of great value.
A.D. 105	The Chinese find methods to use common plants in the production of paper.
150	Parchment is folded instead of rolled, creating the "book" style that is familiar today.
300	Monks work in scriptoria during the Dark Ages to preserve information by copying and illuminating manuscripts.
1456	Johann Gutenberg prints the first book by means of a moveable-type mechanical press. The work is the Bible. Many consider this to be the beginning of the first Information Revolution.
1609	One of the first weekly newspapers begins publishing in Strasbourg, France.
1623	Wilhelm Schickard creates the very first mechanical calculator.
1768	The *Encyclopaedia Britannica* is published.
1776	The Virginia Bill of Rights calls the press the "bulwark of liberty."
1784	The first mail sent by coaches goes from London to Bristol.
1791	Thomas Paine's *Rights of Man* is published.
	The First Amendment to the U.S. Constitution guarantees freedom of the press.

1794   Claude Chappe, an engineer, develops a semaphore that can carry a message 144 miles from the town of Lille, France, to Paris in about two minutes. His system consists of a series of towers set five to ten miles apart but within sight of each other. Each tower is equipped with a pivoted beam that will swing into sight with an appropriate signal. Operators on each tower use telescopes to see and relay the beam-arm signals.

1800   Joseph Marie Jacquard, a French inventor, develops the first successful commercial loom for weaving. One unique and important contribution of Jacquard's design is the incorporation of punched cards as a system for information storage and retrieval. This innovation allows for instruction sets to be distributed in any order, not simply numerically.

1820   Charles Xavier Thomas produces the first commercially successful mechanical calculator capable of addition, subtraction, multiplication, and division.

1822   British mathematician Charles Babbage designs and builds a prototype of his difference engine. This machine is conceived as a way to automate the drudgery involved in the human computation of repeating mathematical operations (e.g., logarithmic and astronomical tables). The British government funds his research into the development of an operational model of his calculating device, which is to be steam-powered and driven by a fixed instruction program. For the next 12 years he continues to work on the project, although no fully functional model is ever completed.

1824   George Stephenson builds the Stockton & Darlington Railway between 1823 and 1825 in England. This 20-mile rail line is the first public railway in the world to be powered by a steam locomotive.

1828   The first railroad is built in the United States, commissioned by merchants in Baltimore, Maryland. The Baltimore & Ohio Railroad goes into service two years later.

1834   Charles Babbage abandons work on his difference engine to spend more time developing the concept of his analytical engine. This machine was to be the first fully programmable automatic mechanical digital computer. With this concept, Babbage establishes himself as a man fully one century ahead of his time. His analytical engine can operate on 50 decimal digits and can even store 1,000 such numbers. Instructions are to be input from punched cards, and they can be entered at various remote stations. However, this device is never constructed.

1837   William F. Cooke and Charles Wheatstone perfect and install the first railway telegraph in England. This same year, Samuel F. B. Morse invents the Morse code (an early digital language) and develops a prototype electromagnetic telegraph receiver with Alfred Vail.

1839   Louis J. M. Daguerre develops the light-sensitive daguerreotype, a photographic plate on which a camera image can be held and fixed permanently. This same year, a French firm begins to manufacture the first commercial camera.

1844   Hutton Gregory's electrified modification of Claude Chappe's semaphore signaling system includes 500 stations in a telegraph network that connects 29 French cities.

            In the United States, a telegraph line joins Washington, D.C., and Baltimore, Maryland. Morse demonstrates his magnetic telegraph receiver by sending the message, "What hath God wrought," the first words to be transmitted electronically.

1858   The first transatlantic telegraph cable is stretched along the ocean floor between Newfoundland and Ireland mostly due to the persistence of Cyrus W. Field, an American promoter. Queen Victoria sends the first official transatlantic message to President James Buchanan, but three weeks later the insulation on the line deteriorates to the point where it becomes useless.

1865   James Clerk Maxwell theorizes that an oscillating electric charge produces an electromagnetic field.

1866   The Atlantic cable is successfully reinstalled when Field employs the largest steamship of its time, the *Great Eastern*, to lay the 2,000 miles of line.

1868   Christopher Latham Sholes patents a typewriter with his partners Samuel W. Soule and Carlos Glidden. Sholes, a printer, politician, and journalist from Wisconsin, continues to improve his device over the next decade and eventually sells the rights to the Remington Arms Company.

1872   Englishman Eadweard Muybridge, the famous Yosemite landscape photographer, is hired by Leland Stanford to win a bet. Stanford, the former governor of California, wagers that once in every stride, all the hoofs of a horse are off the ground at once. It will take five years for Muybridge's pictures, shot as sequential frames of the horse's running action, to prove Stanford right. The research project leads to Muybridge's development in 1879 of the zoopraxiscope, a machine that simulates motion from photographs. These are the first "moving pictures."

Thomas Alva Edison perfects the duplex telegraph, which allows for simultaneous two-way transmissions of signals.

1874   Alexander Graham Bell develops the idea for the telephone by accident as he attempts to make improvements on the telegraph.

1876   "Mr. Watson, come here; I want you" is transmitted over the line of the new telephone communication device that Bell demonstrates.

1877   The first telephones become available to the public.

Edison announces his tinfoil cylinder "sound writer," the first phonograph.

1879   Edison exhibits his incandescent electric lightbulb. By 1882 he develops the first power station to run public lighting in New York City.

1884   George Eastman develops and patents the first practical sensitized photographic film in roll form.

1887   Heinrich Hertz experiments with James Maxwell's electromagnetic theories, leading to the development of wireless communication and radio.

1888   George Eastman perfects his box camera, which he names Kodak. It is the first camera designed specifically to use roll film.

Nikola Tesla constructs the alternating current (AC) electric motor, which is to prove a more capable power source for Edison's light.

Emile Berliner demonstrates his "gramophone," a phonographic device that etches sound waves in a spiral groove on the surface of a flat disc. He will license his patent to the Victor Talking Machine Company in 1901.

1889   Eastman develops flexible transparent film, an image storage medium that proves vital to the development of motion pictures.

1890   Herman Hollerith, an employee of the U.S. Census Bureau, devises a way to automate the population count by developing a method to store data in a series of punched holes in cards. With the help of James Powers, he develops a machine that can read the cards by passing them through electrical contacts.

1892   The automatic telephone switchboard is introduced.

1895   Guglielmo Marconi invents the radio-signaling system, which is first applied to the wireless telegraph.

Sir William Crookes invents the cathode-ray tube (CRT), the basis for luminescent display devices like television screens and computer monitors.

Auguste and Louis Lumière perfect a camera that also serves as a projector. They call their system cinematographe. The first film, *La Sortie des usines Lumière (Quitting Time at the Lumière Factory)*, is shown in Paris.

1896   Hollerith starts the Tabulating Machine Company, which is to evolve into the International Business Machines Corporation (IBM).

1900   Reginald Fessenden designs a high-frequency alternator with which he transmits speech by radio waves.

1904   The first telegraphic transmission of photographs is accomplished.

            Sir J. Ambrose Fleming invents the electronic vacuum tube, based on a principle demonstrated by Edison. It proves to be a great advance in the technology of radio telegraphy.

1906   Fessenden is responsible for the first program of speech and music ever transmitted by radio. He also establishes the first two-way transatlantic wireless telegraph communication in this year.

            The Haloid Corporation is founded. This company will eventually change its name to Xerox.

1907   Lee De Forest develops the triode, initially called the audion, making amplification of radio signals possible. His invention is the basis for radar and television devices.

1913   There are over a half million telephones in homes in New York and 90,000 in Paris.

1915   Thomas A. Watson receives the first transcontinental phone call from his collaborator, Alexander Graham Bell.

1918   The United States War Department starts the first regular airmail service on routes between New York, Philadelphia, and Washington, D.C.

1920   KDKA in Pittsburgh begins service as the first regularly scheduled radio station.

1923   Russian-American Vladmir Zworykin patents the iconoscope kinescope devices for the sending and receiving of television signals.

1926   Kodak produces the first 16mm movie film, and the motion picture *Metropolis*, Fritz Lang's work, is released.

1927   Warner Brothers releases *The Jazz Singer*, the first "talkie."

Transatlantic telephone service is initiated.

1928   George Eastman demonstrates color motion pictures, and J. L. Baird demonstrates color television. The NBC and CBS networks establish the first scheduled television broadcasts.

1929   *Lights of New York* is the first all-talking motion picture to be produced.

1930   Vannevar Bush and other scientists at the Massachusetts Institute of Technology (MIT) create the differential analyzer, the precursor of the analog computer.

1933   Bell Telephone Laboratories develops stereophonic sound reproduction.

1937   Alan Turing publishes "On Computable Numbers," a paper in which he first conceives of a machine that can change states following a rigorous set of rules. His Turing machine foreshadows modern digital computation.

1939   Howard Aiken and others at IBM begin to develop the Harvard Mark I, a computer driven by punch cards that can perform all four arithmetic operations.

John Vincent Atanasoff finishes the prototype of the first electronic digital computer. His work proves to be the basis for basic digital techniques that are eventually used in the first fully functional electronic digital computer, ENIAC.

Konrad Zuse invents the first electromechanical binary computer.

1942   Magnetic recording tape is invented.

1943   ENIAC development is begun under the direction of J. Presper Eckert and John W. Mauchly at the University of Pennsylvania, under contract to the U.S. War Department. Its task is to calculate trajectories of ballistic missiles.

1944   Aiken's Harvard Mark I computer debuts, as does the Colossus Mark II and Bell Labs' Computer Model IV.

1945   Vannevar Bush writes the article "As We May Think" for the *Atlantic Monthly*. This is the first public proposal for a way to improve the world through the improved application of knowledge.

1946   Jay Forrester begins work on the Whirlwind computer for digital flight simulation at MIT.

1947   The concept of artificial intelligence is first introduced in an article written by Alan Turing. The first computer-related organization is formed when the Association for Computing Machinery has its first meeting.

1948   William Shockley, John Bardeen, and Walter Brattain invent the transistor at Bell Telephone Laboratories. This advance means that larger electrical relay and vacuum tubes can be replaced to control electric current in devices that transmit information.

        Dennis Gabor creates holography, a process for producing a three-dimensional image. Polaroid develops "instant" photography.

        The microgroove long-play record (LP) is invented.

1949   Link Corporation signs an agreement with the Air Force to develop the first jet flight simulator.

1951   The color television is introduced into the U.S. market, which now has sold 15 million sets.

        Eckert and Mauchly, developers of ENIAC, sell 46 of their new UNIVAC I computers in the United States.

1954   The microchip, or microprocessor, is invented. This breakthrough allows for the development of solid-state integrated circuitry, which eventually leads to the creation of central processing units, the brains of computers.

1955   TAT-1, the first transatlantic cable capable of carrying telephone calls, is laid between the United States and Europe. The capacity is 52 simultaneous calls.

1956   A patent is issued for the first head-mounted video viewing device.

1957   The Advanced Research Projects Agency is established by order of President Dwight D. Eisenhower in response to the progress demonstrated by the Soviets in their launch of the satellite *Sputnik*.

1958   Ampex develops a videotape recorder that will record in color.

1959   Jack Kilby, of Texas Instruments, announces the first integrated circuit. Robert Noyce at Fairchild Semiconductor develops his own idea for integrated circuits at the same time.

1960   The 914 xerographic copier, from Xerox, is the first commercial copier available. Lasers are invented.

             Digital Equipment Corporation introduces its first computer.

1962   Douglas Englebart invents the light pen and the use of "windows" as a computer interface.

             North Americans own almost 60 million television sets.

             The *Telstar* satellite transmits its first TV signal from North America to Europe. By using radio signals, technicians on the ground are able to repair the satellite's "brain," which is some 2,500 miles away in space.

1963   MIT implements the Compatible Time Sharing System, a system by which operators in various locations can access the most powerful computers via dumb terminals.

1964   *Understanding Media: The Extensions of Man*, by Marshall McLuhan, is published.

AT&T introduces the Picturephone, and IBM markets the magnetic Tape Selectric Typewriter, the first word processor.

1965   Ted Nelson coins the word *hypertext*.

IBM unveils its 360/30 and 360/40 computers.

1966   Bob Taylor, working at DARPA, introduces the idea of developing and building a broad-based computer network.

Ivan Sutherland begins work on the first head-mounted display at MIT's Lincoln Lab.

1967   McLuhan's *The Medium Is the Massage* is published.

1968   Network development makes great strides with the following events: A packet-switching network proposal is made to the Advanced Research Products Agency (ARPA), Bob Taylor is given $1 million to build an experimental network, Larry Roberts designs a small packet-switching network, Wes Clark invents the Interface Message Processor (IMP), and Bolt, Beranik, and Newman (BBN) builds the first commercial IMP.

1969   ARPAnet, the first wide-area network, is commissioned by the Department of Defense for the purpose of research. The first protocols (software to interact on the network) are developed at the same time. These applications include Vint Cerf and Bob Kahn's development of transmission control protocol and Internet protocol (TCP/IP) and Jon Postel's Telnet program. In short order the first four network nodes are activated at the University of California, Los Angeles; Stanford Research Institute; the University of Utah; and the University of California, Santa Barbara.

1969
cont.

Intel Corporation creates the first 1-KB random-access memory (RAM) chip.

1970

The University of Hawaii implements ALOHAnet.

1971

Lexitron introduces a word processor that uses a video display screen, and Intel introduces the first microprocessor.

"Computer Space," the first arcade-type computer video game, is introduced.

ARPAnet expands to 15 nodes.

1972

Sun Microsystems is incorporated. The personal computer concept is introduced, and the term PC becomes widely used.

Forty computers are connected on ARPAnet in a public demonstration of the power of the infrastructure. BBN implements an e-mail program.

Cray Research, Inc. is formed. Intel releases the 8008 chip with 16 KB of memory. Atari is started and ships its first video game, "Pong." Philips markets the first consumer videocassette recorder.

1973

Odyssey by Magnavox is the first home video game system to be marketed.

ARPAnet makes its first international connections to Norway and England.

The first microcomputer, a French-built Micral (the first nonkit computer using a microprocessor), appears.

A fax machine for general use is developed.

1974

The first answering machines and first digital watches are announced.

Intel releases the 8080 chip with 64 KB of memory.

The terms *hypermedia* and *artificial reality* are coined.

1975   Intel founder Gordon Moore states Moore's Law, which predicts that the number of transistors on chips will double every two years.

                 The computer language BASIC, written by Bill Gates and Paul Allen, is sold for the Altair 8800, and Microsoft is founded.

                 Martin Hellman and Whitfield Diffie develop public-key cryptography at Stanford University.

1976   Apple Computer is formed, and the first Apple is sold in kit form. The founders' proposal for the development of a personal desktop computer is turned down by several companies.

                 Queen Elizabeth of England sends the first royal e-mail message.

1977   The Apple II is introduced, selling for $1,300. Commodore Business Machines, Inc. releases the Commodore PET for $600.

1978   Ward Christenson and Randy Suess create the first personal computer bulletin board system.

                 Philips develops the laser disc.

1979   Richard Bartle and Roy Trubshaw create the first multiuser domain. Tom Truscott and Steve Bellovin create Usenet.

                 The Source, a telecommunications service, goes online for the first time. MicroNet goes on-line; it will later become CompuServe.

                 Philips announces compact disc (CD) digital audio.

                 Cellular telephones are introduced.

1980   Minitel, the French telecommunications network, is started by French Telecom.

                 Alvin Toffler's *The Third Wave* is published.

                 There are more than 1 million computers in the United States.

1981	Hayes Microcomputer Products releases the Smart-modem 300. IBM announces the IBM Personal Computer with 64 KB of RAM for $3,000. Epson releases the first laptop computer.
	Microsoft buys all rights to DOS, a disc operating system, from Seattle Computer Products and introduces MS-DOS.
	Eighteen percent of schools have some kind of computer on site.
1982	*Tron*, from Disney, is the first film to make extensive use of computer graphics.
	AT&T is broken up by court order, creating 22 regional phone companies.
1983	Myron Krueger's *Artificial Reality* is published.
	The TAT-7 cable is deployed to carry 9,000 telephone conversations back and forth across the Atlantic.
1984	Apple's famous commercial is shown during the Super Bowl, and the company introduces the Macintosh personal computer, with its graphical user interface, for $2,500.
	Many companies begin selling a 2,400-baud modem for around $850. The first wristwatch computer is marketed by Seiko Instruments. Microsoft starts selling Windows and its first mouse.
	The word *cyberspace* is used for the first time by William Gibson in his novel, *Neuromancer*.
	There are now more than 1,000 nodes on ARPAnet.
1985	Desktop publishing becomes a reality with the release of PageMaker by Aldus. Initially, it runs on the Macintosh only.
	The Whole Earth 'Lectronic Link computer bulletin board system is operational.
1986	There are over 30 million computers in the United States, and 95 percent of the software is in the form of video games.

The Electronic Communications Privacy Act is passed by Congress.

The NSFnet is created with a backbone speed of 56 kbps. The Cleveland Freenet is started.

Intel starts selling the 80386 chip, and computer manufacturers start shipping machines with the new microprocessor.

1987   ARPAnet is now connected with over 10,000 hosts.

IBM and Microsoft jointly announce the OS/2 operating system.

1988   VPL makes and markets the first commercial virtual reality system.

AT&T deploys the first fiber-optic transatlantic cable (TAT-8), which can carry 40,000 simultaneous telephone calls.

1989   NSFnet's backbone increases its capacity and upgrades to T1 status (1.544 kbps). Tim Berners-Lee submits the first proposal for his World Wide Web idea. The number of hosts on the ARPAnet is over 100,000. Chip Morningstar and F. Randall Farmer create Habitat for Lucasfilm Games, an on-line community that is the first to use the "avatar" concept.

MIT's Media Lab creates the first real-time holographic 3-D images.

1990   ARPAnet is no longer needed because of the NSFnet, and it is shut down.

The Electronic Frontier Foundation is founded by the CEO of Lotus Development Corporation in response to what many consider to be an unwarranted FBI "hacker crackdown."

Work begins on the first command-line World Wide Web browser. The first object-oriented multiuser computer network environment, or MOO, is opened.

1991   The U.S. High Performance Computing Act establishes the National Research and Education Network,

1991 *cont.*	which is the government's philosophical basis for the Internet. At the same time, a consortium of commercial network service providers joins forces in the Commercial Internet Exchange (CIX) Association, Inc.

Ninety-eight percent of the schools in the United States have computers, but most do not have up-to-date or useful software.

The gopher protocol is developed at the University of Minnesota, and HTTP (World Wide Web) servers are created at Stanford University. The new Web protocol is announced to the public.

1992	The Internet Society is formed, and the NSFnet carrying capacity is increased to the T3 (44,736 mbps) level. The first MBONE multicast takes place, providing audio and video capabilities on the Net. The first graphical World Wide Web browser is introduced, and there are now over a million host computers connected to the Internet.

The first all-digital telephone network is deployed.

1993	The new telephone cable laid across the Atlantic can carry over 22,000 phone calls.

Mark Pesce and Tony Parisi begin working on the first 3-D space browser. NSF creates the InterNIC registration service. Marc Andreessen, working at NCSA, releases the Mosaic Web browsers for multiple platforms. CU-SeeMe, the free Internet videoconferencing program, is released by Cornell University.

The National Academy of Science sponsors the nationwide convocation "Reinventing Schools: The Technology Is Now."

The White House comes on-line, and Bill Clinton becomes the first U.S. president to send an e-mail message.

Voyager distributes *A Hard Day's Night* on a CD, the first full-length movie to be transcribed into hypertext. *Wired* magazine begins publishing.

1994 Vice President Al Gore gives a speech at UCLA in which he makes reference to the Information Super-highway, a term that is picked up and exploited by the media.

The World Wide Web traffic on NSFnet is now great-er than gopher use. Jim Clark and Marc Andreessen launch Netscape Communications (originally Mosaic Communications Corporation), and the first Net-scape browser for the Web is released.

Nintendo releases the first head-mounted display game system, called "Virtual Boy." The first marriage ceremony using virtual reality equipment takes place.

1995 Ninety-five percent of U.S. homes have a television set, and 36 percent have a computer.

The NSFnet is ended, and all responsibility for carry-ing Internet traffic moves to commercial systems.

Netscape Communications becomes a publicly traded corporation with an initial public offering price set under $20. It begins trading at $72 and hits $150 less than two months later.

Toy Story, the first totally computer-generated anima-tion film, is created by Pixar, a company headed by Apple founder Steven Jobs.

1996 The Telecommunications Reform Act is passed, allowing for increased competition between hereto-fore segregated arms of the communication industry. Along with it are the provisions of the Communi-cations Decency Act, characterized by some as a threat to First Amendment rights.

A federal panel strikes down the provisions of the Communications Decency Act less than six months after it is signed into law.

Biographical Sketches 3

I ncluded here are brief descriptions of the lives, relevant activities, and important publications of some of the people who have been instrumental in establishing the technical possibilities of the Communication Age or who have attempted to influence the debate that is swirling around their application.

Charles Babbage (1792–1871)

Most readers undoubtedly will not have heard of this nineteenth-century mathematician, but it was his theoretical work on a "difference engine" that laid the foundation for today's digital computers.

Charles Babbage was born in 1792, and he attended Cambridge University. In 1827 he became Lucasian Professor of Mathematics at Cambridge, where he never taught, but rather studied a variety of scientific, technological, and economic problems. The British Association for the Advancement of Science was established because of his work in 1831. His real obsession, however, was in the area of the computation of logarithms. He saw that human computation was drudgery and often less than accurate. He sought a mechanical means by which much of that work could be accomplished.

Babbage spent his family's fortune on an attempt to create such a machine. He never succeeded before his death in 1871. His son Henry finally assembled six difference engines in 1879 that were based on an automated textile loom, which used punched cardboard cards to control woven patterns. Though the machines never proved practical, Babbage's ideas about digitally controlled computation are credited as the basis for modern computing devices.

John Perry Barlow (b. 1947)

John Perry Barlow, currently vice chairman of the Electronic Frontier Foundation (EFF), helps to educate the public about the threat to privacy, First Amendment rights, and proposed changes to copyright law that many in EFF feel will alter the landscape of cyberspace forever.

Barlow was raised on a cattle ranch in Wyoming, where he was born in 1947. His early years were filled with mischief as his parents tended to ranching and Republican state politics and left the raising of their boy to employees. At age 15 he was enrolled in a military academy in Colorado where he continued to get into trouble. Now, however, he had an accomplice named Bob Weir. Barlow wrote poetry and Weir played his guitar. Both of them gained reputations as troublemakers. In 1965 Barlow graduated from the school to begin work in comparative religions at Wesleyan University. Weir, who had been expelled from the academy, was in San Francisco starting a band called the Grateful Dead.

In 1970, two years after graduating from college and traveling through India, Barlow visited Weir in San Francisco. His friend encouraged him to try using his gift for poetry to supply lyrics for the band's songs. He eventually did contribute 30 sets of lyrics, many of which became Grateful Dead concert favorites, but Barlow would not take up the rock-and-roll lifestyle. Responding to a request for help from his father, who suffered a stroke years before, he returned to Wyoming to manage the family ranch in 1971.

In 1987 he began using the personal computer to keep track of expenses on the ranch. He sold the ranch the next year but got more involved with his computer by connecting to the Internet. There he discovered what he found to be as exciting and wide-open an environment as he'd known on the plains of Wyoming. Not that he could not tell the difference between "information and experience," but the possibilities of the cybersociety did intrigue him. He began to post articles and messages to news-groups, mail lists, and on-line conferences that explored the new realities of electronic interaction. He soon picked up the title of poet laureate of cyberspace.

In 1990 his growing reputation on the Net brought a call from the FBI, which wanted to discuss the activity of some dangerous hackers who were distributing source code for the Apple Macintosh computer. It quickly became apparent to Barlow that the government agents knew almost nothing about computer technology, and that their misinformation was leading them into acting against U.S. citizens who were probably not guilty of anything. On-line discussions with others on the Whole Earth 'Lectronic Link conferencing system, including Lotus Development Corporation founder Mitch Kapor, led to the establishment of EFF.

More current information about Barlow can be discovered at http://www.eff.org/~barlow/.

Bonnie Bracey (b. 1939)

Bonnie Bracey is a superior teacher, one who has always made the classroom a comfortable and exciting place for her elementary-aged students. She has numerous awards that prove this. When she was introduced to the computer in the 1980s, she did not appreciate the capabilities of that tool. Soon, through a patient and thorough analysis of and immersion into the technology, she came to see how the computer could be used to keep her teaching fresh and her students involved. One could say that this was just the beginning.

In 1988 Bracey took part in training sponsored by the National Geographic Society that showed how the teaching of geography could be integrated into an inquiry about physical science. The training was carried out on an interactive computer network called KidsNetwork. This was her first exposure to this type of digital communication. Again Bracey was skeptical about using such new modalities in the classroom, but once more she was willing to expand her vision and dedicate the time it took to understand what connectivity like this could mean for her students.

In no time she was training other teachers in her school, buying her own software, establishing network accounts with her own money, and cajoling and pushing to get her administration to adapt some of the new tools. She wasn't always popular with those who wanted to keep the status quo in the schoolhouse. She even had software and new materials thrown away by a principal when she moved to a different assignment, but her advocacy for excellent teaching using the newest technologies caught the attention of many who appreciated her efforts. In 1994 she was named to represent all K–12 educators on the National Information Infrastructure Advisory Council (NIIAC).

Bracey believes that teachers will not embrace the new technologies of the Communication Age if they are not adequately prepared to use the new tools. She knows that many otherwise fine educators will resist this change because of the retraining burden it imposes. She has done much to get the word out to the greater community about the needs of teachers. "On the Committee [NIIAC] I fight for the teachers, I speak up."

She was one of the voices of the average citizen as the NIIAC met over the two years of its existence. She was never bashful about raising the issues that she felt might especially impact the poor and the unrepresented as the plans for the NII were being laid. She continues to speak out and to write about the needs of teachers and students who require training and cheap access to the Information Highway of opportunities.

Stewart Brand (b. 1939)

Stewart Brand found phenomenal success in the traditional publishing world by producing one of the most successful magazines to hit the newsstands, *The Whole Earth Catalog*. That compendium of environmentally based resources and writings lasted from 1968 until 1972 and sold more than 2.5 million copies of each issue. However, it was in the new emerging world of information technology that he had found an exciting outlet for his creative spirit.

Brand had already experienced the capabilities of the computer as far back as 1962, when he saw what researchers at Stanford University were doing with the mainframe there. He noticed that they were playing a computer game, Space War, and he surmised something important about the development of technology then. In his words, "The future of technology can be predicted by looking at what researchers are discouraged from doing...the cool stuff is still disapproved of." So when the last *Whole Earth Catalog* was finished, he was happy to take an assignment to report on game players for *Rolling Stone* magazine.

The research for this article took Brand to the most advanced digital information research facilities of the day, and he discovered ARPAnet. A new idea was born. Though it would not happen for 12 more years, Brand eventually founded the Whole Earth 'Lectronic Link, an on-line conferencing facility for the San Francisco area that is better known as the WELL. This computer agora now boasts over 10,000 members worldwide, and it has been mentioned in books like Howard Rheingold's *The Virtual Community* as an example of how digital domains can facilitate intimacy among the participants.

Brand works as a consultant for businesses on the use of information technologies. But his most important contribution to the inquiry about where the new age is headed has to do with the humanizing effects of computer-mediated communication.

Vannevar Bush (1890–1974)

Interest in Vannevar Bush increased on the fiftieth anniversary of the publication of his article, "As We May Think," in 1995. Originally published in the July 1945 issue of *The Atlantic Monthly*, this visionary work was the first to lay out the possibilities of an information future for the general populace. In that article he predicted the development of a "memex," or a "device in which an individual stores all his books, records, and communications, and which is mechanized so that it may be consulted with exceeding speed and flexibility.... It consists of a desk, and while it can presumably be operated from a distance, it is primarily the piece of furniture at which he works. On the top are slanting translucent screens, on which material can be projected for convenient reading. There is a keyboard, and sets of buttons and levers."

Dr. Bush was born in 1890 in Massachusetts. He earned his doctorate in engineering at the Massachusetts Institute of Technology (MIT) and Harvard. For most of the years leading up to World War II, he held the position of dean of engineering at MIT. During this time he directed work on several inventions, the most important of which was the differential analyzer, one of the first analog computing devices.

Dr. Bush served as director of the Office of Scientific Research and Development (OSRD), an organization that brought 6,000 scientists together to apply their discoveries to the war effort against the Nazis and the Japanese. He wrote "As We May Think" after his work with the OSRD had come to an end. In 1945 he wanted the country to redirect its energy in similar ways to enhance the powers of the intellect rather than the might of machines. The National Science Foundation was created in 1950 as a response to Bush-led initiatives.

Dr. Bush died in 1974, having lived long enough to see some of the predictions of his memex come true.

Esther Dyson (b. 1951)

According to *Vanity Fair* magazine in 1995, Esther Dyson is one of the "Fifty Leaders of the Information Age." One of the few women to hold a position of power in the information industry, her opinion is highly respected and her time always in demand. She currently serves as a member of the National Information Infrastructure Advisory Council, and she is the president of the Electronic Frontier Foundation. In addition, she serves on the board of several nonprofit organizations and industry forums.

Dyson graduated from Harvard in 1972 with a B.A. degree in economics and experience as a journalist for the college's newspaper. She parlayed the combination into a job with *Forbes* magazine as a reporter from 1974 until 1977, then worked as a Wall Street securities analyst until 1982. She went on to start her own company, EDventure Holdings, which focuses on the emerging information technologies in the Western nations, but with a special emphasis on Eastern European markets. Dyson speaks fluent Russian and makes regular trips to former Soviet bloc countries to consult, give presentations, and stage industry forums.

EDventure Holdings also sponsors PC Forum, one of the most important gatherings for industry leaders in the United States, which has met yearly since 1978. Through these conferences and her widely read newsletter, *RELEASE 1.0*, Dyson has proven to be one of the brilliant thinkers and true visionaries of an exciting age.

Bill Gates (b. 1955)

There is an excellent chance that Microsoft CEO Bill Gates will continue to be one of the most influential participants in the design of the digital information realm.

William Henry Gates III was born in Seattle, Washington, in 1955 to a family of some wealth and prestige in that city. He attended the private and academically elite Lakeside School in north Seattle, where his interest in computers motivated him to start programming when he was just 13 years old. In 1974, when he was an undergraduate at Harvard University and his interest in computers had only become more intense, he developed the programming language known as BASIC for MIT's Altair. This

first microcomputer helped launch the era of hobbyist computing in America.

Gates left college a year later to join his friend Paul Allen in
founding Microsoft, the first microcomputer software company.
Microsoft's big break, reflecting what many say is the genius of
Gates, came in 1980 with the contract to provide the operating
software for the new personal computer then under development at IBM. That company wasn't interested in owning the
software; personal computing was simply too new a business
for many to see the potential. Gates saw that potential, and he
has been driven by the dream of seeing a "computer on every
office desktop and in every home." He negotiated a deal with
IBM and subsequently with almost every other PC manufac-
turer in the world to pay a royalty for including his Microsoft
Disk Operating System (MS-DOS) in their machines.

Eventually, Microsoft developed other application software
to run on top of MS-DOS, and their programming became the de
facto standard for the new industry. Today, some 85 percent of
the computers in existence run on Microsoft platforms. Gates
himself was the first person in history to achieve billionaire status by the age of 31. Because of its near-monopolistic position in
the computer software industry, Microsoft is watched very
closely for the latest in innovation and possible trends. Other
software companies must write their applications to work in
MS-DOS or Windows environments if they expect to be successful in this highly competitive world.

Lately Gates has made many pronouncements about the
importance of the Internet for the future of computing and digital information exchange, and his company has begun to develop software that will utilize the Internet protocol. He is not
about to stop there, however, as he sees the potential of the Net
developing well beyond these first stages. He has signed agreements with entertainment companies like Disney and Steven
Spielberg's Amblin Entertainment to develop content. He has
partnered with NBC-TV to develop an interactive news service,
and there are plans to launch a series of low-altitude communication satellites in the next century.

George Gilder (b. 1939)

George Gilder is a Senior Fellow of the Discovery Institute in
Seattle. He directs the program on high technology and public
policy at the nonprofit think tank.

Gilder first gained a reputation as Ronald Reagan's most frequently quoted living author. He has a long history as an advisor to the Republican Party, and his advocacy normally falls within what most would consider the conservative side of the political spectrum. After graduating from Exeter Academy in 1958, he studied under Henry Kissinger as an undergraduate at Harvard University. He began to write speeches for prominent Republicans soon after his graduation and the subsequent publishing of his political history, *The Party That Lost Its Head*. Some of his most important speeches were written for Nelson Rockefeller, George Romney, and Richard Nixon.

By the 1970s Gilder was doing independent research and writing on the causes of poverty. He is widely regarded as the man who formulated the theory of supply-side economics, and his books on economics, *Men and Marriage* (1972), *Visible Man* (1978), and the best-selling *Wealth and Poverty* (1981), reflect his thinking in regard to wealth and the lack thereof. In the 1980s he broadened the scope of his inquiry to include an investigation of those who had become highly successful entrepreneurs, especially in the high-technology industries. His analysis of the roots of these new electronics businesses, *Microcosm* (1989), became another best-seller. This was followed by the 1992 publication of a book that is a prophecy of the future of telecommunications, *Life after Television*.

Gilder is a widely sought-after speaker throughout the world, and he is called often by congressional committees to testify as one of the nation's foremost authorities on information technology and the future. He is one of House Speaker Newt Gingrich's favorite advisors. His latest published work, *Telecosm* (1996), continues his analysis of the changes occurring in society and its institutions due to the application of information technology. He is also credited as one of the contributors to the Progress and Freedom Foundation's "Cyberspace and the American Dream: A Magna Carta for the Knowledge Age," which is reprinted in chapter 4.

Gilder can be reached via e-mail at gg@gilder.com.

Mitchell Kapor (b. 1950)

Mitchell Kapor founded the Electronic Frontier Foundation (EFF) in 1990 with John Perry Barlow, and EFF has become the most well-respected public interest organization on or about the Net. Kapor is much in demand as a consultant and public speaker regarding the law versus privacy issues that are now being defined. He was asked by President Clinton to sit as one of the members of the National Information Infrastructure Advisory Council so that his expertise might be available to the policymakers in Washington, D.C.

Kapor graduated from Yale in 1971 with a major in cybernetics. The Brooklyn native, born there in 1950, went on to do postgraduate work in management at the Sloan School of Management of the Massachusetts Institute of Technology (MIT). In 1995 he was named an adjunct professor, media arts and sciences, at MIT.

After graduating from Yale, Kapor became a software developer, achieving success on the Apple II platform, among other applications. His great success, however, came when he started the Lotus Development Corporation in 1982 to market and distribute his own application, called Lotus 1-2-3. With that integrated package as the core of the company, Lotus became the largest independent software developer of its time. Kapor later sold his interest in Lotus to found a new company called On Technology, a firm specializing in the production of groupware applications.

Though he has achieved considerable success as an information entrepreneur, Kapor has made valuable contributions to the understanding of information technologies. He is a regular speaker on policy panels, at congressional hearings, and in the mass media. His writings have appeared in *Wired* magazine, *Scientific American*, and *The Whole Earth Review*, among others. He seems to work tirelessly in the cause of maintaining individual rights for the denizens of cyberspace.

For more information about Kapor, log on to http:// www.kei.com/homepages/mkapor/.

Herbert Marshall McLuhan (1911–1980)

Marshall McLuhan was a Canadian writer and teacher whose work is being revived of late as a reference for these new times. Much of the research and publication from his Centre for Culture and Technology is being reexamined, and his writings are in demand again.

McLuhan was born in Edmonton, Alberta, Canada, on 21 July 1911 and died from complications of a stroke in 1980. He had been a respected professor of English literature at the University of Toronto until age 40, when he surprisingly began to publish a series of books about communication and mass media. No one before had analyzed the relationship between "content" (what was being transmitted), the "medium" (what was doing the transmitting), and the human nervous system (the receptor of the transmissions). His "medium is the message" became the bumper-sticker answer for many disaffected souls trying to cope with the sixties, but his work went well beyond this to place him at the center of an inquiry that has even more meaning today, when digital multimedia is poised to reinvent our institutions.

What seemed controversial in the 1960s now may just prove to be some sort of blueprint or mapping of the encroaching cyberspace. McLuhan wrote his first book on the subject, *The Mechanical Bride: Folklore of Industrial Man*, in 1952. *Understanding Media: The Extensions of Man, The Gutenberg Galaxy*, and *The Medium Is the Massage: An Inventory of Effects*, among others, followed and are highly recommended.

Gordon Moore (b. 1928)

Founder of Intel, Gordon Moore is the author of Moore's Law, the central assumption about computing power that governs much of the planning for future software and hardware capabilities in the industry. Moore's Law explains why there is no stability in the computing business, and why change is becoming the only constant in so many of our lives. In 1965 Moore wrote an article for *Electronics* magazine in which he predicted that the complexity of the silicon microchip would double every 18 months while the cost would drop proportionately. In practical terms, computing power has been increased by a factor of two at least every two years, and the cost of a typical PC has dropped steadily since it was introduced in the 1970s.

Moore has been one of the most instrumental of the computer entrepreneurs in the creation of that scenario, although he had no intention of going into business when he graduated with a Ph.D. from the California Institute of Technology in 1954. The quiet man had planned a life of teaching and research in academia. However, finding teaching positions scarce on the West Coast and a short stint doing weapons research at Johns Hopkins unsatisfactory, he decided to join the team at Shockley Semiconductor in 1956. William Shockley, the coinventor of the transistor, personally recruited Moore. Shockley proved to be a poor manager, however, and the company soon went under.

After starting Fairchild Semiconductor with fellow Shockley employee Robert Noyce and six others in 1957, Moore led the development of the first integrated circuit. This advance allowed many electrical functions to occur on a single chip. It was the beginning of what would become a $100 billion business, but not at Fairchild. Moore and Noyce were able to raise $2.5 million with their new partner, Arthur Rock, and they started their own company, Intel.

The first product Intel produced was a static memory chip, and the company gained a substantial advantage in the industry. By 1985 the rest of the world was catching up, and they moved to producing the brains of a computer, the microprocessor. Intel's 80286, 80386, 80486, and Pentium—the "Intel inside"—have become the standards of an industry that seems boundless.

Nicholas Negroponte (b. 1943)

Nicholas Negroponte is one of the chief speakers for the new time. He is a cheerleader of the digital domain. His column for *Wired* magazine is read for his analysis of new technologies, his take on legislation and events that might work to slow the process of change, and his insights into the future.

Negroponte was born in 1943. His first love was architecture, in which he received his initial career training, but love of science and the possibilities of what engineering might accomplish led him to the Massachusetts Institute of Technology. There he founded a unique institution in 1986 called the Media Laboratory with initial funding from publishers and the media industry elite. His vision was the development of a multimedia mix concocted from the wealth of information found in the best published works, the audiovisual experience of the entertainment sector, and the interactivity of digital computers.

A decade later, the Media Laboratory stands as an example of a type of commercial-academic research partnership that may prove to be a model for other disciplines as top scientists attempt to reinvent the world in the Third Wave. At any given moment, there may be scores of projects under way at the lab, directed by teachers and their elite students looking for processes that will help industry and individuals migrate out of Industrial Age thinking and expectations.

Negroponte embodies that vision. His *Being Digital* was a best-seller for months, and it is available in many languages. The book is one of the best starting points for anyone trying to make sense of these unstable but exciting times.

Howard Rheingold (b. 1947)

Howard Rheingold is one of the most important writers and reporters about the times in which we live. Rheingold is best known as the editor of *The Whole Earth Review*, a publication dedicated to finding the latest information about issues that include environmental restoration, community-building, whole systems thinking, and medical self-care. His last association with that magazine was as editor of *The Millennium Whole Earth Catalog*, which was published by HarperSanFrancisco in 1994. In that work some of the best tools of the past 25 years of the magazine were revisited, but Rheingold also made certain that readers had access to information and new tools that would help them succeed in the new world of cyberspace.

Rheingold was born in Tucson, Arizona, in 1947. He graduated from Reed College with a degree in psychology in 1968, the year of the first *Whole Earth Catalog*. His interests have always been piqued by the relationship between human thought and the intelligent machine, and what it means for the individual, community-building, and true democracy when that relationship becomes more intimate. He has studied this relationship in several books in which he tried to make the emerging technology understandable to a broader audience, including *Talking Tech: A Conversational Guide to Science and Technology* with Howard Levine (1982), *Higher Creativity* with Willis Harman (1984), and *Tools for Thought* (1985). In 1988 he experienced virtual reality with top scientists at the University of North Carolina for the first time, and his book *Virtual Reality* (1991) tries to make sense of what this new tool will mean for our society.

It was during Rheingold's work with the Whole Earth 'Lectronic Link, one of the most important electronic bulletin board conferencing systems, that the ideas of on-line communities started to come together. He reported on the interactions of that new type of neighborhood in *The Virtual Community* in 1993, and true to the promise of the type of relationship he sees occurring there, he has made the full text of the work available on-line.

Rheingold's syndicated column is called "Tomorrow." It is worth reading for his insight into the probable electronic future. More information about the author is available on his home page at http://www.well.com/user/hlr/.

Facts and Statistics

4

This chapter presents some empirical data in three different formats: charts and graphs, excerpts and reprints of selected text, and interesting quotations. The first section includes graphic representation of demographic information about the Internet, the World Wide Web, and digital communication in general. The second section includes reproductions of the work of important authors who are writing about the issues of cyberspace development. The documents include: (1) "Cyberspace and the American Dream: A Magna Carta for the Knowledge Age"; (2) "Cyberspace Inc. and the Robber Baron Age," an analysis of the above "Magna Carta"; (3) "Proposed Declaration of the Rights of Netizens"; (4) Executive Summary of the NIIAC final report to the president on the important issues relating to the development, deployment, and regulation of the National Information Infrastructure; (5) title page and table of contents from the 1996 Telecommunications Act; (6) an excerpt from the Communications Decency Act (the so-called Exxon Amendment), Title V—Obscenity and Violence, a section of the full Telecommunications Act; (7) John Perry Barlow's "A Cyberspace Independence Declaration"; and (8) excerpts from the legal opinion that struck down the

Communications Decency Act on 11 June 1996. The final section of this chapter is comprised of a wide array of quotations taken from both contemporary and historic sources. Its purpose is to illustrate the changing attitudes toward the Information Revolution.

Demographic Presentations

While it may be obvious that the Information Superhighway is just down the road in most of the industrialized world, Third World peoples may not even have access to a phone yet. The areas in black on the map on the following page (Figure 4.1) show where access to the Internet is available throughout the world as of 1994.

Hard statistics on the development of the Internet and what will become the Information Superhighway are very difficult to obtain. It is widely held that there are approximately 30 million users on the Net, but the modalities employed to create this estimate are suspect. Currently, several institutions are conducting surveys to attempt to quantify some aspects of the on-line population. Criticism about the techniques used by the A.C. Nielsen Company—a well-known television ratings group—were rampant when it attempted to measure the public's use of the Internet in 1995. A.C. Nielsen Company's most recent survey, done in 1996, seems to have been more widely accepted, but no one really knows for certain how many people surf the Net. It is an accepted fact, however, that the number is climbing at a tremendous pace.

The Georgia Tech Research Corporation is another institution that is attempting to quantify some aspects of the on-line population. Their well-respected World Wide Web Surveys have been conducted since 1994. They have agreed to the publication of some of their data on Web use that were obtained in the April 1996 Fifth World Wide Web Survey. A requirement for their participation in this book is the inclusion of the following information, which covers the data that were used to generate Figures 4.2 through 4.16:

> Copyright 1996 GTRC, all rights reserved, contact:www-survey@cc.gatech.edu. The complete report of this and subsequent surveys is available at http://www.cc.gatech/gvu/ user_surveys.

Figure 4.1 Internet Connectivity Map

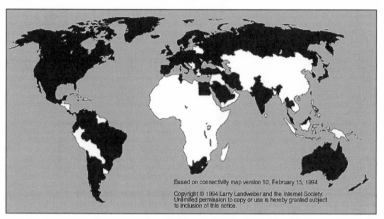

Note: Based on connectivity map version 10, 15 February 1994.

Source: Copyright © 1994 Larry Landweber and the Internet Society. Unlimited permission to copy or use is hereby granted subject to inclusion of the notice.

The Graphics, Visualization & Usability (GVU) Center at Georgia Tech has noted that some interesting trends are beginning to emerge over the course of the two years of their research.

GVU researchers note that the 31.5 percent of the WWW users are female and the other 68.5 percent are male. This is a small increase in the number of females using the Web, with the United States leading the way in this trend. Younger women in particular are more likely to be on-line. See Figure 4.2.

Figure 4.3 indicates the average age of all the Web users that responded to the Fifth Georgia Tech Survey is 33 years old, which is an increase in age from the last survey conducted in 1995. Other results confirmed that the U.S. users are older than Europeans who access the Web.

Figure 4.4 indicates that educational occupations account for 29.6 percent of Web users, with computer-related occupations running a close second at 27.8 percent. This is a change from previous results that showed that respondents were from computer-related occupations.

The next two graphs (Figures 4.5 and 4.6) display the responses from participants indicating their feelings about being connected to other individuals who might share their views

Figure 4.2 Gender of WWW Users by Location

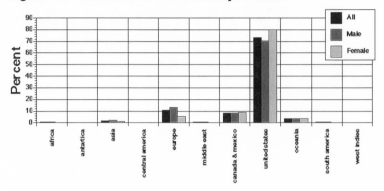

Figure 4.3 Age Distribution of WWW Users

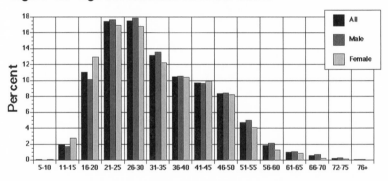

Figure 4.4 Occupation of WWW Users by Gender

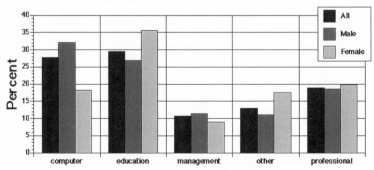

Figure 4.5 Level of Connectivity by Age

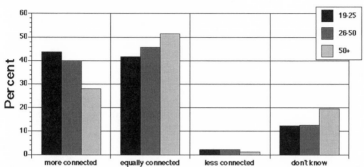

Figure 4.6 Level of Connectivity by Gender

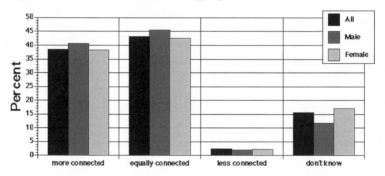

about important issues since they went on-line. Overall, 38.6 percent reported feeling more connected to people who share similar views.

The following three graphs (Figures 4.7, 4.8, and 4.9) show the results of respondents' answers to the question of whether their involvement with political issues has changed since going on-line. Nearly half—40.3 percent of the respondents—reported that they are more involved. Europeans report being even more involved than those in the United States.

The next four graphs (Figures 4.10, 4.11, 4.12, and 4.13) show how the political activity is manifested on-line. Over 52.2 percent of the users report engaging in some "other" on-line political activity that does not fall into any of the defined categories. Of

Figure 4.7 Level of Issues Involvement On-Line by Age

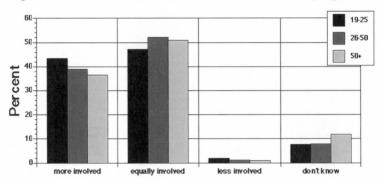

Figure 4.8 Level of Issues Involvement On-Line by Gender

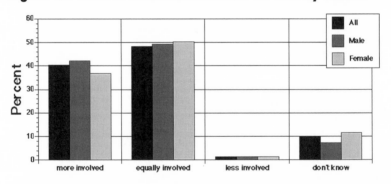

Figure 4.9 Level of Issues Involvement On-Line by Location

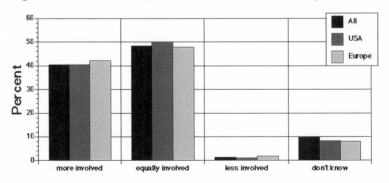

Figure 4.10 Type of On-Line Political Activity by Age

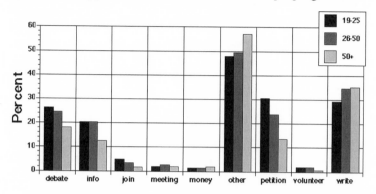

Figure 4.11 Type of On-Line Political Activity by Gender

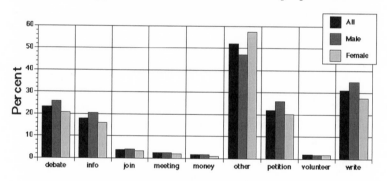

Figure 4.12 Type of On-Line Political Activity by Location

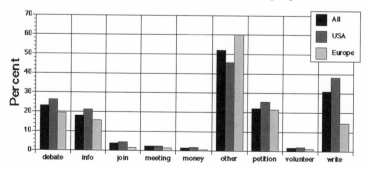

Figure 4.13 WWW Users' Political Affiliation by Location

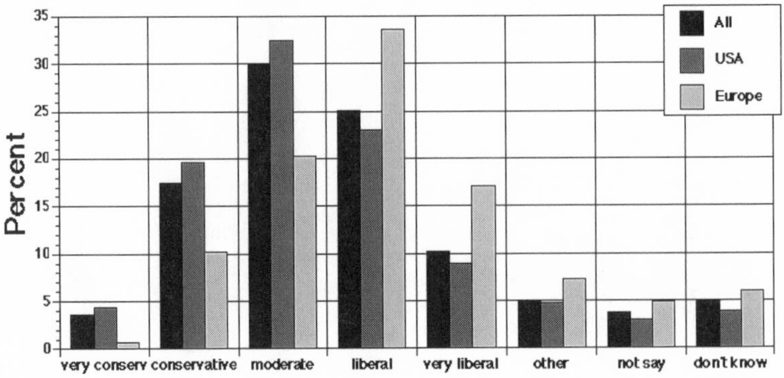

those others they could choose, the most popular were "writing a government official," "discussing political issues," and "signing petitions."

The survey notes that the largest category of respondents considered themselves moderate in their political views (30.1 percent), 21.1 percent considered themselves to be conservative or very conservative, while 35.18 percent were liberal or very liberal. In Europe, the curve peaked at liberal (33.6 percent). The GVU researchers caution that the terms *liberal* and *conservative* may have different definitions in different cultures.

The survey respondents were allowed to choose more than one category to describe where they get their news and political information: either from on-line or more traditional sources such as local newspapers (62.6 percent), network television news (58.2 percent), on-line news (52.7 percent), and news television channels, such as CNN, C-Span, etc. (51.4 percent), were the most popular across age groups (see Figure 4.14). In other findings, females reported a higher use of local newspapers, network television news, and off-line discussions as their source for news and political information. Males report more use of national newspapers and electronic news. (Note that in Figure 4.14 offline d and on-line d refer to discussion groups.)

Figures 4.15 and 4.16 show the habits of the respondents in regard to their use of the Web as a replacement for time they would normally be watching television. One highlight, note the GVU researchers, is that almost 36 percent of respondents claim that they use the Web instead of watching television on a daily basis. Females are less likely than males to use the Web instead

Figure 4.14 FT Source of News by Age

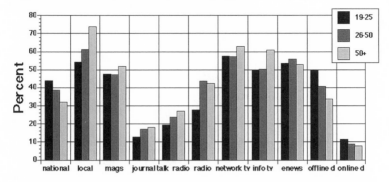

Figure 4.15 Use of WWW versus Television by Age

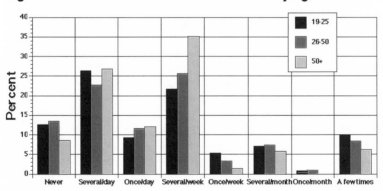

Figure 4.16 Use of WWW versus Television by Gender

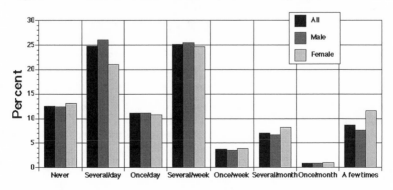

Figure 4.17 Student Use of Computers in Schools (1989 and 1993)

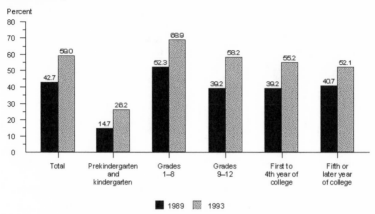

Percent

■ 1989 ▨ 1993

Source: U.S Department of Commerce, Bureau of Census, Current Population Survey, October 1989 and 1993

of television several times a day, but they are nearly equal in all other categories. Related results show that Europeans are far less likely to use the Web instead of television.

The final graph (Figure 4.17) was compiled from data gathered by the United States Census Bureau that shows the trend for computer use in schools over the recent past. One of the most important issues that experts name regarding equity of access and training has to do with educational uses of computers. It is also an important issue as the FCC meets to define "universal access" and "discounted connections" for education.

Documents

According to the Progress & Freedom Foundation, the organization that commissioned the following work, "This statement represents the cumulative wisdom and innovation of many dozens of people. It is based primarily on the thoughts of four 'coauthors': Ms. Esther Dyson; Mr. George Gilder; Dr. George Keyworth; and Dr. Alvin Toffler. This release 1.2 has the final 'imprimatur' of no one. In the spirit of the age: It is copyrighted solely for the purpose of preventing someone else from doing so. If you have it, you can use it any way you want."

Cyberspace and the American Dream: A Magna Carta for the Knowledge Age, Release 1.2, 22 August 1994

The Progress & Freedom Foundation is a not-for-profit research and educational organization dedicated to creating a positive vision of the future founded in the historic principles of the American idea.

PREAMBLE

The central event of the Twentieth century is the overthrow of matter. In technology, economics, and the politics of nations, wealth—in the form of physical resources—has been losing value and significance. The powers of mind are everywhere ascendant over the brute force of things.

In a First Wave economy, land and farm labor are the main "factors of production." In a Second Wave economy, the land remains valuable while the "labor" becomes massified around machines and larger industries. In a Third Wave economy, the central resource—a single word broadly encompassing data, information, images, symbols, culture, ideology, and values—is actionable knowledge.

The industrial age is not fully over. In fact, classic Second Wave sectors (oil, steel, auto-production) have learned how to benefit from Third Wave technological breakthroughs—just as the First Wave's agricultural productivity benefited exponentially from the Second Wave's farm-mechanization.

But the Third Wave, and the Knowledge Age it has opened, will not deliver on its potential unless it adds social and political dominance to its accelerating technological and economic strength. This means repealing Second Wave laws and retiring Second Wave attitudes. It also gives to leaders of the advanced democracies a special responsibility— to facilitate, hasten, and explain the transition.

As humankind explores this new "electronic frontier" of knowledge, it must confront again the most profound questions of how to organize itself for the common good. The meaning of freedom, structures of self-government, definition of property, nature of competition, conditions for cooperation, sense of community and nature of progress will each be redefined for the Knowledge Age—just as they were redefined for a new age of industry some 250 years ago.

What our Twentieth-century countrymen came to think of as the "American dream," and what resonant thinkers referred to as "the promise of American life" or "the American Idea," emerged from the turmoil of Nineteenth-century industrialization. Now it's our turn: The knowledge revolution, and the Third Wave of historical change it powers, summon us to renew the dream and enhance the promise.

THE NATURE OF CYBERSPACE

The Internet—the huge (2.2 million computers), global (135 countries), rapidly growing (10–15% a month) network that has captured the American imagination—is only a tiny part of cyberspace. So just what is cyberspace?

More ecosystem than machine, cyberspace is a bioelectronic environment that is literally universal: It exists everywhere there are telephone wires, coaxial cables, fiber-optic lines or electromagnetic waves.

This environment is "inhabited" by knowledge, including incorrect ideas, existing in electronic form. It is connected to the physical environment by portals which allow people to see what's inside, to put knowledge in, to alter it, and to take knowledge out. Some of these portals are one-way (e.g. television receivers and television transmitters); others are two-way (e.g. telephones, computer modems).

Most of the knowledge in cyberspace lives the most temporary (or so we think) existence: Your voice, on a telephone wire or microwave, travels through space at the speed of light, reaches the ear of your listener, and is gone forever.

But people are increasingly building cyberspatial "warehouses" of data, knowledge, information and misinformation in digital form, the ones and zeros of binary computer code. The storehouses themselves display a physical form (discs, tapes, CD-ROMs)—but what they contain is accessible only to those with the right kind of portal and the right kind of key.

The key is software, a special form of electronic knowledge that allows people to navigate through the cyberspace environment and make its contents understandable to the human senses in the form of written language, pictures and sound.

People are adding to cyberspace—creating it, defining it, expanding it—at a rate that is already explosive and getting faster. Faster computers, cheaper means of electronic storage, improved software and more capable communication channels (satellites, fiber-optic lines)—each of these factors independently add to cyberspace. But the real explosion comes from the combination of all of them, working together in ways we still do not understand.

The bioelectronic frontier is an appropriate metaphor for what is happening in cyberspace, calling to mind as it does the spirit of invention and discovery that led ancient mariners to explore the world, generations of pioneers to tame the American continent and, more recently, to man's first exploration of outer space.

But the exploration of cyberspace brings both greater opportunity, and in some ways more difficult challenges, than any previous human adventure.

Cyberspace is the land of knowledge, and the exploration of that land can be a civilization's truest, highest calling. The opportunity is now before us to empower every person to pursue that calling in his or her own way.

The challenge is as daunting as the opportunity is great. The Third Wave has profound implications for the nature and meaning of property, of the marketplace, of community and of individual freedom. As it emerges, it shapes new codes of behavior that move each organism and institution—family, neighborhood, church group, company, government, nation—inexorably beyond standardization and centralization, as well as beyond the materialist's obsession with energy, money and control.

Turning the economics of mass-production inside out, new information technologies are driving the financial costs of diversity—both product and personal—down toward zero, "demassifying" our institutions and our culture. Accelerating demassification creates the potential for vastly increased human freedom.

It also spells the death of the central institutional paradigm of modern life, the bureaucratic organization. (Governments, including the American government, are the last great redoubt of bureaucratic power on the face of the planet, and for them the coming change will be profound and probably traumatic.)

In this context, the one metaphor that is perhaps least helpful in thinking about cyberspace is—unhappily—the one that has gained the most currency: The Information Superhighway. Can you imagine a phrase less descriptive of the nature of cyberspace, or more misleading in thinking about its implications? Consider the following set of polarities:

Information Superhighway	/	Cyberspace
Limited Matter	/	Unlimited Knowledge
Centralized	/	Decentralized
Moving on a grid	/	Moving in space
Government ownership	/	A vast array of ownerships
Bureaucracy	/	Empowerment
Efficient but not hospitable	/	Hospitable if you customize it
Withstand the elements	/	Flow, float and fine-tune
Unions and contractors	/	Associations and volunteers
Liberation from First Wave	/	Liberation from Second Wave
Culmination of Second Wave	/	Riding the Third Wave

"The highway analogy is all wrong," explained Peter Huber in *Forbes* this spring, "for reasons rooted in basic economics. Solid things obey immutable laws of conservation—what goes south on the highway must go back north, or you end up with a mountain of cars in Miami. By the same token, production and consumption must balance. The average Joe can consume only as much wheat as the average Jane can grow. Information is completely different. It can be replicated at almost no cost—so every individual can (in theory) consume society's entire output. Rich and poor alike, we all run information deficits. We all take in more than we put out."

THE NATURE AND OWNERSHIP OF PROPERTY

Clear and enforceable property rights are essential for markets to work. Defining them is a central function of government. Most of us have "known" that for a long time. But to create the new cyberspace environment is to create new property—that is, new means of creating goods (including ideas) that serve people.

The property that makes up cyberspace comes in several forms: Wires, coaxial cable, computers and other "hardware"; the electromagnetic spectrum; and "intellectual property"—the knowledge that dwells in and defines cyberspace.

In each of these areas, two questions must be answered. First, what does "ownership" mean? What is the nature of the property itself, and what does it mean to own it? Second, once we understand what ownership means, who is the owner? At the level of first principles, should ownership be public (i.e. government) or private (i.e. individuals)?

The answers to these two questions will set the basic terms upon which America and the world will enter the Third Wave. For the most part, however, these questions are not yet even being asked. Instead, at least in America, governments are attempting to take Second Wave concepts of property and ownership and apply them to the Third Wave. Or they are ignoring the problem altogether.

For example, a great deal of attention has been focused recently on the nature of "intellectual property"—i.e. the fact that knowledge is what economists call a "public good," and thus requires special treatment in the form of copyright and patent protection.

Major changes in U.S. copyright and patent law during the past two decades have broadened these protections to incorporate "electronic property." In essence, these reforms have attempted to take a body of law that originated in the Fifteenth century, with Gutenberg's invention of the printing press, and apply it to the electronically stored and transmitted knowledge of the Third Wave.

A more sophisticated approach starts with recognizing how the Third Wave has fundamentally altered the nature of knowledge as a "good," and that the operative effect is not technology per se (the shift from printed books to electronic storage and retrieval systems), but rather the shift from a mass-production, mass-media, mass-culture civilization to a demassified civilization.

The big change, in other words, is the demassification of actionable knowledge.

The dominant form of new knowledge in the Third Wave is perishable, transient, customized knowledge: The right information, combined with the right software and presentation, at precisely the right time. Unlike the mass knowledge of the Second Wave—"public good" knowledge that was useful to everyone because most people's information needs were standardized—Third Wave customized knowledge is by nature a private good.

If this analysis is correct, copyright and patent protection of knowledge (or at least many forms of it) may no longer be unnecessary. In fact, the marketplace may already be creating vehicles to compensate creators of customized knowledge outside the cumbersome copyright/patent process, as suggested last year by John Perry Barlow:

> "One existing model for the future conveyance of intellectual property is real-time performance, a medium currently used only in theater, music, lectures, stand-up comedy and pedagogy. I believe the concept of performance will expand to include most of the information economy, from multicasted soap operas to stock analysis. In these instances, commercial exchange will be more like ticket sales to a continuous show than the purchase of discrete bundles of that which is being shown. The other model, of course, is service. The entire professional class—doctors, lawyers, consultants, architects, etc.—are already being paid directly for their intellectual property. Who needs copyright when you're on a retainer?"

Copyright, patent and intellectual property represent only a few of the "rights" issues now at hand. Here are some of the others:

- Ownership of the electromagnetic spectrum, traditionally considered to be "public property," is now being "auctioned" by the Federal Communications Commission to private companies. Or is it? Is the very limited "bundle of rights" sold in those auctions really property, or more in the nature of a use permit—the right to use a part of the spectrum for a limited time, for limited purposes? In either case, are the rights being auctioned defined in a way that makes technological sense?
- Ownership over the infrastructure of wires, coaxial cable and fiber-optic lines that are such prominent features in the geography of cyberspace is today much less clear than might be imagined. Regulation, especially price regulation, of this property can be tantamount to confiscation, as America's cable operators recently learned when the Federal government imposed price limits on them and effectively confiscated an estimated $___ billion of their net worth. (Whatever one's stance on the FCC's decision and the law behind it, there is no disagreeing with the proposition that one's ownership of a good is less meaningful when the government can step in, at will, and dramatically reduce its value.)
- The nature of capital in the Third Wave—tangible capital as well as intangible—is to depreciate in real value much faster than industrial-age capital—driven, if nothing else, by Moore's Law, which states that the processing power of the microchip doubles at least every eighteen months. Yet accounting and tax regulations still require property to be depreciated over periods as

long as thirty years. The result is a heavy bias in favor of "heavy industry" and against nimble, fast-moving baby businesses.
- Who will define the nature of cyberspace property rights, and how? How can we strike a balance between interoperable open systems and protection of property?

THE NATURE OF THE MARKETPLACE

Inexpensive knowledge destroys economies-of-scale. Customized knowledge permits "just in time" production for an ever rising number of goods. Technological progress creates new means of serving old markets, turning one-time monopolies into competitive battlegrounds.

- These phenomena are altering the nature of the marketplace, not just for information technology but for all goods and materials, shipping and services. In cyberspace itself, market after market is being transformed by technological progress from a "natural monopoly" to one in which competition is the rule. Three recent examples:
- The market for "mail" has been made competitive by the development of fax machines and overnight delivery—even though the "private express statutes" that technically grant the U.S. Postal Service a monopoly over mail delivery remain in place.
- During the past 20 years, the market for television has been transformed from one in which there were at most a few broadcast TV stations to one in which consumers can choose among broadcast, cable and satellite services.
- The market for local telephone services, until recently a monopoly based on twisted-pair copper cables, is rapidly being made competitive by the advent of wireless service and the entry of cable television into voice communication. In England, Mexico, New Zealand and a host of developing countries, government restrictions preventing such competition have already been removed and consumers actually have the freedom to choose.

The advent of new technology and new products creates the potential for dynamic competition—competition between and among technologies and industries, each seeking to find the best way of serving customers' needs. Dynamic competition is different from static competition, in which many providers compete to sell essentially similar products at the lowest price.

Static competition is good, because it forces costs and prices to the lowest levels possible for a given product. Dynamic competition is better, because it allows competing technologies and new products to challenge the old ones and, if they really are better, to replace them. Static competition might lead to faster and stronger horses. Dynamic competition gives us the automobile.

Such dynamic competition—the essence of what Austrian economist Joseph Schumpeter called "creative destruction"—creates winners and losers on a massive scale. New technologies can render instantly obsolete billions of dollars of embedded infrastructure, accumulated over decades. The transformation of the U.S. computer industry since 1980 is a case in point.

In 1980, everyone knew who led in computer technology. Apart from the minicomputer boom, mainframe computers were the market, and America's dominance was largely based upon the position of a dominant vendor—IBM, with over 50% world market-share.

Then the personal-computing industry exploded, leaving older-style big-business-focused computing with a stagnant piece of a burgeoning total market. As IBM lost market-share, many people became convinced that America had lost the ability to compete. By the mid-1980s, such alarmism had reached from Washington all the way into the heart of Silicon Valley.

But the real story was the renaissance of American business and technological leadership. In the transition from mainframes to PCs, a vast new market was created. This market was characterized by dynamic competition consisting of easy access and low barriers to entry. Start-ups by the dozens took on the larger established companies—and won.

After a decade of angst, the surprising outcome is that America is not only competitive internationally, but, by any measurable standard, America dominates the growth sectors in world economics—telecommunications, microelectronics, computer networking (or "connected computing") and software systems and applications.

The reason for America's victory in the computer wars of the 1980s is that dynamic competition was allowed to occur, in an area so breakneck and pell-mell that government would've had a hard time controlling it even had it been paying attention. The challenge for policy in the 1990s is to permit, even encourage, dynamic competition in every aspect of the cyberspace marketplace.

THE NATURE OF FREEDOM

Overseas friends of America sometimes point out that the U.S. Constitution is unique—because it states explicitly that power resides with the people, who delegate it to the government, rather than the other way around.

This idea—central to our free society—was the result of more than 150 years of intellectual and political ferment, from the Mayflower Compact to the U.S. Constitution, as explorers struggled to establish the terms under which they would tame a new frontier.

And as America continued to explore new frontiers—from the Northwest Territory to the Oklahoma land-rush—it consistently returned to this fundamental principle of rights, reaffirming, time after time, that power resides with the people.

Cyberspace is the latest American frontier. As this and other societies make ever deeper forays into it, the proposition that ownership of this frontier resides first with the people is central to achieving its true potential.

To some people, that statement will seem melodramatic. America, after all, remains a land of individual freedom, and this freedom clearly extends to cyberspace. How else to explain the uniquely American phenomenon of the hacker, who ignored every social pressure and violated every rule to develop a set of skills through an early and intense exposure to low-cost, ubiquitous computing.

Those skills eventually made him or her highly marketable, whether in developing applications-software or implementing networks. The hacker became a technician, an inventor and, in case after case, a creator of new wealth in the form of the baby businesses that have given America the lead in cyberspatial exploration and settlement.

It is hard to imagine hackers surviving, let alone thriving, in the more formalized and regulated democracies of Europe and Japan. In America, they've become vital for economic growth and trade leadership. Why? Because Americans still celebrate individuality over conformity, reward achievement over consensus and militantly protect the right to be different.

But the need to affirm the basic principles of freedom is real. Such an affirmation is needed in part because we are entering new territory, where there are as yet no rules—just as there were no rules on the American continent in 1620, or in the Northwest Territory in 1787.

Centuries later, an affirmation of freedom—by this document and similar efforts—is needed for a second reason: We are at the end of a century dominated by the mass institutions of the industrial age. The industrial age encouraged conformity and relied on standardization. And the institutions of the day—corporate and government bureaucracies, huge civilian and military administrations, schools of all types— reflected these priorities. Individual liberty suffered—sometimes only a little, sometimes a lot:

- In a Second Wave world, it might make sense for government to insist on the right to peer into every computer by requiring that each contain a special "clipper chip."
- In a Second Wave world, it might make sense for government to assume ownership over the broadcast spectrum and demand massive payments from citizens for the right to use it.
- In a Second Wave world, it might make sense for government to prohibit entrepreneurs from entering new markets and providing new services.
- And, in a Second Wave world, dominated by a few old-fashioned, one-way media "networks," it might even make sense for government to influence which political viewpoints would be carried over the airwaves.

All of these interventions might have made sense in a Second Wave world, where standardization dominated and where it was assumed that the scarcity of knowledge (plus a scarcity of telecommunications capacity) made bureaucracies and other elites better able to make decisions than the average person.

But, whether they made sense before or not, these and literally thousands of other infringements on individual rights now taken for granted make no sense at all in the Third Wave.

For a century, those who lean ideologically in favor of freedom have found themselves at war not only with their ideological opponents, but with a time in history when the value of conformity was at its peak. However desirable as an ideal, individual freedom often seemed impractical. The mass institutions of the Second Wave required us to give up freedom in order for the system to "work."

The coming of the Third Wave turns that equation inside-out. The complexity of Third Wave society is too great for any centrally planned bureaucracy to manage. Demassification, customization, individuality, freedom—these are the keys to success for Third Wave civilization.

THE ESSENCE OF COMMUNITY

If the transition to the Third Wave is so positive, why are we experiencing so much anxiety? Why are the statistics of social decay at or near all-time highs? Why does cyberspatial "rapture" strike millions of prosperous Westerners as lifestyle rupture? Why do the principles that have held us together as a nation seem no longer sufficient—or even wrong?

The incoherence of political life is mirrored in disintegrating personalities. Whether 100% covered by health plans or not, psychotherapists and gurus do a land-office business, as people wander aimlessly amid competing therapies. People slip into cults and covens or, alternatively, into a pathological privatism, convinced that reality is absurd, insane or meaningless. "If things are so good," *Forbes* magazine asked recently, "why do we feel so bad?"

In part, this is why: Because we constitute the final generation of an old civilization and, at the very same time, the first generation of a new one. Much of our personal confusion and social disorientation is traceable to conflict within us and within our political institutions—between the dying Second Wave civilization and the emergent Third Wave civilization thundering in to take its place.

Second Wave ideologues routinely lament the breakup of mass society. Rather than seeing this enriched diversity as an opportunity for human development, they attach it as "fragmentation" and "balkanization." But to reconstitute democracy in Third Wave terms, we need to jettison the frightening but false assumption that more diversity automatically brings more tension and conflict in society.

Indeed, the exact reverse can be true: If 100 people all desperately want the same brass ring, they may be forced to fight for it. On the other hand, if each of the 100 has a different objective, it is far more rewarding for them to trade, cooperate, and form symbiotic relationships. Given appropriate social arrangements, diversity can make for a secure and stable civilization.

No one knows what the Third Wave communities of the future will look like, or where "demassification" will ultimately lead. It is clear, however, that cyberspace will play an important role knitting together in the diverse communities of tomorrow, facilitating the creation of "electronic neighborhoods" bound together not by geography but by shared interests.

Socially, putting advanced computing power in the hands of entire populations will alleviate pressure on highways, reduce air pollution, allow people to live further away from crowded or dangerous urban areas, and expand family time.

The late Phil Salin (in Release 1.0 11/25/91) offered this perspective: "[B]y 2000, multiple cyberspaces will have emerged, diverse and increasingly rich. Contrary to naive views, these cyberspaces will not all be the same, and they will not all be open to the general public. The global network is a connected 'platform' for a collection of diverse communities, but only a loose, heterogeneous community itself. Just as access to homes, offices, churches and department stores is controlled by their owners or managers, most virtual locations will exist as distinct places of private property."

"But unlike the private property of today," Salin continued, "the potential variations on design and prevailing customs will explode, because many variations can be implemented cheaply in software. And the 'externalities' associated with variations can drop; what happens in one cyberspace can be kept from affecting other cyberspaces."

"Cyberspaces" is a wonderful pluralistic word to open more minds to the Third Wave's civilizing potential. Rather than being a centrifugal force helping to tear society apart, cyberspace can be one of the main forms of glue holding together an increasingly free and diverse society.

THE ROLE OF GOVERNMENT

The current Administration has identified the right goal: Reinventing government for the Twenty-first century. To accomplish that goal is another matter, and for reasons explained in the next and final section, it is not likely to be fully accomplished in the immediate future. This said, it is essential that we understand what it really means to create a Third Wave government and begin the process of transformation.

Eventually, the Third Wave will affect virtually everything government does. The most pressing need, however, is to revamp the policies and programs that are slowing the creation of cyberspace. Second Wave programs for Second Wave industries—the status quo for the status quo—will do little damage in the short run. It is the government's efforts to apply its Second Wave modus operandi to the fast-moving, decentralized creatures of the Third Wave that is the real threat to progress. Indeed, if there is to be an "industrial policy for the knowledge age," it should focus on removing barriers to competition and massively deregulating the fast-growing telecommunications and computing industries.

One further point should be made at the outset: Government should be as strong and as big as it needs to be to accomplish its central functions effectively and efficiently. The reality is that a Third Wave government will be vastly smaller (perhaps by 50% or more) than the current one—this is an inevitable implication of the transition from the centralized power structures of the industrial age to the dispersed, decentralized institutions of the Third. But smaller government does not imply weak government; nor does arguing for smaller government require being "against" government for narrowly ideological reasons.

Indeed, the transition from the Second Wave to the Third Wave will require a level of government activity not seen since the New Deal. Here are five proposals to back up the point.

1. **The Path to Interactive Multimedia Access**

    The "Jeffersonian Vision" offered by Mitch Kapor and Jerry Berman has propelled the Electronic Frontier Foundation's campaign for an "open platform" telecom architecture:

    > "The amount of electronic material the superhighway can carry is dizzying, compared to the relatively narrow range of broadcast TV and the limited number of cable channels. Properly constructed and regulated, it could be open to all who wish to speak, publish and communicate. None of the interactive services will be possible, however, if we have an eight-lane data superhighway rushing into every home and only a narrow footpath coming back out. Instead of settling for a multimedia version of the same entertainment that is increasingly dissatisfying on today's TV, we need a superhighway that encourages the production and distribution of a broader, more diverse range of programming" (*New York Times* 11/24/93, p. A25).

    The question is: What role should government play in bringing this vision to reality? But also: Will incentives for the openly-accessible, "many to many," national multimedia network envisioned by EFF harm the rights of those now constructing thousands of nonopen local-area networks?

    These days, interactive multimedia is the daily servant only of avant-garde firms and other elites. But the same thing could have been said about word-processors twelve years ago, or phone-line networks six years ago. Today we have, in effect, universal access to personal computing—which no political coalition ever subsidized or "planned." And America's networking menu is in a hyper-growth phase. Whereas the accessing software cost $50 two years ago, today the same companies hand it out free—to get more people on-line.

This egalitarian explosion has occurred in large measure because government has stayed out of these markets, letting personal computing take over while mainframes rot (almost literally) in warehouses, and allowing (no doubt more by omission than commission) computer networks to grow, free of the kinds of regulatory restraints that affect phones, broadcast and cable.

All of which leaves reducing barriers to entry and innovation as the only effective near-term path to Universal Access. In fact, it can be argued that a near-term national interactive multimedia network is impossible unless regulators permit much greater collaboration between the cable industry and phone companies. The latter's huge fiber resources (nine times as extensive as industry fiber and rising rapidly) could be joined with the huge asset of 57 million broadband links (i.e. into homes now receiving cable-TV service) to produce a new kind of national network—multimedia, interactive and (as costs fall) increasingly accessible to Americans of modest means.

That is why obstructing such collaboration—in the cause of forcing a competition between the cable and phone industries—is socially elitist. To the extent it prevents collaboration between the cable industry and the phone companies, present federal policy actually thwarts the Administration's own goals of access and empowerment.

The other major effect of prohibiting the "manifest destiny" of cable preserves the broadcast (or narrowband) television model. In fact, stopping an interactive multimedia network perpetuates John Malone's original formula—which everybody (especially Vice President Gore and the FCC) claims to oppose because of the control it leaves with system owners and operators.

The key condition for replacing Malone's original narrowband model is true bandwidth abundance. When the federal government prohibits the interconnection of conduits, the model gains a new lease on life. In a world of bandwidth scarcity, the owner of the conduit not only can but must control access to it—thus the owner of the conduit also shapes the content. It really doesn't matter who the owner is. Bandwidth scarcity will require the managers of the network to determine the video programming on it.

Since cable is everywhere, particularly within cities, it would allow a closing of the gap between the knowledge-rich and knowledge-poor. Cable's broadband "pipes" already touch almost two-thirds of American households (and are easily accessible to another one-fourth). The phone companies have broadband fiber. A hybrid network—co-ax plus fiber—is the best means to the next generation of cyberspace expansion. What if this choice is blocked?

In that case, what might be called cyberspace democracy will be confined to the computer industry, where it will arise from the Internet over the years, led by corporate and suburban/exurban interests. While not a technological calamity, this might be a social perversion equivalent to what "Japan Inc." did to its middle and lower classes for decades: Make them pay 50% more for the same quality vehicles that were gobbling up export markets.

Here's the parallel: If Washington forces the phone companies and cable operators to develop supplementary and duplicative networks, most other advanced industrial countries will attain cyberspace democracy—via an interactive multimedia "open platform"—before America does, despite this nation's technological dominance.

Not only that, but the long-time alliance of East Coast broadcasters and Hollywood glitterati will have a new lease on life: If their one-way video empires win new protection, millions of Americans will be deprived of the tools to help build a new interactive multimedia culture.

A contrived competition between phone companies and cable operators will not deliver the two-way, multimedia and more civilized tele-society Kapor and Berman sketch. Nor is it enough to simply "get the government out of the way." Real issues of antitrust must be addressed, and no sensible framework exists today for addressing them. Creating the conditions for universal access to interactive multimedia will require a fundamental rethinking of government policy.

2. Promoting Dynamic Competition

Technological progress is turning the telecommunications marketplace from one characterized by "economies of scale" and "natural monopolies" into a prototypical competitive market. The challenge for government is to encourage this shift—to create the circumstances under which new competitors and new technologies will challenge the natural monopolies of the past.

Price-and-entry regulation makes sense for natural monopolies. The tradeoff is a straightforward one: The monopolist submits to price regulation by the state, in return for an exclusive franchise on the market.

But what happens when it becomes economically desirable to have more than one provider in a market? The continuation of regulation under these circumstances stops progress in its tracks. It prevents new entrants from introducing new technologies and new products, while depriving the regulated monopolist of any incentive to do so on its own.

Price-and-entry regulation, in short, is the antithesis of dynamic competition.

The alternative to regulation is antitrust. Antitrust law is designed to prevent the acts and practices that can lead to the creation of new monopolies, or harm consumers by forcing up prices, limiting access to competing products or reducing service quality. Antitrust law is the means by which America has, for over 120 years, fostered competition in markets where many providers can and should compete.

The market for telecommunications services—telephone, cable, satellite, wireless—is now such a market. The implication of this simple fact is also simple, and price/entry regulation of telecommunications services—by state and local governments as well as the Federal government—should therefore be replaced by antitrust law as rapidly as possible.

This transition will not be simple, and it should not be instantaneous. If antitrust is to be seriously applied to telecommunications, some government agencies (e.g. the Justice Department's Antitrust Division) will need new types of expertise. And investors in regulated monopolies should be permitted time to re-evaluate their investments given the changing nature of the legal conditions in which these firms will operate—a luxury not afforded the cable industry in recent years.

This said, two additional points are important. First, delaying implementation is different from delaying enactment. The latter should be immediate, even if the former is not. Secondly, there should be no half steps. Moving from a regulated environment to a competitive one is—to borrow a cliché—like changing from driving on the left side of the road to driving on the right: You can't do it gradually.

3. **Defining and Assigning Property Rights**

In 1964, libertarian icon Ayn Rand wrote:

> "It is the proper task of government to protect individual rights and, as part of it, formulate the laws by which these rights are to be implemented and adjudicated. It is the government's responsibility to define the application of individual rights to a given sphere of activity—to define (i.e. to identify), not create, invent, donate, or expropriate. The question of defining the application of property rights has arisen frequently, in the wake of oil rights, vertical space rights, etc. In most cases, the American government has been guided by the proper principle: It sought to protect all the individual rights involved, not to abrogate them" ("The Property Status of the Airwaves," Objectivist Newsletter, April 1964).

Defining property rights in cyberspace is perhaps the single most urgent and important task for government information policy. Doing so will be a complex task, and each key area—the electromagnetic spectrum, intellectual property, cyberspace itself (including the right to privacy)—involves unique challenges. The important points here are:

First, this is a "central" task of government. A Third Wave government will understand the importance and urgency of this undertaking and begin seriously to address it; to fail to do so is to perpetuate the politics and policy of the Second Wave.

Secondly, the key principle of ownership by the people—private ownership—should govern every deliberation. Government does not own cyberspace, the people do.

Thirdly, clarity is essential. Ambiguous property rights are an invitation to litigation, channeling energy into courtrooms that serve no customers and create no wealth. From patent and copyright systems for software, to challenges over the ownership and use of spectrum, the present system is failing in this simple regard.

The difference between America's historic economic success can, in case after case, be traced to our wisdom in creating and allocating clear, enforceable property rights. The creation and exploration of cyberspace requires that wisdom to be recalled and reaffirmed.

4. **Creating Pro-Third-Wave Tax and Accounting Rules**

We need a whole set of new ways of accounting, both at the level of the enterprise, and of the economy.

"GDP" and other popular numbers do nothing to clarify the magic and muscle of information technology. The government has not been very good at measuring service-sector output, and almost all institutions are incredibly bad at measuring the productivity of information. Economists are stuck with a set of tools designed during, or as a result of, the 1930s. So they have been measuring less and less important variables with greater and greater precision.

At the level of the enterprise, obsolete accounting procedures cause us to systematically overvalue physical assets (i.e. property) and undervalue human-resource assets and intellectual assets. So, if you are an inspired young entrepreneur looking to start a software company, or a service company of some kind, and it is heavily information-intensive, you will have a harder time raising capital than the guy next door who wants to put in a set of beat-up old machines to participate in a topped-out industry.

On the tax side, the same thing is true. The tax code always reflects the varying lobbying pressures brought to bear on government. And the existing tax code was brought into being by traditional manufacturing enterprises and the allied forces that arose during the assembly line's heyday.

The computer industry correctly complains that half their product is depreciated in six months or less—yet they can't depreciate it for tax purposes. The U.S. semiconductor industry faces five-year depreciation timetables for products that have three-year lives (in contrast to Japan, where chipmakers can write off their fabrication plants in one year). Overall, the tax advantage remains with the long, rather than the short, product life-cycle, even though the latter is where all design and manufacturing are trending.

It is vital that accounting and tax policies—both those promulgated by private-sector regulators like the Financial Accounting Standards Board and those promulgated by the government at the IRS and elsewhere—start to reflect the shortened capital life-cycles of the Knowledge Age, and the increasing role of intangible capital as "wealth."

5. **Creating a Third Wave Government**

Going beyond cyberspace policy per se, government must remake itself and redefine its relationship to the society at large. No single set of policy changes can create a future-friendly government. But there are some yardsticks we can apply to policy proposals. Among them:

- Is it based on the factory model, i.e. on standardization, routine and mass-production? If so, it is a Second Wave policy. Third Wave policies encourage uniqueness.
- Does it centralize control? Second Wave policies centralize power in bureaucratic institutions; Third Wave policies work to spread power—to empower those closest to the decision.
- Does it encourage geographic concentration? Second Wave policies encourage people to congregate physically; Third Wave policies permit people to work at home, and to live wherever they choose.
- Is it based on the idea of mass culture—of everyone watching the same sitcoms on television—or does it permit, even encourage, diversity within a broad framework of shared values? Third Wave policies will help transform diversity from a threat into an array of opportunities.

A serious effort to apply these tests to every area of government activity—from the defense and intelligence community to health care and education—would ultimately produce a complete transformation of government as we know it. Since that is what's needed, let's start applying.

GRASPING THE FUTURE

The conflict between Second Wave and Third Wave groupings is the central political tension cutting through our society today. The more basic political question is not who controls the last days of industrial society, but who shapes the new civilization rapidly rising to replace it.

Who, in other words, will shape the nature of cyberspace and its impact on our lives and institutions?

Living on the edge of the Third Wave, we are witnessing a battle not so much over the nature of the future—for the Third Wave will arrive—but over the nature of the transition. On one side of this battle are the partisans of the industrial past. On the other are growing millions who recognize that the world's most urgent problems can no longer be resolved within the massified frameworks we have inherited.

The Third Wave sector includes not only high-flying computer and electronics firms and biotech start-ups. It embraces advanced, information-driven manufacturing in every industry. It includes the increasingly data-drenched services—finance, software, entertainment, the media, advanced communication, medical services, consulting, training and learning. The people in this sector will soon be the dominant constituency in American politics.

And all of those confront a set of constituencies made frightened and defensive by their mainly Second Wave habits and locales: Command-and-control regulators, elected officials, political opinion-molders, philosophers mired in materialism, traditional interest groups, some broadcasters and newspapers—and every major institution (including corporations) that believes its future is best served by preserving the past.

For the time being, the entrenched powers of the Second Wave dominate Washington and the state houses—a fact nowhere more apparent than in the 1993 infrastructure bill: Over $100 billion for steel and cement, versus one lone billion for electronic infrastructure. Putting aside the question of whether the government should be building electronic infrastructure in the first place, the allocation of funding in that bill shows the Second Wave swamping the Third.

Only one political struggle so far contradicts the landscape offered in this document, but it is a big one: Passage of the North American Free Trade Agreement last November. This contest carried both sides beyond partisanship, beyond regionalism, and—after one climactic debate on CNN—beyond personality. The pro-NAFTA coalition opted to serve the opportunity instead of the problem, and the future as opposed to the past. That's why it constitutes a standout model for the likely development of a Third Wave political dialectic.

But a "mass movement" for cyberspace is still hard to see. Unlike the "masses" during the industrial age, this rising Third Wave consti-tuency is highly diverse. Like the economic sectors it serves, it is demassified—composed of individuals who prize their differences. This very heterogeneity contributes to its lack of political awareness. It is far harder to unify than the masses of the past.

Yet there are key themes on which this constituency-to-come can agree. To start with, liberation—from Second Wave rules, regula-tions, taxes and laws laid in place to serve the smokestack barons and bureaucrats of the past. Next, of course, must come the creation—creation of a new civilization, founded in the eternal truths of the American Idea.

It is time to embrace these challenges, to grasp the future and pull ourselves forward. If we do so, we will indeed renew the American Dream and enhance the promise of American life.

Reprinted with permission, the Progress & Freedom Foundation, 1301 K Street, N.W., Suite 650 West, Washington, DC 20005.

This analysis by Richard K. Moore, dated 19 August 1995, is a critique of "Cyberspace and the American Dream: A Magna Carta for the Knowledge Age." Further information is available at their Web site: http://www.ics.uci.edu/~kling.

Cyberspace Inc. and the Robber Baron Age, an Analysis of PFF's "Magna Carta"

The manifesto "Cyberspace and the American Dream: A Magna Carta for the Knowledge Age," published by the Progress and Freedom Foundation (PFF), is a document of considerable significance. Its very title reveals much about its intent. Its promoters—both alleged and concealed—are indicative of its propagandistic mission. Its contents have accurately prophesied the legislative agenda and rhetoric which have unfolded subsequent to the manifesto's publication.

Given the powerful telecommunications interests behind PFF—and the close ties of that organization to Speaker Newt Gingrich—a detailed analysis of the manifesto can provide insight into what may (unfortunately) be the most likely scenario for the future of cyberspace....

The title invites direct comparison with the original Magna Carta, which is defined in *The Cassell Concise English Dictionary* as follows:

> Magna Carta—The Great Charter of English liberties, sealed by King John on 15 June, 1215.

With due respect to Cassell's, this is a misleading definition. The Magna Carta did not grant liberties generally to "the English," but rather devolved powers and privileges exclusively to an elite aristocracy. As shall be shown in this article, PFF's "Magna Carta" is similarly misleading: much of its rhetoric seems to imply a concern with individual liberties, but its substance would devolve power and privilege exclusively to the biggest corporate players in the telecommunications industry.

Just as the Magna Carta supported the power of the Nobles—with each to have autocratic power in his own domain—so PFF's manifesto supports the power of communications monopolies—with each to have unregulated control over its own cyberspace fiefdom. Rather than being a charter of liberties, the manifesto promotes a regime of robber barons in cyberspace.

Instead of an infrastructure for public communication—like the current Internet, or the American highway system—cyberspace would be developed as a corporate owned monopoly—priced at whatever the traffic will bear. Instead of providing a "space" in which citizens are free to speak and associate (like Internet), cyberspace would become a profit-machine and propaganda channel for media conglomerates. PFF's manifesto is a formula for neo-feudalism in the "Knowledge Age"—it is a charter for what could aptly be dubbed "Cyberspace Inc.". . .

The ultimate promoters of the manifesto are concealed. Its introduction claims:

> This statement represents the cumulative wisdom and innovation of many dozens of people. It is based primarily on the thoughts of four "coauthors": Ms. Esther Dyson; Mr. George Gilder; Dr. George Keyworth; and Dr. Alvin Toffler. This release 1.2 has the final "imprimatur" of no one.

The implication would seem to be that enlightened individuals spontaneously composed the manifesto, in the interests, presumably, of progress and freedom. The true authorship is uncertain. According to Mark Stahlman of New Media Associates, a scheduled speaker at an upcoming PFF conference:

> The "author" of this rambling camel-of-a-report is Frank Gregorsky. He's a journalist working for PFF who does their newsletter. None of the listed contributors actually did any work directly on the document. That's why it's simply not coherent. [posted to telecomreg@relay.doit.wisc.edu on Sun., 5 Feb. 1995]

The "coherence" of the manifesto will be discussed in some detail below. As for the authorship, it would appear that PFF itself must be considered the source of the manifesto.

PFF turns out to be a typical industry-front organization. Characterized by Mr. Stahlman as "Newt's 'think tank,'" PFF is funded by a panoply of corporate sponsors. The February 6, 1995 issue of *The Nation* carries an article by David Corn, entitled "CyberNewt." Here's an excerpt:

> There is nothing particularly futuristic about the funding sources behind the PFF and its conference. Telecommunications firms subsidize the group: AT&T, BellSouth, Turner Broadcasting System, Cox Cable Communications. Other donors to the PFF's $1.9 million bank account include conservative foundations, *Wired* magazine, high-tech firms, military

contractors, and drug companies (another foundation passion is attacking the Food and Drug Administration).

When Senator Phil Gramm spoke at the [PFF] conference luncheon, the tables closest to the podium were reserved for corporate benefactors: Eli Lilly, Seagram's, Phillip Morris, S.B.C. Communications (formerly Southwestern Bell).

Brock N. Meeks published an article in Inter@ctive Week, dated April 28, 1995, entitled "Freedom Foundation Faces Scrutiny." These brief excerpts from the article outline Mr. Meeks' understanding of how PFF funds are used, and how it seeks to hide its link to Mr. Gingrich:

> ... Among I@W's findings:
>
> - PFF spent $483,000 to underwrite a college course taught by Gingrich...
> - PFF spent $148,000 to underwrite The Progress Report, Gingrich's weekly cable talk show carried on his own National Empowerment Television....

The PFF links to Gingrich and his own political action committee, called GOPAC, have drawn the interest of the Ethics Committee and the IRS, which is "reevaluating" PFF's nonprofit status, according to an IRS source.

The PFF link to Gingrich's rising political currency has proved lucrative. From March 1993 to March 1994 the group raised $611,000. During the remainder of 1994, when it became clear that the Republicans stood a good chance to capture both the House and the Senate for the first time in 40 years, an additional $1.07 million poured into PFF coffers, according to its financial records....

The latest PFF tax returns do not make any link to GOPAC or Gingrich. Any such linking would violate IRS tax exemption rules. However, Eisenach is on record acknowledging that he did the basic groundwork of setting up PFF while running GOPAC.

The money trail apparently goes from media/telecommunications conglomerates, to PFF, and finally to Mr. Gingrich's projects, which seem to be heavily focused on propaganda ventures. Small wonder that PFF's manifesto, and Mr. Gingrich's legislative agenda, promote excessive deregulation of the telecommunications industry, and pave the way for monopolistic control. Evidently the Lords of Cyberspace Inc. are to include the likes of AT&T, BellSouth, Turner Broadcasting System, and Cox Cable Communications. Mr. Gingrich's famous pledges to "empower the individual" and "provide laptops for ghetto dwellers" should be seen for what they are: a shallow populist veneer covering a corporate-pandering agenda....

The text of PFF's manifesto is an artful piece of propaganda. Clouded in cyber-jargon, illogical in its flow of argument, and disjoint in its presentation—it does superficially appear to be a "rambling camel-of-a-report," as Mr. Stahlman observes. But beneath the deceptive rhetoric—if one digs patiently—there can indeed be found a coherent set of proposals for the commercial exploitation of cyber-space.The rhetoric is grandiose. It talks about the original American experience, characterized as daring pioneers conquering a new land—based on the principles of individual initiative and freedom. Cyberspace is described as a similar frontier, and a rallying cry is raised to reaffirm freedom for the individual—especially from government control. The preservation of the American heritage itself, the manifesto argues, hangs in the balance: freedom for the individual in cyberspace must be protected!

But the manifesto makes no mention whatever of protections for *individual* freedoms. There's no discussion, for example, of guaranteeing freedom of expression or of protecting privacy. In addition, there's no discussion of preserving the viability of Internet mailing lists and bulletin boards—which have proven to be cyberspace's equivalent of "freedom of association" and "freedom of the press."

What the manifesto does discuss—at great length—is the protection of freedoms for *telecommunications & media conglomerates*: freedom to form monopolies, freedom to set arbitrary price rates and structures, freedom to control content, and freedom from fair taxation, through special accounting procedures. This is a formula which harks back to the robber-baron capitalism of the late Nineteenth century, when railroad, oil, and steel monopolies ran roughshod over America's economy and political system.

Hence the rhetoric of PFF's manifesto is aimed at accomplishing a clear propaganda mission. It aims to stir up sentiment for freedom of the individual, and then to deftly shift the ground under the manifesto's audience. The pro-freedom sentiment is subtly transferred from the *individual* to the *corporation*, not explicitly, but by deceptive turns of phrase. "The corporation" is subtly equated to the "the individual," so that "deregulation of conglomerates" *seems* to be synonymous with "freedom for the individual."

Implementation of the manifesto's agenda would not lead to individual freedom at all. It would lead to subjugation of the individual by corporate media monopolies. The right to access services, the price of the services, the definition of what services would be provided, the content of "news" and entertainment—these would all be decided entirely by media conglomerates, based on their business interests and political agendas. Neither individuals nor their elected representatives would have any say over how cyberspace is to be developed or used, under PFF's charter for Cyberspace Inc.

Most of the remainder of this article is devoted to examining representative excerpts of the manifesto text, in order to substantiate and illustrate the summary analysis above. At the end there's a brief discussion of the relationship between the manifesto and the current legislative agenda in Washington. . . .

In its Preamble, the manifesto sets forth its grandiose characterization of cyberspace as the next frontier of the American Dream:

What our Twentieth-century countrymen came to think of as the "American dream," and what resonant thinkers referred to as "the promise of American life" or "the American Idea," emerged from the turmoil of Nineteenth-century industrialization. Now it's our turn: The knowledge revolution, and the Third Wave of historical change it powers, summon us to renew the dream and enhance the promise.

In the first section, "The Nature of Cyberspace," the emphasis on cyberspace as a delivery media for information products is introduced:

Cyberspace is the land of knowledge, and the exploration of that land can be a civilization's truest, highest calling. The opportunity is now before us to empower every person to pursue that calling in his or her own way.

As is typical throughout the manifesto, the substance is hidden within fluff rhetoric. The operative phrases in this paragraph, confirmed by the rest of the manifesto, are "land of knowledge" and "exploration." Cyberspace is to be primarily a source of "knowledge"—meaning commercial media products—and the role of the *consumer* will be to "explore" it—meaning to navigate the purchasing options.

This first section also introduces the theme that government is inconsistent with cyberspace pioneering:

[Cyberspace] spells the death of the central institutional paradigm of modern life, the bureaucratic organization. (Governments, including the American government, are the last great redoubt of bureaucratic power on the face of the planet, and for them the coming change will be profound and probably traumatic.)

As you might expect, nowhere does the manifesto acknowledge that Internet was established due to government initiative and sponsorship. And interestingly enough, the word "Internet" occurs only twice in the manifesto, and the Internet precedent is seldom cited as a source of models for how cyberspace might evolve. Also, the authors are evidently blind to the possibility that *corporations* might be "redoubts of bureaucratic power."

The next section, "The Nature and Ownership of Property," introduces a number of complex topics regarding ownership of hardware infrastructure, intellectual property, and the electromagnetic spectrum. This section also introduces the issue of pricing regulation, and touches on preferential taxation.

The main propaganda theme, intentionally confusing the individual with corporations, is introduced at this point:

At the level of first principles, should ownership be public (i.e. government) or private (i.e. individuals)?

The hook is set here, favoring private over government owner-ship—in the name of the individual. But in all that follows, it is the corporation that is granted privileges, not the individual. As part of the same deceptive dichotomy, "public/government" is everywhere equated to central bureaucracy, with no acknowledgment that any kind of regulation could ever be useful, nor that any kind of public agency, even if highly decentralized, could possibly be beneficial. And there is no hint that individuals might ever need to be protected from corpora-tions, or that government might play some role in such protection.

The ownership of hardware infrastructure is mentioned, but not discussed. It is patently obvious, evidently, to both the authors and the presumed readers, that this level of infrastructure is to be privately owned. State operated telecommunications systems are so far beyond the pale as to be unimaginable. Again the precedent of Internet (until very recently supported by a public backbone network) is conspicu-ously absent from the manifesto.

The discussion of intellectual property is interesting, and appears to have some merit. Patents and copyrights are described as being a "public good" approach to intellectual property, outdated and cumber-some in the age of cyberspace:

> Third Wave customized knowledge is by nature a private good.

The manifesto's favored approach to intellectual property is described in a quotation from John Perry Barlow:

> One existing model for the future conveyance of intellectual property is real-time performance.... In these instances, commercial exchange will be more like ticket sales to a contin-uous show.... The other model, of course, is service.... Who needs copyright when you're on a retainer?

Apparently the model is that authors would sell their services or their rights to a commercial distributor, who would then charge the consumer on a "pay per view" basis.

Dealing with copyrights in electronic media has indeed proven to be a thorny problem. Journalists have complained about not being remunerated by electronic republishing services; rap musicians have allegedly "sampled" previous material without payment; copyrighted articles are forwarded around Internet on a free basis. New mecha-nisms are needed, and the private sector *is* likely to be a creative source of solutions, such as metering technologies.

This model makes no mention of royalties. Many authors would prefer royalties, based on distributor revenues, rather than being forced to sell their services or works on a fixed-price basis. This is a time-honored practice in pre-electronic media, and a fully accountable and enforceable royalty scheme would be a desirable part of any cyberspace solution for intellectual property.

With regard to ownership of the electromagnetic spectrum, ominous questions are raised, but a specific agenda is not developed. Existing channel auctioning practices are criticized as being too limiting. Perhaps PFF's corporate backers are seeking outright permanent ownership of this presumably public resource:

> ...Is the very limited "bundle of rights" sold in those auctions really property, or more in the nature of a use permit—the right to use a part of the spectrum for a limited time, for limited purposes?...

Thus far, the manifesto has "established" that private ownership of infrastructure, intellectual property, and the electromagnetic spectrum should be strengthened and extended, with the root justification hanging on the thin thread of deception equating corporation with individual.

Next, the specter of evil regulation is raised:

> Regulation, especially price regulation, of this property can be tantamount to confiscation, as America's cable operators recently learned when the Federal government imposed price limits on them...there is no disagreeing with the proposition that one's ownership of a good is less meaningful when the government can step in, at will, and dramatically reduce its value.

Thus the manifesto proposes that every aspect of cyberspace is to be corporate owned, and that no price regulation should be imposed. If adequate measures were taken to insure healthy competition, this formula *might* serve the public welfare. But the monopoly proposals, to be discussed further on, make this a dangerous formula indeed. Note above the use of the phrase "one's ownership," reinforcing the confusion of individual and corporate identity. Notice also, there was no discussion of the consumer complaints that led to the regulation, nor of the immense profits that the cable operators continue to reap subsequent to the "confiscation."

Next is raised the issue of property depreciation. The precedent of microchips is used to claim that cyberspace investments should be depreciated rapidly. Current capital depreciation practices are denigrated:

> ...Yet accounting and tax regulations still require property to be depreciated over periods as long as 30 *years*. The result is a heavy bias in favor of "heavy industry" and against nimble, fast-moving baby businesses.

The comparison with microchips and small entrepreneurial ventures is patently absurd. Cyberspace Inc. is aiming to consolidate ownership of existing infrastructures, and to deploy new cable, fiber, and coax. These are long-range hardware investments by big players, and the above argument for accelerated depreciation makes no sense. Such inappropriate tax treatment would amount to yet another give-away to rich corporations, at the expense of the oft-touted individual. Perhaps small, risk-taking, nimble companies *should* enjoy more rapid depreciation, but not these corporate giants, aiming as they are to exploit already proven technologies.

In the next section, "The Nature of the Marketplace," the principle of "dynamic competition" is discussed. The principle is very simple, essentially that new kinds of products should be allowed to capture markets from outmoded products, just as the automobile replaced the horse and buggy. The manifesto attempts to present the idea as if it were a major breakthrough in economic theory. It then issues a rallying cry for bold new directions:

> The challenge for policy in the 1990s is to permit, even encourage, dynamic competition in every aspect of the cyber-space marketplace.

What the manifesto fails to mention is that the American communications industry is already experiencing *dramatic* dynamic competition. Cable, cellular, satellite, telephone, and broadcast modalities are increasingly overlapping, evolving, competing, shifting markets around, and bringing down prices. By a strange twist of logic, as we shall see later, the *concept* of dynamic competition will be used as an argument for increased monopoly control over markets—for reducing the *actual* dynamic competition that is working so well today.

The next section, "The Nature of Freedom," develops several threads. It presents a revisionist version of U.S. and Internet history; it continues the blurring of individual and corporate interests; it continues the demonization of government; it restates the corporate goal of gaining outright ownership of the electromagnetic spectrum; it hints at the monopolist agenda.

In a Second Wave world, it might make sense for government to assume ownership over the broadcast spectrum and demand massive payments from citizens for the right to use it.

Broadcast license fees (hardly massive, by the way) are paid by corporate broadcasters, not citizens. Having laid its propaganda groundwork, the manifesto now freely interchanges individualist and corporate terms with Orwellian impunity. By an incredible stretch of doublethink, handing over the public airwaves to corporate ownership is to be a victory for the individual!

In a Second Wave world, it might make sense for government to prohibit entrepreneurs from entering new markets and providing new services.

In a single sweeping revisionist fantasy, America's remarkable record of supporting innovative entrepreneurs vanishes from history! And the manifesto would have us swallow the premise that billion-dollar telecommunications and media giants are poor, struggling entrepreneurs. However desirable as an ideal, individual freedom often seemed impractical. The mass institutions of the Second Wave required us to give up freedom in order for the system to "work."

In yet another revisionist fantasy, America's world-famous history of freedom is discounted. And once again individual freedom is praised, as if that had some connection to the corporate agenda being espoused.

The next section, "The Essence of Community," proclaims the notion of distributed communities—long common on Internet—as if they were a bold new idea:

> No one knows what the Third Wave communities of the future will look like.... It is clear, however, that cyberspace will play an important role knitting together in the diverse communities of tomorrow, facilitating the creation of "electronic neighborhoods" bound together not by geography but by shared interests.

Why does "no one know?" Why aren't Internet lists and newsgroups cited as living prototypes for distributed communities of the future? Such frequent and glaring omission of the Internet precedent is disturbing. Just as the American pioneer (so often praised by the manifesto) saw the New World (falsely) as a virgin land ready for exploitation, so the manifesto seems to see cyberspace as an empty frontier, yet to be explored and developed. Are the "natives" of this frontier—today's extensive Internet culture—to be similarly decimated and pushed onto bleak reservations? Just as the Magna Carta metaphor reveals much about the manifesto's robber-baron objectives, perhaps the darker implications of the pioneering metaphor should be taken seriously as well.

Given the monopoly-priced environment proposed by the manifesto (in the next section), the kind of informal, citizen-oriented virtual communities popular on Internet are highly unlikely to be viable. PFF's notion of distributed communities (called "cyberspaces") seems to resemble today's internal corporate networks, as described in a quote from Phil Salin:

> ...Contrary to naive views, these cyberspaces will not all be the same, and they will not all be open to the general public. The global network is a connected 'platform' for a collection of diverse communities, but only a loose, heterogeneous community itself. Just as access to homes, offices, churches and department stores is controlled by their owners or managers, most virtual locations will exist as distinct places of private property.

Those groups which can afford to pay the monopolist prices—such as corporations and well-funded associations—can enjoy the benefits which today are affordable to millions of individuals and groups. Perhaps nowhere else in the manifesto is the pro-individualist rhetoric so clearly revealed to be the lie that it is. Instead of promoting individual freedom in cyberspace, existing freedoms and privileges are likely to be taken away. The ominous precedent implicit in the "pioneer" metaphor threatens to recur as cyberspace is cleared for commercial development.

The next section, "The Role of Government," reiterates previously stated corporate objectives—no price regulation, corporate ownership of spectra, new definition of intellectual property, favored tax treatment—and proclaims a new objective: enabling total monopoly control over communications markets.

Much is made of the distinction between one-way and two-way communications, the implication apparently being that phone companies are better prepared to develop cyberspace than cable operators:

> ... None of the interactive services will be possible, however, if we have an eight-lane data superhighway rushing into every home and only a narrow footpath coming back out. . . .

The claim is made that the multimedia future depends on greater collaboration between phone and cable companies:

> ... it can be argued that a near-term national interactive multimedia network is impossible unless regulators permit much greater collaboration between the cable industry and phone companies. . . . That is why obstructing such collaboration—in the cause of forcing a competition between the cable and phone industries—is socially elitist.

Next, it is claimed that dynamic competition requires that regulated-monopoly mechanisms (which govern today's RBOCs and cable companies) should be abolished. Price and entry regulation are to be replaced by new antitrust law:

> Antitrust law is the means by which America has . . . fostered competition in markets where many providers can and should compete. . . . The market for telecommunications services— telephone, cable, satellite, wireless—is now such a market. . . . price/entry regulation of telecommunications services . . . should therefore be replaced by antitrust law as rapidly as possible.

The obvious likely consequences of such an agenda are conspicuously not discussed by the manifesto. If entry regulation is removed, and phone/cable collaboration is encouraged, then the obvious alternatives for collaboration would be interconnection, joint venture, and acquisition. Given the multibillion dollar capital reserves of the phone companies, the best business opportunity would presumably be for phone companies to simply acquire cable companies, thus establishing total monopolies over wires coming into the home.

Antitrust law would be largely irrelevant to this scenario. To begin with, antitrust enforcement seems to be a thing of the past—especially with the Republican radicals in Congress. More important, perhaps, is the current anti-trust stance toward the RBOCs: partitioning them into separate turfs seems to be the most that antitrust enforcers demand. Within their turfs, they're allowed be as monopolistic as they can get by with.

If price-regulation is removed, then we would be left with *totally* unregulated telecommunications monopolies in each RBOC region—controlling phone, television, multimedia, and messaging services, and charging whatever the traffic will bear. Hence the appropriateness of this article's title: "Cyberspace Inc and the Robber Baron Age." America's total communications infrastructure would be divided into feudal fiefdoms, and the economic regime would resemble the railroad cartels of the Nineteenth century.

All the manifesto's rhetoric about individual freedom and dynamic competition is deception—the agenda is totally anticompetitive, anti-individual, and anti-free enterprise. A century's progress in achieving dynamic, competitive, and diverse communications industries—based on appropriate and nonstifling regulation—would be thrown out the window all at once.

The final section of the manifesto, "Grasping the Future," is mostly devoted to reiterating the grandiose rhetorical visions of the mythical "Third Wave." The phrase "grasping the future" is an apt conclusion to the manifesto: the conglomerates behind PFF are indeed grasping at the future with both hands, ready to pocket monopolistic windfall profits, presumably enhanced by favored tax advantages.... Despite the strongly adversarial attitude this article has taken toward the "Magna Carta," not all of the points made in that manifesto are considered by this author to be wrong-headed. Creative initiatives to the problems posed by cyberspace are indeed needed, and the manifesto offers some constructive ideas in that regard. A pay-per-view model of intellectual property may have merit—if original authors are fairly and account-ably compensated, and if noncommercial material is also accommo-dated at reasonable cost. Close collaboration among existing installed bases of coax, cable, and satellite may be desirable—if appropriately regulated with respect to price and common-carrier status. And new paradigms and visions for understanding the meaning of communica-tions in the "information age" are needed—but with more honesty about the metaphors to be embraced and how they actually map onto cyberspace realities.

What *is* highly objectionable in the manifesto is the deceptive manipulation of libertarian/individualist sentiment, the ignoring of the Internet precedent and the lessons to be learned from that, the absence of provisions for freedom of communication and privacy for individ-uals, the discounting of the proven constructive role for appropriate regulation, and the disguised corporate power-grab inherent in the proposed package of policies.

This is not the place to analyze or even enumerate the plethora of competing legislative proposals currently before Congress regarding telecommunications. Suffice it to say that the agenda promulgated by the "Magna Carta" is finding widespread expression in that legislation. This fact—along with the manifesto's close connection to the communications industry and to Speaker Gingrich—indicates that the "Magna Carta" should be taken very seriously, as regards both its agenda, and the kind of rhetoric and deception employed. The "Magna Carta" provides a rare insight into the threat facing America's future from corporate power grabbers, and simplifies the task of seeing through the propaganda smokescreen being employed by legislators and industry spokespeople.

Richard K. Moore rkmoore@internet-eireann.ie (USA Citizen) Moderator: Cyberjournal Wexford, Ireland, http://www.internet-eireann.ie/cyberlib

Reprinted with permission from *The Information Society* 12, no. 3 (1996).

The following is a draft chapter from Michael Hauben and Ronda Hauben's Netbook, The Netizens and the Wonderful World of the Net. *For the on-line version, log on to http://www.columbia.edu/~hauben/netbook/.*

Proposed Declaration of the Rights of Netizens

We Netizens have begun to put together a Declaration of the Rights of Netizens and are requesting from other Netizens contributions, ideas, and suggestions of what rights should be included. Following are some beginning ideas.

The Declaration of the Rights of Netizens:

In recognition that the Net represents a revolution in human communications that was built by a cooperative noncommercial process, the following Declaration of the Rights of the Netizen is presented for Netizen comment. As Netizens are those who take responsibility and care for the Net, the following are proposed to be their rights:

- Universal access at no or low cost
- Freedom of Electronic Expression to promote the exchange of knowledge without fear of reprisal
- Uncensored Expression
- Access to Broad Distribution
- Universal and Equal access to knowledge and information
- Consideration of one's ideas on their merits
- No limitation to access to read, to post and to otherwise contribute
- Equal quality of connection
- Equal time of connection

- No Official Spokesperson
- Uphold the public grassroots purpose and participation
- Volunteer Contribution—no personal profit from the contribution freely given by others
- Protection of the public purpose from those who would use it for their private and money making purposes.

The Net is not a Service, it is a Right. It is only valuable when it is collective and universal. Volunteer effort protects the intellectual and technological common-wealth that is being created.

DO NOT UNDERESTIMATE THE POWER OF THE NET and NETIZENS. Inspiration from: RFC 3 (1969), Thomas Paine, *Declaration of Independence* (1776), *Declaration of the Rights of Man and of the Citizen* (1789), NSF Acceptable Use Policy, Jean Jacques Rousseau, and the current cry for democracy worldwide.

Reprinted with the authors' permission from *The Amateur Computerist* 6, nos. 2–3 (Fall/Winter 1994/1995).

The National Information Infrastructure Advisory Council (NIIAC) was appointed by President Clinton to advise him regarding the many issues arising from the deployment of what the government calls the National Information Infrastructure (NII). This excerpt is from their extensive final report.

Executive Summary of the National Information Infrastructure Advisory Council Final Report

I. The Council's Vision

The United States stands today in the midst of one of the great revolutions in recorded history: the Information Age. The Information Superhighway provides the infrastructure that enables enormous benefits in education, economic well-being, and quality of life.

The Council urges that the Nation adopt the following five fundamental goals.

First, let us find ways to make information technology work for us, the people of this country, by ensuring that these wondrous new resources advance American constitutional precepts, our diverse cultural values, and our sense of equity.

Second, let us ensure, too, that getting America on-line results in stronger communities, and a stronger sense of national community.

Third, let us extend to every person in every community the opportunity to participate in building the Information Superhighway. The Information Superhighway must be a tool that is available to all individuals—people of all ages, those from a wide range of economic, social, and cultural backgrounds, and those with a wide range of functional abilities and limitations—not just a select few. It must be affordable, easy to use, and accessible from even the most disadvantaged or remote neighborhood.

Fourth, let us ensure that we Americans take responsibility for the building of the Superhighway—private sector, government at all levels, and individuals.

And, fifth, let us maintain our world leadership in developing the services, products, and an open and competitive market that lead to deployment of the Information Superhighway. Research and development will be an essential component of its sustained evolution.

In charting a course to meet these goals for the Information Superhighway, the Advisory Council identified what it believes are four critical issues that must be addressed and must be addressed early:

- What are the key areas of American life and work that will be impacted?
- What is the role of universal access in the digital age?
- What are the rules of the road regarding intellectual property, privacy, and security?
- Who are the key stakeholders, and what are their roles?

The following recommendations reflect the Council's major proposals for addressing those issues.

II. Recommendations

A. Impact on Key Areas of American Life and Work

1. Electronic Commerce.

   The Federal Government, in conjunction with others, should take steps to identify and resolve, wherever possible, legal, regulatory, and policy issues that restrict the development of electronic commerce on the Information Superhighway.

2. Education and Lifelong Learning.

   Create targeted Federal, State, and local initiatives, in full cooperation with the private sector, to accelerate access to the Information Superhighway and to facilitate the effective integration of Information Superhighway technologies and resources into all lifelong learning environments. Such initiatives should encourage the development and wide availability of quality Information Superhighway learning resources and stimulate the development of a viable market for Information Superhighway-related educational products and services.

3. Emergency Management and Public Safety.

   The Federal Government should convene a broad-based committee composed of those entities involved in standard setting, those involved with the development of new technology, and relevant State, local, and Tribal agencies to meet the needs of the emergency management, public safety, and criminal justice communities. The Federal Government also should involve local governments in regional planning and review to ensure the best possible coordination of resources within a region and involve community-based organizations for more effective gathering and dissemination of public information.

4. Health.

The Federal Government, in conjunction with Tribal, State, regional, and local governments, should take steps to resolve, wherever possible, conflicting legal or regulatory barriers to the delivery and reimbursement of health information and health care across State borders. Such efforts should be accompanied by government funding of evaluation of telemedicine applications in the areas of cost, access, and quality.

Since protection of health information is a primary concern to everyone, the Council's recommendations on privacy and security should apply to the area of health information and should ensure both that information can be protected, and that it is available in properly authorized treatment situations.

5. Government Information and Services.

All levels of government should use information infrastructure technologies to provide basic pointers* to government information and services, thus simplifying public access to relevant government information; improving delivery of government services and the management and use of government information; and enabling the private sector to develop and provide enhanced and expanded value-added information products and services.

B. Ensuring Access for All

1. Information Superhighway Deployment.

Commercial and competitive forces should drive the development of the Information Superhighway. Regulatory disincentives to Information Superhighway development should be removed. All subsidies should be made explicit and applied in a competitively neutral manner.

2. Universal Access and Service.

The definition of universal service should evolve to accommodate converging technologies. All individuals should have

---

* The term "pointers" in this context refers to information sources that would enable individuals and organizations in both the public and private sectors to identify and access government information and services. The pointers are not the sought-after information and services themselves. Rather, they provide direct pathways to the desired government information and services. Current examples include the Federal Register, the Government Information Locator Services, and legislative calendars.

affordable, ubiquitous, convenient, and functional access to Information Superhighway services. All individuals should be able to be both consumers and producers of information. Design of its components should accommodate the needs of disabled individuals.

3. Government's Role.

Government should act when commercial and competitive forces are failing to achieve the goals of universal access and universal service. Government should lead by example in the use of the Information Superhighway for offering and using information and services.

C. **Rules of the Road**

1. Intellectual Property.

All levels of government should promote ongoing public education about the meaning and importance of intellectual property, including copyright and the fair use doctrine.

The Federal Government should strive to have other countries implement consistent, effective, and appropriate policies and protections for intellectual property in the digital environment.

2. Privacy.

The Federal Government should follow through on privacy policy issues with the initial task of reviewing existing laws and practices to implement the Council's privacy principles and the recommendations of the IITF Privacy Working Group.

3. Security.

The Federal Government should encourage private sector awareness of security issues, initiate a public-private security consultation process, and foster mechanisms to promote private accountability for proper use of security measures.

The Federal Government should not inhibit the development and deployment of encryption by the private sector.

4. Free Speech.

The government should not be in the business of regulating content on the Information Superhighway. It should defer to the use of privately provided filtering, reviewing, and rating mechanisms and parental supervision as the best means of preventing access by minors to inappropriate materials.

D. **Key Roles**

1. The Private Sector Must Be the Builder.

The private sector—defined broadly to include an array of nongovernmental entities—must have the primary responsibility for the continued design, deployment, and operation of the Information Superhighway.

2. Communities Are Key to Access and Learning.

   As demonstrated in the Council's companion volume, KickStart Initiative: Connecting America's Communities to the Information Superhighway, it is the access at local institutions, especially schools, libraries, and community centers, that will continue to facilitate the Superhighway at the neighborhood level and open new opportunities to young students, working people, and older persons alike.

3. Government Has a Critical Role as Catalyst.

   Although not the primary builders of the Information Superhighway, all levels of government have a significant role to play in ensuring its effective development and deployment.

4. Individuals Must Take Charge.

   To realize the benefits of the Information Superhighway, individuals must be its champions at the local level, learn about and seize its opportunities, and respect the rights of others.

Reprinted below are the title page and table of contents of the Telecommunications Act of 1996, a historic reform of the 1934 telecommunications statute that will help to define information technologies for the new millennium.

Telecommunications Act of 1996

One Hundred Fourth Congress
of the United States of America.

At the Second Session

Begun and held at the City of Washington on Wednesday, the third day of January, one thousand nine hundred and ninety-six

An Act

To promote competition and reduce regulation in order to secure lower prices and higher quality services for American telecommunications consumers and encourage the rapid deployment of new telecommunications technologies.

Be it enacted by the Senate and House of Representatives of the United States of America in Congress assembled,

SECTION 1. SHORT TITLE; REFERENCES.

(a) SHORT TITLE—This Act may be cited as the Telecommunications Act of 1996.

(b) REFERENCES—Except as otherwise expressly provided, whenever in this Act an amendment or repeal is expressed in terms of an amendment to, or repeal of, a section or other provision, the reference shall be considered to be made to a section or other provision of the Communications Act of 1934 (47 U.S.C. 151 et seq.).

SEC. 2. TABLE OF CONTENTS.

The table of contents for this Act is as follows:

Sec. 403. Elimination of unnecessary Commission regulations and functions.

TITLE V—OBSCENITY AND VIOLENCE
SUBTITLE A—OBSCENE, HARASSING, AND WRONGFUL UTILIZA-TION OF TELECOMMUNICATIONS FACILITIES

Sec. 501. Short title.
Sec. 502. Obscene or harassing use of telecommunications facilities under the Communications Act of 1934.
Sec. 503. Obscene programming on cable television.
Sec. 504. Scrambling of cable channels for nonsubscribers.
Sec. 505. Scrambling of sexually explicit adult video service programming.
Sec. 506. Cable operator refusal to carry certain programs.
Sec. 507. Clarification of current laws regarding communication of obscene materials through the use of computers.
Sec. 508. Coercion and enticement of minors.
Sec. 509. Online family empowerment.

SUBTITLE B—VIOLENCE

Sec. 551. Parental choice in television programming.
Sec. 552. Technology fund.

SUBTITLE C—JUDICIAL REVIEW

Sec. 561. Expedited review.

TITLE VI—EFFECT ON OTHER LAWS

Sec. 601. Applicability of consent decrees and other law.
Sec. 602. Preemption of local taxation with respect to direct-to-home services.

TITLE VII—MISCELLANEOUS PROVISIONS

Sec. 701. Prevention of unfair billing practices for information or services provided over toll-free telephone calls.
Sec. 702. Privacy of customer information.
Sec. 703. Pole attachments.
Sec. 704. Facilities siting; radio frequency emission standards.
Sec. 705. Mobile services direct access to long distance carriers.
Sec. 706. Advanced telecommunications incentives.
Sec. 707. Telecommunications Development Fund.
Sec. 708. National Education Technology Funding Corporation.
Sec. 709. Report on the use of advanced telecommunications services for medical purposes.
Sec. 710. Authorization of appropriations.

The portion of the Telecommunications Act reprinted on the next page is the "Exon Amendment," or the Communications Decency Act, which had become the most controversial portion of the legislation. Widespread protest was initiated the day it was signed into law, and its eventual fate lies in the hands of the courts.

Communications Decency Act of 1996

TITLE V—OBSCENITY AND VIOLENCE

SUBTITLE A—OBSCENE, HARASSING, AND WRONGFUL UTILIZA-TION OF TELECOMMUNICATIONS FACILITIES
SEC. 501. SHORT TITLE.

This title may be cited as the 'Communications Decency Act of 1996.'

SEC. 502. OBSCENE OR HARASSING USE OF TELECOMMUNI-CATIONS FACILITIES UNDER THE COMMUNICATIONS ACT OF 1934.

Section 223 (47 U.S.C. 223) is amended—
(1) by striking subsection (a) and inserting in lieu thereof:
(a) Whoever—
(1) in interstate or foreign communications—
(A) by means of a telecommunications device knowingly—
(i) makes, creates, or solicits, and
(ii) initiates the transmission of any comment, request, suggestion, proposal, image, or other communication which is obscene, lewd, lascivious, filthy, or indecent, with intent to annoy, abuse, threaten, or harass another person;
(B) by means of a telecommunications device knowingly—
(i) makes, creates, or solicits, and
(ii) initiates the transmission of any comment, request, suggestion, proposal, image, or other communication which is obscene or indecent, knowing that the recipient of the communication is under 18 years of age, regardless of whether the maker of such communication placed the call or initiated the communication;
(C) makes a telephone call or utilizes a telecommunications device, whether or not conversation or communication ensues, without disclosing his identity and with intent to annoy, abuse, threaten, or harass any person at the called number or who receives the communications;
(D) makes or causes the telephone of another repeatedly or continuously to ring, with intent to harass any person at the called number; or
(E) makes repeated telephone calls or repeatedly initiates communication with a telecommunications device, during which conversation or communication ensues,

solely to harass any person at the called number or who receives the communication; or

(2) knowingly permits any telecommunications facility under his control to be used for any activity prohibited by paragraph (1) with the intent that it be used for such activity, shall be fined under title 18, United States Code, or imprisoned not more than two years, or both; and (2) by adding at the end the following new subsections:

(d) Whoever—

   (1) in interstate or foreign communications knowingly—

      (A) uses an interactive computer service to send to a specific person or persons under 18 years of age, or

      (B) uses any interactive computer service to display in a manner available to a person under 18 years of age, any comment, request, suggestion, proposal, image, or other communication that, in context, depicts or describes, in terms patently offensive as measured by contemporary community standards, sexual or excretory activities or organs, regardless of whether the user of such service placed the call or initiated the communication; or

   (2) knowingly permits any telecommunications facility under such person's control to be used for an activity prohibited by paragraph (1) with the intent that it be used for such activity, shall be fined under title 18, United States Code, or imprisoned not more than two years, or both.

(e) In addition to any other defenses available by law:

   (1) No person shall be held to have violated subsection (a) or (d) solely for providing access or connection to or from a facility, system, or network not under that person's control, including transmission, downloading, intermediate storage, access software, or other related capabilities that are incidental to providing such access or connection that does not include the creation of the content of the communication.

   (2) The defenses provided by paragraph (1) of this subsection shall not be applicable to a person who is a conspirator with an entity actively involved in the creation or knowing distribution of communications that violate this section, or who knowingly advertises the availability of such communications.

   (3) The defenses provided in paragraph (1) of this subsection shall not be applicable to a person who provides access or connection to a facility, system, or network engaged in the violation of this section that is owned or controlled by such person.

   (4) No employer shall be held liable under this section for the actions of an employee or agent unless the employee's or

agent's conduct is within the scope of his or her employ-
ment or agency and the employer (A) having knowledge
of such conduct, authorizes or ratifies such conduct, or
(B) recklessly disregards such conduct.

(5) It is a defense to a prosecution under subsection (a)(1)(B) or
(d), or under subsection (a)(2) with respect to the use of a
facility for an activity under subsection (a)(1)(B) that a
person—

(A) has taken, in good faith, reasonable, effective, and
appropriate actions under the circumstances to restrict
or prevent access by minors to a communication specified in such subsections, which may involve any appropriate measures to restrict minors from such
communications, including any method which is
feasible under available technology; or

(B) has restricted access to such communication by
requiring use of a verified credit card, debit account,
adult access code, or adult personal identification
number.

The article below is John Perry Barlow's response to the Commu-
nications Decency Act on the day it was signed into law by President
Clinton. As a codirector of the Electronic Frontier Foundation, he speaks
for many cybercitizens in his new declaration of independence.

A Cyberspace Independence Declaration

John Perry Barlow, e-mail distribution, February, 8, 1996

Governments of the Industrial World, you weary giants of flesh and
steel, I come from Cyberspace, the new home of Mind. On behalf of
the future, I ask you of the past to leave us alone. You are not welcome
among us. You have no sovereignty where we gather.

We have no elected government, nor are we likely to have one, so
I address you with no greater authority than that with which liberty
itself always speaks. I declare the global social space we are building to
be naturally independent of the tyrannies you seek to impose on us.
You have no moral right to rule us nor do you possess any methods of
enforcement we have true reason to fear.

Governments derive their just powers from the consent of the
governed. You have neither solicited nor received ours. We did not
invite you. You do not know us, nor do you know our world.
Cyberspace does not lie within your borders. Do not think that you can
build it, as though it were a public construction project. You cannot. It
is an act of nature and it grows itself through our collective actions.

You have not engaged in our great and gathering conversation, nor
did you create the wealth of our marketplaces. You do not know our

culture, our ethics, or the unwritten codes that already provide our society more order than could be obtained by any of your impositions.

You claim there are problems among us that you need to solve. You use this claim as an excuse to invade our precincts. Many of these problems don't exist. Where there are real conflicts, where there are wrongs, we will identify them and address them by our means. We are forming our own Social Contract. This governance will arise according to the conditions of our world, not yours. Our world is different.

Cyberspace consists of transactions, relationships, and thought itself, arrayed like a standing wave in the web of our communications. Ours is a world that is both everywhere and nowhere, but it is not where bodies live.

We are creating a world that all may enter without privilege or prejudice accorded by race, economic power, military force, or station of birth.

We are creating a world where anyone, anywhere may express his or her beliefs, no matter how singular, without fear of being coerced into silence or conformity.

Your legal concepts of property, expression, identity, movement, and context do not apply to us. They are based on matter. There is no matter here.

Our identities have no bodies, so, unlike you, we cannot obtain order by physical coercion. We believe that from ethics, enlightened self-interest, and the commonweal, our governance will emerge. Our identities may be distributed across many of your jurisdictions. The only law that all our constituent cultures would generally recognize is the Golden Rule. We hope we will be able to build our particular solutions on that basis. But we cannot accept the solutions you are attempting to impose.

In the United States, you have today created a law, the Telecommunications Reform Act, which repudiates your own Constitution and insults the dreams of Jefferson, Washington, Mill, Madison, DeToqueville, and Brandeis. These dreams must now be born anew in us.

You are terrified of your own children, since they are natives in a world where you will always be immigrants. Because you fear them, you entrust your bureaucracies with the parental responsibilities you are too cowardly to confront yourselves. In our world, all the sentiments and expressions of humanity, from the debasing to the angelic, are parts of a seamless whole, the global conversation of bits. We cannot separate the air that chokes from the air upon which wings beat.

In China, Germany, France, Russia, Singapore, Italy and the United States, you are trying to ward off the virus of liberty by erecting guard posts at the frontiers of cyberspace. These may keep out the contagion for a small time, but they will not work in a world that will soon be blanketed in bit-bearing media.

Your increasingly obsolete information industries would perpetuate themselves by proposing laws, in America and elsewhere, that
claim to own speech itself throughout the world. These laws would
declare ideas to be another industrial product, no more noble than
pig iron. In our world, whatever the human mind may create can be
reproduced and distributed infinitely at no cost. The global conveyance
of thought no longer requires your factories to accomplish.

These increasingly hostile and colonial measures place us in the
same position as those previous lovers of freedom and self-determination
who had to reject the authorities of distant, uninformed powers. We must
declare our virtual selves immune to your sovereignty, even as we continue to consent to your rule over our bodies. We will spread ourselves
across the Planet so that no one can arrest our thoughts. We will create a
civilization of the Mind in Cyberspace. May it be more humane and fair
than the world your governments have made before.

Davos, Switzerland
February 8, 1996

*On 11 June 1996, the United States Court of Appeals for the
Third Circuit, meeting in Philadelphia, handed down a decision in a
case brought by the American Civil Liberties Union and several other
plaintiffs seeking to stop the enactment of the Communications
Decency Act provision of the Telecommunications Act of 1996. The
three-judge panel found unanimously for the plaintiff, effectively delet-
ing the language from the law. Most experts now believe that the so-
called Exon Amendment will be held to be unconstitutional by the
Supreme Court if the government chooses to appeal this decision.
Excerpts from the opinion are reprinted below.*

American Civil Liberties Union, Civil Action et al. v. United States Department of Justice et al. No. 96-1458

Before: Sloviter, Chief Judge, United States Court of Appeals for the
Third Circuit; Buckwalter and Dalzell, Judges, United States District
Court for the Eastern District of Pennsylvania

June 11, 1996

ADJUDICATION ON MOTIONS
FOR PRELIMINARY INJUNCTION

I.   INTRODUCTION

Procedural Background

Before us are motions for a preliminary injunction filed by
plaintiffs who challenge on constitutional grounds provisions of

the Communications Decency Act of 1996 (CDA or "the Act"), which constitutes Title V of the Telecommunications Act of 1996, signed into law by the President on February 8, 1996. [1] telecommunications Act of 1996, Pub. L. No. 104-104, • 502, 110 Stat. 56, 133-35.

Plaintiffs include various organizations and individuals who, inter alia, are associated with the computer and/or communications industries, or who publish or post materials on the Internet, or belong to various citizen groups. See ACLU Complaint (•• 7-26), ALA First Amended Complaint (•• 3, 12-33).

The defendants in these actions are Janet Reno, the Attorney General of the United States, and the United States Department of Justice. For convenience, we will refer to these defendants as the Government. Plaintiffs contend that the two challenged provisions of the CDA that are directed to communications over the Internet which might be deemed "indecent" or "patently offensive" for minors, defined as persons under the age of eighteen, infringe upon rights protected by the First Amendment and the Due Process Clause of the Fifth Amendment. Plaintiffs in Civil Action Number 96-963, in which the lead plaintiff is the American Civil Liberties Union (the ACLU), [2] filed their action in the United States District Court for the Eastern District of Pennsylvania on the day the Act was signed, and moved for a temporary restraining order to enjoin enforcement of these two provisions of the CDA. On February 15, 1996, following an evidentiary hearing, Judge Ronald L. Buckwalter, to whom the case had been assigned, granted a limited temporary restraining order, finding in a Memorandum that 47 U.S.C. • 223(a)(1)(B) ("the indecency provision" of the CDA) was unconstitutionally vague. On the same day, Chief Judge Dolores K. Sloviter, Chief Judge of the United States Court of Appeals for the Third Circuit, having been requested by the parties and the district court to convene a three-judge court, pursuant to • 561(a) of the CDA, appointed such a court consisting of, in addition to Judge Buckwalter, Judge Stewart Dalzell of the same district, and herself, as the circuit judge required by 28 U.S.C. • 2284.

After a conference with the court, the parties entered into stipulation, which the court approved on February 26, 1996, wherein the Attorney General agreed that she will not initiate any investigations or prosecutions for violations of 47 U.S.C. 223(d) for conduct occurring after enactment of this provision until the three-judge court hears Plaintiffs' Motion for Preliminary Injunction and has decided the motion.

[Substantial text was deleted here, much of which deals with the technology of Internet communications and the history of the development of the network infrastructure. The following excerpts are from the opinion written by Sloviter, Chief Judge, Court of Appeals for the Third Circuit.]

D. **The Nature of the Government's Interest**

The government asserts that shielding minors from access to indecent materials is the compelling interest supporting the CDA. It cites in support the statements of the Supreme Court that "[i]t is evident beyond the need for elaboration that a State's interest in 'safeguarding the physical and psychological well-being of a minor' is 'compelling,'" *New York v. Ferber*, 458 U.S. 747, 757 (1982) (quoting *Globe Newspaper Co. v. Superior Court*, 457 U.S. 596, 607 (1982), and "there is a compelling interest in protecting the physical and psychological well-being of minors. This interest extends to shielding minors from the influence of literature that is not obscene by adult standards." *Sable*, 492 U.S at 126. It also cites the similar quotation appearing in *Fabulous Assoc., Inc. v. Pennsylvania Public Utility Commission*, 896 F.2d 780, 787 (3d Cir. 1990).

Those statements were made in cases where the potential harm to children from the material was evident. Ferber involved the constitutionality of a statute which prohibited persons from knowingly promoting sexual performances by children under 16 and distributing material depicting such performances. Sable and Fabulous involved the FCC's ban on "dial-a-porn" (dealing by definition with pornographic telephone messages). In contrast to the material at issue in those cases, at least some of the material subject to coverage under the "indecent" and "patently offensive" provisions of the CDA may contain valuable literary, artistic or educational information of value to older minors as well as adults. The Supreme Court has held that "minors are entitled to a significant measure of First Amendment protection, and only in relatively narrow and well-defined circumstances may government bar public dissemination of protected materials to them." *Erznoznik v. City of Jacksonville*, 422 U.S. 205, 212-213 (1975) (citations omitted).

In Erznoznik, the Court rejected an argument that an ordinance prohibiting the display of films containing nudity at drive-in movie theatres served a compelling interest in protecting minor passersby from the influence of such films. The Court held that the prohibition was unduly broad, and explained that "[s]peech that is neither obscene as to youths nor subject to some other legitimate proscription cannot be suppressed solely to protect the young from ideas or images that a legislative body thinks unsuitable for them." 422 U.S. at 213-14. As Justice Scalia noted in *Sable*, "[t]he more pornographic what is embraced within the . . . category of 'indecency,' the more reasonable it becomes to insist upon greater assurance of insulation from minors." *Sable*, 492 U.S. at 132 (Scalia, J., concurring). It follows that where non-pornographic, albeit sexually explicit, material also falls within the sweep of the statute, the interest will not be as compelling.

In part, our consideration of the government's showing of a "compelling interest" trenches upon the vagueness issue, discussed in detail in Judge Buckwalter's opinion but equally pertinent to First Amendment analysis. Material routinely acceptable according to the standards of New York City, such as the Broadway play Angels in America which concerns homosexuality and AIDS portrayed in graphic language, may be far less acceptable in smaller, less cosmopolitan communities of the United States. Yet the play garnered two Tony Awards and a Pulitzer prize for its author, and some uninhibited parents and teachers might deem it to be material to be read or assigned to eleventh and twelfth graders. If available on the Internet through some libraries, the text of the play would likely be accessed in that manner by at least some students, and it would also arguably fall within the scope of the CDA.

There has been recent public interest in the female genital mutilation routinely practiced and officially condoned in some countries. News articles have been descriptive, and it is not stretching to assume that this is a subject that occupies news groups and chat rooms on the Internet. We have no assurance that these discussions, of obvious interest and relevance to older teenage girls, will not be viewed as patently offensive—even in context—in some communities.

Other illustrations abound of non-obscene material likely to be available on the Internet but subject to the CDA's criminal provisions. Photographs appearing in National Geographic or a travel magazine of the sculptures in India of couples copulating in numerous positions, a written description of a brutal prison rape, or Francesco Clemente's painting "Labirinth," see Def. Exh. 125, all might be considered to "depict or describe, in terms patently offensive as measured by contemporary community standards, sexual or excretory activities or organs." 47 U.S.C. • 223(d)(1). But the government has made no showing that it has a compelling interest in preventing a seventeen-year-old minor from accessing such images.

By contrast, plaintiffs presented testimony that material that could be considered indecent, such as that offered by Stop Prisoner Rape or Critical Path AIDS project, may be critically important for certain older minors. For example, there was testimony that one quarter of all new HIV infections in the United States is estimated to occur in young people between the ages of 13 and 20, an estimate the government made no effort to rebut. The witnesses believed that graphic material that their organizations post on the Internet could help save lives, but were concerned about the CDA's effect on their right to do so.

The government counters that this court should defer to legislative conclusions about this matter. However, where First

Amendment rights are at stake, "[d]eference to a legislative finding cannot limit judicial inquiry." *Sable*, 492 U.S. at 129 (quoting *Landmark Communications, Inc. v. Virginia*, 435 U.S. 829, 843 (1978)). "[W]hatever deference is due legislative findings would not foreclose our independent judgment of the facts bearing on an issue of constitutional law." Id.

Moreover, it appears that the legislative "findings" the government cites concern primarily testimony and statements by legislators about the prevalence of obscenity, child pornography, and sexual solicitation of children on the Internet. Similarly, at the hearings before us the government introduced exhibits of sexually explicit material through the testimony of Agent Howard Schmidt, which consisted primarily of the same type of hard-core pornographic materials (even if not technically obscene) which concerned Congress and which fill the shelves of "adult" book and magazine stores. Plaintiffs emphasize that they do not challenge the Act's restrictions on speech not protected by the First Amendment, such as obscenity, child pornography or harassment of children. Their suit is based on their assertion, fully supported by their evidence and our findings, that the CDA reaches much farther.

I am far less confident than the government that its quotations from earlier cases in the Supreme Court signify that it has shown a compelling interest in regulating the vast range of online material covered or potentially covered by the CDA. Nonetheless, I acknowledge that there is certainly a compelling government interest to shield a substantial number of minors from some of the online material that motivated Congress to enact the CDA, and do not rest my decision on the inadequacy of the government's showing in this regard.

E. The Reach of the Statute

Whatever the strength of the interest the government has demonstrated in preventing minors from accessing "indecent" and "patently offensive" material online, if the means it has chosen sweeps more broadly than necessary and thereby chills the expression of adults, it has overstepped onto rights protected by the First Amendment. *Sable*, 492 U.S. at 131.

The plaintiffs argue that the CDA violates the First Amendment because it effectively bans a substantial category of protected speech from most parts of the Internet. The government responds that the Act does not on its face or in effect ban indecent material that is constitutionally protected for adults. Thus one of the factual issues before us was the likely effect of the CDA on the free availability of constitutionally protected material. A wealth of persuasive evidence, referred to in detail in the Findings of Fact, proved that it is either technologically impossible or economically prohibitive for many of the plaintiffs to comply with the CDA without seriously impeding their posting of online material which adults have a constitutional right to access.

With the possible exception of an e-mail to a known recipient, most content providers cannot determine the identity and age of every user accessing their material. Considering separately content providers that fall roughly into two categories, we have found that no technology exists which allows those posting on the category of newsgroups, mail exploders or chat rooms to screen for age. Speakers using those forms of communication cannot control who receives the communication, and in most instances are not aware of the identity of the recipients. If it is not feasible for speakers who communicate via these forms of communication to conduct age screening, they would have to reduce the level of communication to that which is appropriate for children in order to be protected under the statute. This would effect a complete ban even for adults of some expression, albeit "indecent," to which they are constitutionally entitled, and thus would be unconstitutional under the holding in *Sable*, 492 U.S. at 131.

Even as to content providers in the other broad category, such as the World Wide Web, where efforts at age verification are technically feasible through the use of Common Gateway Interface (cgi) scripts (which enable creation of a document that can process information provided by a Web visitor), the Findings of Fact show that as a practical matter, non-commercial organizations and even many commercial organizations using the Web would find it prohibitively expensive and burdensome to engage in the methods of age verification proposed by the government, and that even if they could attempt to age verify, there is little assurance that they could successfully filter out minors.

The government attempts to circumvent this problem by seeking to limit the scope of the statute to those content providers who are commercial pornographers, and urges that we do likewise in our obligation to save a congressional enactment from facial unconstitutionality wherever possible. But in light of its plain language and its legislative history, the CDA cannot reasonably be read as limited to commercial pornographers. A court may not impose a narrowing construction on a statute unless it is "readily susceptible" to such a construction. *Virginia v. American Booksellers Association*, 484 U.S. 383, 397 (1988). The court may not "rewrite a . . . law to conform it to constitutional requirements." Id. Although we may prefer an interpretation of a statute that will preserve the constitutionality of the statutory scheme, *United States v. Clark*, 445 U.S. 23, 27 (1980), we do not have license to rewrite a statute to "create distinctions where none were intended." *American Tobacco Co. v. Patterson*, 456 U.S. 63, 72 n.6 (1982); see also *Consumer Party v. Davis*, 778 F.2d 140, 147 (3d Cir. 1985). The Court has often stated that "absent a clearly expressed legislative intention to the contrary, [statutory] language must ordinarily be regarded as conclusive." *Escondido Mut. Water Co. v. La Jolla Band of Mission Indians*, 466 U.S. 765, 772 (1984) (quoting *North Dakota v. United States*, 460 U.S. 300, 312 (1983)).

It is clear from the face of the CDA and from its legislative history that Congress did not intend to limit its application to commercial purveyors of pornography. Congress unquestionably knew how to limit the statute to such entities if that was its intent, and in fact it did so in provisions relating to dial-a-porn services. See 47 U.S.C. • 223(b)(2)(A) (criminalizing making any indecent telephone communication "for commercial purposes"). It placed no similar limitation in the CDA. Moreover, the Conference Report makes clear that Congress did not intend to limit the application of the statute to content providers such as those which make available the commercial material contained in the government's exhibits, and confirms that Congress intended "content regulation of both commercial and non-commercial providers." Conf. Rep. at 191. See also, 141 Cong. Rec. S8089 (daily ed. June 9, 1995) (Statement of Senator Exxon).

The scope of the CDA is not confined to material that has a prurient interest or appeal, one of the hallmarks of obscenity, because Congress sought to reach farther. Nor did Congress include language that would define "patently offensive" or "indecent" to exclude material of serious value. It follows that to narrow the statute in the manner the government urges would be an impermissible exercise of our limited judicial function, which is to review the statute as written for its compliance with constitutional mandates.

I conclude inexorably from the foregoing that the CDA reaches speech subject to the full protection of the First Amendment, at least for adults. [1] In questions of the witnesses and in colloquy with the government attorneys, it became evident that even if "indecent" is read as parallel to "patently offensive," the terms would cover a broad range of material from contemporary films, plays and books showing or describing sexual activities (e.g., Leaving Las Vegas) to controversial contemporary art and photographs showing sexual organs in positions that the government conceded would be patently offensive in some communities (e.g., a Robert Mapplethorpe photograph depicting a man with an erect penis).

We have also found that there is no effective way for many Internet content providers to limit the effective reach of the CDA to adults because there is no realistic way for many providers to ascertain the age of those accessing their materials. As a consequence, we have found that "[m]any speakers who display arguably indecent content on the Internet must choose between silence and the risk of prosecution." Such a choice, forced by sections 223(a) and (d) of the CDA, strikes at the heart of speech of adults as well as minors.

[The following excerpted material is from the opinion of Buckwalter, District Judge.]

I believe that plaintiffs should prevail in this litigation.

My conclusion differs in part from my original memorandum filed in conjunction with the request for a Temporary Restraining Order. As part of the expedited review (per • 561 of the CDA), and in contrast to the limited documentation available to me at the time of the T.R.O. hearing, we have now gathered voluminous evidence presented by way of sworn declarations, live testimony, demonstrative evidence, and other exhibits. [1] Based upon our findings of fact derived from careful consideration of that evidence, I now conclude that this statute is overbroad and does not meet the strict scrutiny standard in *Sable Communications of California, Inc. v. FCC,* 492 U.S. 115 (1989).

More specifically, I now find that current technology is inadequate to provide a safe harbor to most speakers on the Internet. On this issue, I concur in Chief Judge Sloviter's opinion. In addition, I continue to believe that the word "indecent" is unconstitutionally vague, and I find that the terms "in context" and "patently offensive" also are so vague as to violate the First and Fifth Amendments. It is, of course, correct that statutes that attempt to regulate the content of speech presumptively violate the First Amendment. See e.g. *R.A.V. v. City of Saint Paul,* 505 U.S. 377, 381 (1992). That is as it should be. The prohibition against Government's regulation of speech cannot be set forth any clearer than in the language of the First Amendment itself. I suspect, however, that it may come as a surprise to many people who have not followed the evolution of constitutional law that, by implication at least, the First Amendment provides that Congress shall make no law abridging the freedom of speech unless that law advances a compelling governmental interest. [2] Our cherished freedom of speech does not cover as broad a spectrum as one may have gleaned from a simple reading of the Amendment. [3] First Amendment jurisprudence has developed into a study of intertwining standards and applications, perhaps as a necessary response to our ever-evolving culture and modes of communication. [4] Essentially, my concerns are these: above all, I believe that the challenged provisions are so vague as to violate both the First and Fifth Amendments, and in particular that Congress' reliance on Pacifica is misplaced. In addition, I believe that technology as it currently exists—and it bears repeating that we are at the preliminary injunction phase only—cannot provide a safe harbor for most speakers on the Internet, thus rendering the statute unconstitutional under a strict scrutiny analysis. I refer to Chief Judge Sloviter's more detailed analysis of this issue.

While I believe that our findings of fact clearly show that as yet no defense is technologically feasible, and while I also have found the present Act to be unconstitutionally vague, I believe it is too early in the development of this new medium to conclude that other attempts to regulate protected speech within the medium will fail a challenge. That is to say that I specifically do not find that any and all statutory regulation of protected speech on the Internet could not survive constitutional scrutiny. Prior cases have established that government regulation to prevent access by minors to speech protected for adults, even in media considered the vanguard of our First Amendment protections, like print, may withstand a constitutional challenge. See e.g. *Ginsberg v. New York*, 390 U.S. 629, 635 (1968) ("'Material which is protected for distribution to adults is not necessarily constitutionally protected from restriction upon its dissemination to children.'") (quoting *Bookcase Inc. v. Broderick*, 18 N.Y.2d 71, 75, 271 N.Y.S.2d 947, 952, 218 N.E.2d 668, 671 (1966), appeal dismissed, sub nom *Bookcase, Inc. v. Leary*, 385 U.S. 12 (1966)). It should be noted that those restrictions that have been found constitutional were sensitive to the unique qualities of the medium at which the restriction was aimed.

[The final excerpts of the opinion for the plaintiffs to stay the execution of the CDA was written by District Judge Dalzell.]

3. **The Effect of the CDA and the Novel Characteristics of Internet Communication**

Over the course of five days of hearings and many hundreds of pages of declarations, deposition transcripts, and exhibits, we have learned about the special attributes of Internet communication. Our Findings of fact—many of them undisputed—express our understanding of the Internet. These Findings lead to the conclusion that Congress may not regulate indecency on the Internet at all. Four related characteristics of Internet communication have a transcendent importance to our shared holding that the CDA is unconstitutional on its face. We explain these characteristics in our Findings of fact above, and I only rehearse them briefly here. First, the Internet presents very low barriers to entry. Second, these barriers to entry are identical for both speakers and listeners. Third, as a result of these low barriers, astoundingly diverse content is available on the Internet. Fourth, the Internet provides significant access to all who wish to speak in the medium, and even creates a relative parity among speakers.

To understand how disruptive the CDA is to Internet communication, it must be remembered that the Internet evolved free of content-based considerations. Before the CDA, it only mattered how, and how quickly, a particular packet of data traveled from one point on the Internet to another. In its earliest incarnation as the ARPANET, the Internet was for many years a private means of access among the military, defense contractors, and defense-related researchers. The developers of the technology focused on creating a medium designed for the rapid transmittal of the information through overlapping and redundant connections, and without direct human involvement. Out of these considerations evolved the common transfer protocols, packet switching, and the other technology in which today's Internet users flourish. The content of the data was, before the CDA, an irrelevant consideration.

It is fair, then, to conclude that the benefits of the Internet to private speakers arose out of the serendipitous development of its underlying technology. As more networks joined the "network of networks" that is the Internet, private speakers have begun to take advantage of the medium. This should not be surprising, since participation in the medium requires only that networks (and the individual users associated with them) agree to use the common data transfer protocols and other medium-specific technology. Participation does not require, and has never required, approval of a user's or network's content.

After the CDA, however, the content of a user's speech will determine the extent of participation in the new medium. If a speaker's content is even arguably indecent in some communities, he must assess, inter alia, the risk of prosecution and the cost of compliance with the CDA. Because the creation and posting of a Web site allows users anywhere in the country to see that site, many speakers will no doubt censor their speech so that it is palatable in every community. Other speakers will decline to enter the medium at all. Unlike other media, there is no technologically feasible way for an Internet speaker to limit the geographical scope of his speech (even if he wanted to), or to "implement a system for screening the locale of incoming" requests. *Sable* 492 U.S. at 125.

The CDA will, without doubt, undermine the substantive, speech-enhancing benefits that have flowed from the Internet. Barriers to entry to those speakers affected by the Act would skyrocket, especially for non-commercial and not-for-profit information providers. Such costs include those attributable to age or credit card verification (if possible), tagging (if tagging is even a defense under the Act[20]), and monitoring or review of one's content.

The diversity of the content will necessarily diminish as a result. The economic costs associated with compliance with the Act will drive from the Internet speakers whose content falls within the zone of possible prosecution. Many Web sites, newsgroups, and chat rooms will shut down, since users cannot discern the age of other participants. In this respect, the Internet would ultimately come to mirror broadcasting and print, with messages tailored to a mainstream society from speakers who could be sure that their message was likely decent in every community in the country.

The CDA will also skew the relative parity among speakers that currently exists on the Internet. Commercial entities who can afford the costs of verification, or who would charge a user to enter their sites, or whose content has mass appeal, will remain unaffected by the Act. Other users, such as Critical Path or Stop Prisoner Rape, or even the ACLU, whose Web sites before the CDA were as equally accessible as the most popular Web sites, will be profoundly affected by the Act. This change would result in an Internet that mirrors broadcasting and print, where economic power has become relatively coterminous with influence.

Perversely, commercial pornographers would remain relatively unaffected by the Act, since we learned that most of them already use credit card or adult verification anyway. Commercial pornographers normally provide a few free pictures to entice a user into proceeding further into the Web site. To proceed beyond these teasers, users must provide a credit card number or adult verification number. The CDA will force these businesses to remove the teasers (or cover the most salacious content with cgi scripts), but the core, commercial product of these businesses will remain in place.

The CDA's wholesale disruption on the Internet will necessarily affect adult participation in the medium. As some speakers leave or refuse to enter the medium, and others bowdlerize their speech or erect the barriers that the Act envisions, and still others remove bulletin boards, Web sites, and newsgroups, adults will face a shrinking ability to participate in the medium. Since much of the communication on the Internet is participatory, i.e., is a form of dialogue, a decrease in the number of speakers, speech fora, and permissible topics will diminish the worldwide dialogue that is the strength and signal achievement of the medium.

It is no answer to say that the defenses and exclusions of • 223(e) mitigate the disruptive forces of the Act. We have already found as facts that the defenses either are not available to plaintiffs here or would impose excessive costs on them. These defenses are also unavailable to participants in specific forms of Internet communication.

I am equally dubious that the exclusions of • 223(e) would provide significant relief from the Act. The "common carrier" exclusion of • 223(e)(1), for example, would not insulate America Online from liability for the content it provides to its subscribers. It is also a tricky question whether an America Online chat room devoted to, say, women's reproductive health, is or is not speech of the service itself, since America Online, at least to some extent, "creat[es] the content of the communication" simply by making the room available and assigning it a topic. Even if America Online has no liability under this example, the service might legitimately choose not to provide fora that led to the prosecution of its subscribers. Similarly, it is unclear whether many caching servers are devoted "solely" to the task of "intermediate storage." The "vicarious liability" exclusion of • 223(e)(4) would not, for example, insulate either a college professor or her employer from liability for posting an indecent online reading assignment for her freshman sociology class.

We must of course give appropriate deference to the legislative judgments of Congress. See *Sable*, 492 U.S. at 129; *Turner*, 114 S. Ct. at 2472-73 (Blackmun, J., concurring). After hearing the parties' testimony and reviewing the exhibits, declarations, and transcripts, we simply cannot in my view defer to Congress's judgment that the CDA will have only a minimal impact on the technology of the Internet, or on adult participation in the medium. As in *Sable*, "[d]eference to a legislative finding cannot limit judicial inquiry when First Amendment rights are at stake." *Sable*, 492 U.S. at 129 (citation omitted). Indeed, the Government has not revealed Congress's "extensive record" in addressing this issue, *Turner*, 114 S. Ct. at 2472 (Blackmun, J., concurring), or otherwise convinced me that the record here is somehow factually deficient to the record before Congress when it passed the Act.

E. Conclusion

Cutting through the acronyms and argot that littered the hearing testimony, the Internet may fairly be regarded as a never-ending worldwide conversation. The Government may not, through the CDA, interrupt that conversation. As the most participatory form of mass speech yet developed, the Internet deserves the highest protection from governmental intrusion.

True it is that many find some of the speech on the Internet to be offensive, and amid the din of cyberspace many hear discordant voices that they regard as indecent. The absence of governmental regulation of Internet content has unquestionably produced a kind of chaos, but as one of [the] plaintiffs' experts put it with such resonance at the hearing:

What achieved success was the very chaos that the Internet is. The strength of the Internet is that chaos.

Just as the strength of the Internet is chaos, so the strength of our liberty depends upon the chaos and cacophony of the unfettered speech the First Amendment protects. For these reasons, I without hesitation hold that the CDA is unconstitutional on its face.

Selected Quotations

This section includes quotations related to issues identified in this Information Revolution. They are in categories to facilitate an understanding of the context in which they were uttered or written.

Education and Information

The Internet is a perfect diversion from learning... [it] opens many doors that lead to empty rooms.

Cliff Stoll,
author of Silicon Snake Oil,
heard at an Electronic Freedom Foundation (EFF) meeting

Everyone has to understand that if you do not have the ability to use computer technology in the twenty-first century, you will be as competitively disadvantaged as if you couldn't read at the turn of the last century. The failure to give kids these tools amounts to economic insanity.

Delaine Eastin,
California superintendent of public instruction,
in *Investor's Business Daily,* 28 September 1995

What information consumes is rather obvious: It consumes the attention of its recipients. Hence a wealth of information creates a poverty of attention, and a need to allocate that attention efficiently among the overabundance of information sources that might consume it.

Herbert Simon,
economist,
in the *Scientific American,* September 1995

It's a truism at this point that if you're looking for information, good information, you don't look for it online. Sure, the thinking goes, there's plenty of information online. Rumors. Rants. Half-baked opinions. What you find online may be interesting—that man-in-the-street stuff has its moments—but by and large it's put together by amateurs. Real journalism comes from professionals. It's been fascinating watching this idea get turned on its head.

Robert Rossney,
in the *San Francisco Chronicle,* July 1995

Cyberporn and Cyberhate

It is no solution to define words as violence[,] or prejudice as oppression, and then by cracking down on words or thoughts pretend that we are doing something about violence and oppression. No doubt it is easier to pass a speech code or hate-crimes law and proclaim the streets safer than actually to make the streets safer, but the one must never be confused with the other...Indeed, equating "verbal violence" with physical violence is a treacherous, mischievous business.

Jonathon Rauch,
in *Harper's Magazine*, May 1995

All fear of "offensive" speech is bourgeois and reactionary. Historically, profane or bawdy language was common in both the upper and lower classes, who lived together in rural areas amid the untidy facts of nature. Notions of propriety and decorum come to the fore in urbanized periods ruled by an expanding middle class, which is obsessed with cleanliness, respectability, and conformism.

Camille Paglia, "Language and the Left,"
in *The Advocate*, 7 March 1995

There are already laws prohibiting the promotion of hatred, and we are now considering new laws to establish limits on the use of the Internet and other forms of communication in a way that might be harmful to us all.

Allan Rock,
Canadian minister of justice,
from a virtual conference, May 1995

This is not politics...it's to protect the innocence of children.

Bob Dole,
former Senate majority leader,
on introducing his bill , the Protection from
Computer Pornography Act of 1995

Children are not being assaulted by images that appear on a computer screen. Any Internet user knows it is quite difficult to stumble across pornography.

Senator Russel Feingold (D-Wisconsin),
in the *Washington Post*, 15 July 1995

Two-point-five million use America Online. That's like a city. Parents wouldn't let their kids go wandering in a city of 2.5 million people without them, or without knowing what they're going to be doing.

> Pam McGraw,
> *America Online spokesperson,*
> in "Children Lured from Home by Internet Acquaintances"
> by David Foster, Associated Press, 13 June 1995

Filtering out [potentially offensive on-line] material at the user end is a more practical, and far less objectionable, approach than limiting a nation of computer users to baby talk.

> Editorial,
> *New York Times,* 28 July 1995

I worry about my child and the Internet all the time, even though she's too young to have logged on yet. Here's what I worry about. I worry that ten or fifteen or twenty years from now she will come to me and say, "Daddy, where were you when they took freedom of the press away from the Internet?"

> Mike Godwin,
> *EFF staff counsel,*
> in "Fear of Freedom: The Backlash against Free Speech
> on the Net," 13 February 1995

Privacy and Regulation

Our problems are not new. We must not sign away our freedom and our reason to make things even easier for the [politicians]. The only cure for bad information is better information. You are in charge now; use your power wisely.

> Jon Carroll,
> in "I Have Met the Enemy. I Have Bad News,"
> *San Francisco Chronicle,* 29 June 1995

I think there are certainly going to be lots of debates about the Internet. My hunch is that the First Amendment rights are going to prevail, and that in fact this is an astonishingly free country and pretty much intends to remain that way, and the Internet will just be one more expression of our freedom.... I think [with encryption] you have a different set of questions. I think clearly no American wants terrorists to be able to have a level of secrecy which enables them to organize ways of killing people; on the other hand people do want the right to confidentiality. I think...that is going to take some time to explore."

Newt Gingrich,
Speaker of the House of Representatives,
in response to a question at the opening ceremony for the
Smithsonian Institution World Wide Web site, May 1995

Business and Information Economy

Stop thinking about it as the "Information Superhighway" and start thinking about it as the "Marketing Superhighway." Doesn't it sound better already?

Don Logan,
CEO of Time Inc.,
in the *New York Times,* 18 October 1994

Have you ever gotten tired of hearing those ridiculous AT&T commercials claiming credit for things that don't even exist yet? You will.

Emmanuel Goldstein,
publisher of 2600: The Hacker Quarterly, 1995

The Department of Justice should resolutely bar monopolizing mergers in all markets, including telecommunications, but they are not in a position, as is the FCC, to promote new competition by selling the airwaves in auctions.

Reed Hundt,
chairman, Federal Communications Commission,
in the *Washington Post,* 14 April 1995

A great deal of information we consider to be highly personal, and of interest to ourselves and the town gossip—our names, telephone numbers, marital status, educational accomplishments, job and credit histories, even medical, dental, and psychiatric records—is now being sold on the open market to anyone who believes he or she might be able to use such information to turn a profit. These transactions usually take place without our knowledge or consent.

Anne Wells Branscomb,
in *Who Owns Information?,* 1994

John [Malone, of cable TV giant TCI] and I were just on a Networked Economy Conference panel together, and we were standing at the urinals talking about things, and Barry Diller comes in and stands between us. And Barry says, "C'mon, you seem like such good friends. Just split the difference."

Ray Smith,
CEO, Bell Atlantic,
on the failed Bell Atlantic/TCI venture, in *Wired,*
February 1995

The Future, Change, and Communities

Cyberspace. A consensual hallucination experienced daily by billions of legitimate operators, in every nation.... A graphical representation of data abstracted from the banks of every computer in the human system. Unthinkable complexity. Lines of light ranged in the nonspace of the mind, clusters and constellations of data. Like city lights, receding...

William Gibson,
in *Neuromancer,* 1984

For the society, the impact will be good or bad depending mainly on the question: Will "to be online" be a privilege or a right? If only a favored segment of the population gets a chance to enjoy the advantage of "intelligence amplification," the network may exaggerate the discontinuity in the spectrum of intellectual opportunity.

J. C. R. Licklider and Robert Taylor,
"The Computer as a Communication Device,"
in *Science and Technology,* April 1968

That [the public's increased access to legislative information] will change over time the entire flow of information and the entire quality of knowledge in the country and it will change the way people will try to play games in the legislative process.

Newt Gingrich,
in *BNA Daily Report for Executives,* 22 November 1994

Directory of Organizations

T he organizations that are described in this chapter have been instrumental in bringing the issues of the information revolution into the mainstream. There are also many groups of professionals in the field of information science who have come together in associations to help their members and interested researchers obtain data and communicate the latest events (technical and social) occurring within the discipline. A selected number are included in this chapter.

Alliance for a Connected Canada
Public Interest Advocacy Centre
(613) 562-4002
Fax: (613) 562-0007
74051.3157@compuserve.com
http://www.lglobal.com/connect/
index.html

The purpose of Alliance for a Connected Canada is to ensure that basic citizens' interests and needs are the primary focus in the public policy debate about Canada's Information Highway. The alliance brings together diverse groups that have an interest in how the information infrastructure is eventually deployed. Their goals are to promote vigorous and open debate regarding communications policy issues, take concerted action to shape Canada's communication policies, influence the design and evolution of basic and enhanced networks, and present policies that represent the public interest in the construction of the Information Highway.

Alliance for Public Technology (APT)
P.O. Box 28578
Washington, DC 20005-2301
(202) 408-1403
Fax: (202) 408-1134
apt@apt.org; http://apt.org/apt/index.html

The Alliance for Public Technology (APT) is a nonprofit coalition of public interest groups that exists to foster broad access to affordable, usable information and communication services. APT provides a grassroots voice for equitable and affordable access to the benefits of telecommunications technology in the Information Age. This is one of the organizations taking a frontline position on the emerging issues of telecommunications.

American Center for the Study of Distance Education (ACSDE)
College of Education
Pennsylvania State University
403 South Allen Street, Suite 206b
University Park, PA 16801-5202
(814) 863-3764
Fax: (814) 865-5878
jxm22@psu.edu
http://www.cde.psu.edu/DE/ACSDE/ACSD.htm

The American Center for the Study of Distance Education (ACSDE) was established in 1988 in the College of Education of Pennsylvania State University to promote distance education research, study, scholarship, and teaching and to serve as a clearinghouse for the dissemination of knowledge about distance education. According to ACSDE's director, "This is an interinstitutional, multidisciplinary center. It aims to facilitate collaboration among individuals and institutions in the United States and overseas."

Publication: The American Journal of Distance Education.

American Society for Information Science (ASIS)
8720 Georgia Avenue, Suite 501
Silver Spring, MD 20910

(301) 495-0900
Fax: (301) 495-0810
info@asis.org
http://www.asis.org/home.html

Founded in 1937, the American Society for Information Science (ASIS) has searched for new and better theories, techniques, and technologies to improve access to information. ASIS is an inter-disciplinary organization that works to sustain new develop-ments in information technology. Its membership of 4,000 includes professionals from such fields as computer science, lin-guistics, management, librarianship, engineering, law, medicine, chemistry, and education, individuals who share a common interest in improving the ways society manipulates information.

Publications: Journal of the American Society for Information Science (JASIS), Bulletin of the American Society for Information Science.

Annenberg Washington Program
The Willard Office Building
1455 Pennsylvania Avenue, NW, Suite 200
Washington, DC 20004-1008
(202) 393-7100; (202) 393-4121 (TDD)
Fax: (202) 638-2745
awp@nwu
http://www.annenberg.nwu.edu/pubs/

Officially known as the Annenberg Washington Program in Communications Policy Studies of Northwestern University, this program was established to provide a neutral forum for assess-ing the impact of communications technologies and public poli-cies. It has brought policymakers, experts, and the public together in forums and other activities since 1984.

Association for Computing Machinery (ACM)
1515 Broadway, 17th Floor
New York, NY 10036-5701
(212) 626-0500
Fax: (212) 944-1318
http://info.acm.org/

Founded in 1947, the Association for Computing Machinery (ACM) is one of the oldest and most respected international sci-entific and educational organizations dedicated to advancing the art, science, engineering, and application of information tech-nology. ACM has nearly a million members today, some 50 years after it was cofounded by John Mauchly, coinventor of ENIAC, the first general-purpose computer.

Publications: Communications of the ACM, Crossroads: The International ACM Student Magazine, Journal of the ACM, and many others, which are available on-line at http://www. acm.org/pubs/.

Association for Information Systems (AIS)
University of Pittsburgh
Katz Graduate School of Business
222 Mervis Hall
Pittsburgh, PA 15260
(412) 648-1588
Fax: (412) 648-1693
oharris@vms.cis.pitt.edu
http://www2.pitt.edu/~ais/

The Association for Information Systems (AIS) is a new professional organization whose stated purpose is to serve as "the premier global organization for academicians specializing in Information Systems."

Publications: Information Systems, Journal of Organizational Computing, and *MIS Quarterly.*

Association for the Advancement of Computing in Education (AACE)
P.O. Box 2966
Charlottesville, VA 22902
(804) 973-3987
Fax: (804) 978-7449
AACE@virginia.edu
http://curry.edschool.Virginia.EDU:80/aace/

Founded in 1981, the Association for the Advancement of Computing in Education (AACE) is an international educational and professional organization dedicated to the advancement of the knowledge, theory, and quality of learning and teaching at all levels with information technology.

Publications: Journal of Computers in Mathematics and Science Teaching (JCMST), Journal of Computing in Childhood Education (JCCE), Journal of Educational Multimedia and Hypermedia (JEMH), Journal of Artificial Intelligence in Education (JAIED), Journal of Technology and Teacher Education (JTATE), International Journal of

Educational Telecommunications (IJET), Educational Technology Review (ED-TECH Review), plus various Journal Special Issues.

Association for the Management of Information Technology in Higher Education (CAUSE)
4840 Pearl East Circle, Suite 302E
Boulder, CO 80301
(303) 449-4430
Fax: (303) 440-0461
info@cause.colorado.edu
http://cause-www.colorado.edu/

The mission of the Association for the Management of Information Technology in Higher Education (CAUSE) is to promote more effective planning, management, and evaluation of information technologies in colleges and universities. A key activity is to help information technology managers on campus enhance their knowledge of the business of higher education, master the ability to think critically, and learn to be creative, innovative, and flexible through the strategic management of the information resource.

Publications: CAUSE/EFFECT, a quarterly journal; a series of position papers and reports on timely issues; *Campus Watch*, a periodic electronic newsletter; plus various databases and related reports.

Association of Research Libraries (ARL)
21 Dupont Circle, NW, Suite 800
Washington, DC 20036
(202) 296-2296
Fax: (202) 872-0884
info@cni.org
http://arl.cni.org/

The Association of Reserach Libraries (ARL) numbers 119 major research libraries in the United States and Canada as members. The mission of the group is to identify and influence forces affecting the future of research libraries in the process of scholarly communication. In regard to the new information technologies, the ARL holds that "the open exchange of public information should be protected. Federal policy should support the integrity and preservation of government electronic databases. Copyright should not be applied to U.S. government information. Diversity of sources of access to U.S. government information is in the public interest, and entrepreneurship should be encouraged. Government information should be available at low cost. A system to provide equitable, no-fee access to basic public information is a requirement of a democratic society."

Center for Civic Networking (CCN)
P.O. Box 53152
Washington, DC 20009
(202) 362-3831
Fax: (202) 244-4380
ccn-info@civicnet.org.
http://civic.net/ccn.html

The Center for Civic Networking (CCN) is a nonprofit organization dedicated to applying information technology for the public good—particularly by putting information infrastructure to work within local communities to improve delivery of local government services and to improve access to information. It initiates projects and conducts policy research toward those ends. Its most visible activity is as sponsor of the National Information Infrastructure Awards.

Publications: Various papers by the staff, including "The Internet and the Poor," by Richard Civille, CCN's executive director; "Models for the Internet Local Loop" and "Life in the Fast Lane: A Municipal Roadmap for the Information Superhighway," by Miles Fidelman, CCN's president.

Center for Democracy and Technology (CDT)
1001 G Street, NW, Suite 700 East
Washington, DC 20001
(202) 637-9800
Fax: (202) 637-0968
info@cdt.org
http://www.cdt.org/index.html

A nonprofit public interest organization based in Washington, D.C., the Center's mission is "to develop and advocate public policies that advance constitutional civil liberties and democratic values in new computer and communications technologies." The Center brings together legal, technical, and public policy expertise on behalf of free speech and the free flow of information. There are many pointers to pertinent public access and privacy issues on their home page. This organization was at the forefront of efforts to repeal the CDA.

Center on Information Technology Accommodation (CITA)
General Services Administration
Center for Information Technology Accommodation
KBA Room 1234
18th & F Streets, NW
Washington, DC 20405
(202) 501-4906; (202) 501-2010 (TDD)
Fax: (202) 501-6269
Susan.Brummel@GSA.GOV
http://www.gsa.gov/coca/cocamain.htm

The General Services Administration (GSA) is a federal government agency that maintains the Center on Information Technology Accommodation (CITA) as a clearinghouse of information on making information systems accessible to all users. The Web site is an effort of GSA's Internet Working Group.

Coalition for Networked Information
21 Dupont Circle, NW
Washington, DC 20036
(202) 296-5098
Fax: (202) 872-0884
joan@cni.
http://www.cni.org/home.html

The Coalition for Networked Information is a partnership of the Association of Research Libraries, CAUSE, and Educom. It was founded in 1990 to enhance the performance of networks and computers for scholarship and enrichment of intellectual pursuits. The coalition operates initiatives in several areas to further the practice of using computer networks to share information. It has established a task force of over 200 institutions to explore shared visions of how information management must change to meet the social and economic realities of the new century. Members include higher education institutions, publishers, infrastructure providers, computer companies, and library organizations.

Committee on Information and Communications (CIC)
National Coordination Office for HPCC
4201 Wilson Boulevard, Suite 665
Arlington, VA 22230
(703) 306-4722

Fax: (703) 306-4727
http://www.whitehouse.gove/WH/EOP/OSTP/NSTC/html/
     CIC/CIC-apd.html

The Committee on Information and Communications (CIC) is
the research and development arm of the president's cabinet-
level agency, the National Science and Technology Council
(NSTC). Its mission is to accelerate technological evolution and
innovation to enable universal, accessible, and affordable applications of information technology to meet America's economic
growth and national security needs.

*Publication: Strategic Planning Document—Information and Com-
munications*, available on-line.

Committee on Institutional Cooperation (CIC)
302 East John Street, Suite 1705
Champaign, IL 61820-5698
(217) 333-8475
Fax: (217) 244-7127
b-sutton@uiuc.edu
http://www.cic.net/cic/cic.html

The Committee on Institutional Cooperation (CIC) is the academic consortium of the "Big Ten" universities and the University
of Chicago. While its focus is on the broadest issues that interact
among these institutions, it is also responsible for CICNet, a network that was formed in 1988 as a part of the NSFnet infrastructure. Today, the organization provides physical connectivity to a
broad population of students, faculty, and researchers in the
Midwest, and it is an active participant in a number of ventures
that are focused on providing access to information resources
and the management of information resources in a wide-area
network environment.

Publication: The *Circuit*, a quarterly newsletter (back issues available at file://ftp.cic.net/pub/cicnet/newsletters).

Communication Institute for Online Scholarship (CIOS)
P.O. Box 57
Rotterdam Junction, NY 12150
(518) 887-2443
Fax: (518) 887-5186
Support@vm.its.rpi.

The nonprofit Communication Institute for Online Scholarship
(CIOS) supports the use of computer and information technologies in the service of communication-related scholarship and

education on a worldwide basis. It runs the Comserve repository of communication-related resources on the Comserve gopher (gopher://cios.llc.rpi.edu). Access is restricted to associated member institutes.

Publications: Electronic Journal of Communication, InterCom.

Communications Policy Project
Benton Foundation
1634 Eye Street, NW, 12th Fl.
Washington, DC 20006
(202) 638-5770
Fax: (202) 638-5771; (800) 254-1671 (fax-on-demand)
benton@benton.org
http://www.benton.org

"Helping nonprofits realize the promise of the national information infrastructure [NII]," is the stated goal of the Benton Foundation's Communications Policy Project, a nonpartisan initiative to strengthen public-interest efforts in shaping the emerging NII. It hopes to help to ensure that public-interest benefits materialize along with the entertainment and commercial options that seem to be in the driver's seat in the deployment of the Information Highway. With the demise of the National Information Infrastructure Advisory Council, the Benton Foundation has agreed to house much of the information and publications generated by that body.

Publications: "What's Going On with the National Information Infrastructure," as well as other policy papers of the foundation or the NIIAC, are updated and available at the Web site.

Community Computer Communication (COM3™)
2033 NW Bobwhite Lane
Silverdale, WA 98383
(360) 613-9554
Fax: (360) 698-3209
COM3@comcomcom.com
http://comcomcom.com

Community Computer Communication (COM3™) is a unique private organization that creates public, private, and government partnerships that help to establish digital and distance learning centers in apartment complexes throughout the United States. Their Community Knowledge Development Centers are model facilities for the delivery of educational and community-focused activities.

Computer Professionals for Social Responsibility (CPSR)
P.O. Box 717
Palo Alto, CA 94302
(415) 322-3778
Fax: (415) 322-4748
cpsr@cpsr.org
http://www.cpsr.org/dox/home.html

Computer Professionals for Social Responsibility (CPSR), founded in 1981 by a group of computer scientists concerned about the use of computers in nuclear weapons systems, is today a public-interest alliance of scientists and others interested in the impact of computer technology on society. The mission is to provide policymakers and the public with realistic assessments of the power, promise, and problems of information technology. General areas of concern include community networks, privacy and civil liberties, caller ID, the clipper chip, and workplace and gender issues.

Publication: CPSR Newsletter.

Computer-Mediated Communication Studies Center (CMC)
154 Third Street
Troy, NY 12180-4039
(518) 271-8469
john@december.com
http://www.december.com/cmc/study/center.html

Under the guidance of John December, a researcher and expert on computer-mediated communication issues and protocols, the Computer-Mediated Communication Studies Center (CMC) is "dedicated to serving the needs of researchers, students, teachers, and practitioners interested in computer-mediated communication." This center helps people share information, make contacts, collaborate, and learn about developments and events.

Publication: CMC Magazine, available on-line at the Web site.

Conseil Europeen pour la Recherche Nucleaire (European Laboratory for Particle Physics) (CERN)
CH-1211
Geneva 23 Switzerland
41 22 767 6111
Fax: 41 22 767 65 55
http://www1.cern.ch/ExpSupport/

The European Laboratory for Particle Physics (CERN) is the birthplace of the World Wide Web. Much of the administration, experimentation, and standard development revolves around this facility.

Consortium for School Networking (CoSN)

1555 Connecticut Avenue, NW, Suite 200
Washington, DC 20036
(202) 466-6296
Fax: (202) 462-9043
membership@cosn.org.
gopher://digital.cosn.org/

The Consortium for School Networking (CoSN) is an active advocate for providing access to the emerging National Information Infrastructure in schools. Their commitment is to equal access, equity and quality of school networking, development and dissemination of networked-based information resources, and utilization of telecommunications to support education.

Discovery Institute

1201 Third Avenue, 40th Floor
Seattle, WA 98101-3099
(206) 287-3144
Fax: (206) 583-8500
discovery@discovery.org
http://www.discovery.org/

The Discovery Institute is a nonprofit organization that believes "in the importance of high ideals in public life, but we also distrust attempts to find perfect solutions for societal problems, especially through government." One of its senior fellows, George Gilder, has become a prophet of the new age of digital telecommunications convergence. A major part of the institute's work revolves around policies of information technology.

Educom

1112 16th Street, NW, Suite 600
Washington, DC 20036
(202) 872-4200
inquiry@educom.edu
http://educom.edu/.index.html

Created in 1964 to serve the leaders who manage information technology in higher education, Educom offers leadership and assistance to its member institutions in order to address critical issues associated with the new tools. It is a nonprofit consortium of education institutions that facilitates the introduction, use, and management of information resources in teaching, learning, scholarship, and research.

Publications: Educom Review, Educom Update, and *Edupage,* one of the Net's most widely read and most often quoted newsletters reporting on information technology issues and trends that might affect education and society.

Electronic Frontier Foundation (EFF)

P.O. Box 170190
San Francisco, CA 94117
(415) 668 7171
Fax: (415) 668 7007
ask@eff.org
http://www.eff.org/

Mitchell D. Kapor, founder of Lotus Development Corporation, and John Perry Barlow started this nonprofit civil liberties organization to work in the public interest to protect privacy, free expression, and access to on-line resources and information in July 1990. Since then, the Electronic Frontier Foundation (EFF) has been at the forefront of the fight for individual freedoms and the right to privacy in cyberspace. The organization produces a very popular guide to the Internet.

Publication: EFFector, the organization's on-line newsletter, is archived at http://www.eff.org/pub/EFF/Newsletters/EFFector/.

Electronic Pathways

3215 Marine Street
CU Campus Box 456
Boulder, CO 80309
(303) 492-5593
Fax: (303) 492-1585
elpath@stripe.colorado.edu
http://hanksville.phast.umass.edu/defs/independent/ElecPat
h/elecpath.html

The mission statement of this Native American organization reads in part, "Electronic Pathways was incorporated in the state of Colorado in 1994 and has minority and women majority ownership. [It] is a nonprofit and tax-exempt organization whose primary mission is to ensure that underserved and underrepresented communities and schools have equal access and opportunity to participate fully in this current information and technological era." It is of critical importance to the members of Electronic Pathways to ensure that the Information Superhighway and its advantages are accessible to all Native Americans in rural, reservation, and urban areas nationwide.

Electronic Privacy Information Center (EPIC)
666 Pennsylvania Avenue, SE, Suite 301
Washington, DC 20003
(202) 544-9240
Fax: (202) 547-5482
info@epic.org
http://epic.org/

The Electronic Privacy Information Center (EPIC) is a nonprofit public-interest research center established in 1994 to focus attention on emerging civil liberties issues relating to the National Information Infrastructure. Important areas of concern for the organization include the clipper chip, the digital telephony proposal, national ID cards, medical record privacy, credit records, and the sale of consumer data.

Publication: The *EPIC Alert* is a free biweekly publication available via e-mail. To subscribe, send the message: SUBSCRIBE CPSR-ANNOUNCE Firstname Lastname to listserv@cpsr.org.

Evergreen TechTeam
P.O. Box 1911
Port Townsend, WA 98368
(360) 379-8651
Fax: (360) 379-0546
martini@olympus.net
http://www.olympus.net/martini/Evergreen.html

The Evergreen TechTeam was formed in Washington State to support public education efforts to train teachers and students about digital information tools through the use of technology-literate volunteers. Initiatives include partnerships with the state's 4-H organization and the Washington State University Extension system.

Global SchoolNet (GSN)
P.O. Box 243
Bonita, CA 91908-0243
(619) 475-4852

Fax: (619) 472-0735
info@gsn.org
http://www.gsn.org/

In operation since 1985, Global SchoolNet (GSN) has been a leader in the instructional applications of telecommunications. The network organization—formerly known as FrEdMail (Free Educational Mail)—originated with a group of teachers in San Diego who pioneered the vision of the "Global Schoolhouse," where teachers, students, business, government, and the community can learn together. Among the services offered is the only professionally managed K–12 newsfeed.

Information Infrastructure Task Force (IITF)
White House Office of Science and Technology Policy
(202) 482-1835
cfranz@ntia.doc.gov
http://iitf.doc.gov/

The Information Infrastructure Task Force (IITF) was convened by the National Economic Council and the White House Office of Science and Technology Policy in 1994. The task force, which was first chaired by Commerce Department Secretary Ron Brown, includes representatives from almost all federal agencies. Its purpose is to coordinate and accelerate the wide range of government activities related to the National Information Infrastructure. Staff work and administrative support for the IITF are carried out by the National Telecommunications and Information Administration (NTIA) of the Department of Commerce. Three IITF committees have been established: Telecommunications Policy, Information Policy, and Applications and Technology.

Information Technology Office (ITO)
Advanced Research Projects Agency
3701 North Fairfax Drive
Arlington, VA 22203-1714
(703) 696-2228
Fax: (703) 696-2207 (ARPA)
http://ftp.arpa.mil/

This Department of Defense Advanced Research Projects Agency (ARPA) office is responsible for research into breakthrough information technologies for potential use in defense applications.

Institute for Academic Technology (IAT)
University of North Carolina at Chapel Hill
2525 Meridian Parkway, Suite 400
Durham, NC 27713
(919) 560-5031
Fax: (919) 560-5047
info.iat@mhs.unc.edu
http://ike.engr.washington.edu/iat/

The Institute for Academic Technology (IAT) is dedicated to the proposition that information technology can be a valuable tool for improving the quality of student learning. To this end, the IAT facilitates the widespread use of effective and affordable technologies in higher education.

Publications: IATNEWS, an e-mail listserve that provides periodic news releases regarding the IAT; and *INFOBITS*, the IAT Information Resources Group's monthly electronic newsletter, which provides short articles related to instruction and information technology worldwide.

Institute of Electrical and Electronics Engineers (IEEE) Communications Society
445 Hoes Lane
Piscataway, NJ 08855-1331
(908) 981-0060
Fax: (908) 981-0345
http://www.ieee.org/

The Institute of Electrical and Electronics Engineers (IEEE) is the world's largest technical professional society. Founded in 1884, today it has a membership of some 320,000 in 147 countries. Its nonprofit mission is to support the application of electrotechnology and allied sciences for the benefit of humanity and the advancement of the profession. Focusing on the technical aspects of deploying information technology, the Communications Society arm of the IEEE addresses the scientific, engineering, technological, and applications issues of transferring information—including voice, data, image, and video—among multiple locations, wired or wireless.

Publications: The IEEE publishes nearly 25 percent of the world's technical papers in the electrical, electronics, and computer engineering fields.

Internet Business Association (IBA)
11160-F South Lakes Drive, Suite 349
Reston, VA 22091
(703) 779-1320
Fax: (703) 779-1362
info@iba.org
gopher://iba.org/

The Internet Business Association (IBA) was conceived in June 1994 by seven companies interested in expanding the possibilities of the Internet for business purposes. The IBA's mission statement notes that it wants "to become the recognized source for public education about the Internet via brochures, speeches, news conferences, and on-line information; to provide legislative and regulatory representation for small- to mid-sized companies by retaining a full-time lobbyist on Capitol Hill; and to provide services for our members that will enhance their businesses and their use of the Internet."

Internet Engineering Task Force (IETF)
c/o Corporation for National Research Initiatives
1895 Preston White Drive, Suite 100
Reston, VA 22091
(703) 620-8990
Fax: (703) 758-5913
ietf-info@cnri.reston.va.us
http://www.ietf.cnri.reston.va.us/home.html

Funded by a National Science Foundation grant, the Internet Engineering Task Force (IETF) is a large international community of network designers, operators, vendors, and researchers concerned with the evolution of the Internet architecture and its smooth operation. This group is the technical end of the operation of the Information Highway. The actual technical development is done in the working groups, which are organized by topic (e.g., routing, network management, security, etc.).

Internet Network Information Center (InterNIC)
505 Huntmar Park Drive
Herndon, VA 22070
(800) 862-0677; (908) 668-6587
Fax: (908) 742-4811
admin@ds.internic.net.
http://internic.net/

The InterNIC is the organization responsible for domain names on the Internet, the top levels of which are education (.edu), governmental (.gov), nonprofit and not-for-profit organizations (.org), commercial (.com), and network (.net). Initiated by the National Science Foundation when it was responsible for the NSFnet backbone that maintained most of the research and academic traffic on the Net, its services were divided in 1995 after NSFnet ceased to exist. The InterNIC project today comprises two distinct services run by separate organizations. These are Directory and Database Services, managed by AT&T Corporation and Registration Services, which are handled by Network Solutions, Inc. (which also provides NIC Support Services).

Internet Society
12020 Sunrise Valley Drive, Suite 210
Reston, VA 20191-3429
(703) 364-9888
Fax: 703-648-9887
membership@isoc.org
http://info.isoc.org

The Internet Society is a nongovernmental international organization for global coordination of the Internet and its Internetworking technologies and protocols. The society, comprising the companies, government agencies, and foundations that created the Net, attempts to maintain the infrastructure's viability as it scales to global proportions.

Kidlink Society
4815 Saltrod
Arendal, Norway
+47 370 31204
Fax: +47 370 27111
opresno@kidlink.org
http://www.kidlink.org/society/

An international nonprofit organization, the Kidlink Society is based in Norway. While memberships are available, participation is open to anyone who will support the goals of the society. There is no cost associated with participation. The key project of the organization is a grassroots effort aimed at getting as many 10–to 15-year-olds as possible involved in a global dialogue. Since the project's start in 1990, over 42,000 kids from 72 countries have participated in the organization's activities.

Loka Institute
P.O. Box 355
Amherst, MA 01004-0355
(413) 253-2828
Fax: (413) 253-4942
loka@amherst.edu

The Loka Institute was founded in 1987 for the purpose of making science and technology more responsive to social and environmental concerns. Their Technology and Democracy Project publishes critical policy analyses, gives public presentations, disseminates a periodic newsletter, and organizes other activities to promote the democratization of technology.

Publication: A newsletter, *Loka Alerts.*

Morino Institute
1801 Robert Fulton Drive, Suite 550
Reston, VA 22091
(703) 620-8971
Fax: (703) 620-4102
http://www.morino.org/

In a broad attempt to "open the doors of opportunity—economic, civic, health, and education," the Morino Institute was formed to improve the lives of people and their communities in the Communication Age. The institute generates papers and policy regarding community networking, and it maintains a list of on-line community networks at the Web site.

Publications: Among its many position papers and fact sheets on issues of importance facing people in the Communication Age are "Opening Doors of Opportunity in the Communications Age," "The Promise and Challenge of a New Communications Age," and "Assessment and Evolution of Community Networking." These are all available for free downloading.

National Coordination Office for High Performance Computing and Communications (HPCC)
4201 Wilson Boulevard, Suite 665
Arlington, VA 22230
(703) 306-4722
Fax: (703) 306-4727
nco@hpcc.gov
http://www.hpcc.gov/

The HPCC is a $1.1 billion federal program to extend U.S. technological leadership in high-performance computing and computer communication; provide wide dissemination and application of the technologies to speed the pace of innovation and to improve the national economic competitiveness, national security, education, health care, and the global environment; and provide key enabling technologies for the National Information Infrastructure (NII) and demonstrate select NII applications.

Publications: Included on-line at the Web site are various blue books, implementation plans, fact sheets, etc., which relate to the deployment of the NII and high-performance computing and communication issues.

National Information Infrastructure Advisory Council (NIIAC)

niiac@niiac-info.org

http://www.uark.edu/~niiac/

Formally established and appointed in early 1994, this 37-member panel was created by executive order no. 12,864 of the president of the United States in 1993. Its diverse membership represents many of the key constituencies with a stake in the National Information Infrastructure (NII), including private industries; state and local governments; community, public interest, education, and labor groups; creators and distributors of content; and privacy and security advocates. The National Information Infrastructure Advisory Council (NIIAC) was an independent body whose official secretariat was the National Telecommunications and Information Administration (NTIA). The council was responsible for advising the secretary of commerce and the administration on a national strategy for promoting the development of the NII as well as the Global Information Infrastructure. The NIIAC issued its final report early in 1996. See entry for the Communications Policy Project.

Members of the NIIAC were Morton Bahr, president, Communications Workers of America, AFL-CIO; Dr. Toni Carbo Bearman, dean and professor, School of Library and Information Science, University of Pittsburgh; Marilyn Bergman, president, American Society of Composers, Authors, and Publishers (ASCAP); Bonnie Laverne Bracey, teacher, Ashlawn Elementary School, Arlington, Virginia; John F. Cooke, president, the Disney Channel; Esther Dyson, president, EDventure Holdings; William C. Ferguson, chairman and chief executive officer, NYNEX

Corporation; Dr. Craig Fields, chairman and chief executive officer, Microelectronics and Computer Technology Corporation; Jack Fishman, publisher, *Citizen-Tribune*, Morristown, Tennessee; Lynn Forester, president and chief executive officer, FirstMark Holdings, Inc.; Carol Fukunaga, senator, state of Hawaii; Jack Golodner, president, Department for Professional Employees, AFL-CIO; Eduardo Gomez, president and general manager, KABQ Radio, Albuquerque, New Mexico; Haynes G. Griffin, president and chief executive officer, Vanguard Cellular Systems, Inc.; LaDonna Harris, president, Americans for Indian Opportunity; Dr. George Heilmeier, president and chief executive officer, Bellcore (Bell Communications Research); Susan Herman, general manager, Department of Telecommunications, city of Los Angeles; James R. Houghton, chairman and chief executive officer, Corning, Inc.; Stanley S. Hubbard, chairman and chief executive officer, Hubbard Broadcasting, Inc. and the United States Satellite Broadcasting Company, Inc.; Robert L. Johnson, founder and president, Black Entertainment Television; Dr. Robert E. Kahn, president, Corporation for National Research Initiatives; Deborah Kaplan, vice president, World Institute on Disability; Mitchell Kapor, chairman, Electronic Frontier Foundation; Delano E. Lewis, president and chief executive officer, National Public Radio; Edward R. McCracken, chairman and chief executive officer, Silicon Graphics, Inc.; Alex J. Mandl, chief executive officer, Communications Services Group, AT&T; Dr. Nathan Myhrvold, senior vice president of advanced technology, Microsoft Corporation; N. M. (Mac) Norton Jr., attorney-at-law, Wright, Lindsey & Jennings; Vance K. Opperman, president, West Publishing Company; Jane Smith Patterson, advisor to the governor of North Carolina for policy, budget and technology; Frances W. Preston, president and chief executive officer, Broadcast Music, Inc. (BMI); Bert C. Roberts Jr., chairman and chief executive officer, MCI Communications Corporation; John Sculley, former chairman, Apple Computers, Inc.; Joan H. Smith, chairman, Oregon Public Utility Commission; Raymond W. Smith, chairman and chief executive officer, Bell Atlantic Corporation; Al Teller, chairman and chief executive officer, MCA Music Entertainment Group; Lawrence Tisch, president and chief executive officer, CBS, Inc.; Jack Valenti, chief executive officer and president, Motion Picture Association of America.

Publications: Various working group and megaproject reports, which are available on-line.

Tech Corps
P.O. Box 832
Sudbury, MA 01776
(508) 820-8100
Fax: (508) 875-4349
info@ustc.org
http://www.ustc.org/index.html

Tech Corps is a national, nonprofit organization of technology volunteers dedicated to helping improve K–12 education at the grass roots, through the effective integration of technology into the learning environment. It was formulated following the ideas generated by Gary Beach, CEO of ComputerWorld. Through a chartering effort that created a branch of the organization in every state, the mission is to place capable technicians in school districts to help teachers and students integrate the new information technologies into their studies.

Trans-European Research and Education Networking Association (TERENA)
Singel 466-468
NL-1017 AW Amsterdam
Netherlands
31 20 639 1131
Fax: 31 20 639 3289
secretariat@terena.nl
http://www.earn.net/

October 1994 marked the start of the Trans-European Research and Education Networking Association (TERENA), as the Réseaux Associés pour la Recherche Européenne (RARE) and European Academic and Research Network (EARN) merged "…to promote and participate in the development of a high-quality international information and telecommunications infrastructure for the benefit of research and education." The group carries out technical activities and provides a platform for discussion and education to encourage the development of a high-quality computer networking infrastructure for the European research community.

USC Information Sciences Institute (ISI)
4676 Admiralty Way
Marina del Rey, CA 90292-6695
(310) 822-1511

Fax: (310) 823-6714
http://www.isi.edu/

A research facility of the USC School of Engineering, the Information Sciences Institute (ISI) is involved in a broad spectrum of information processing research and the development of advanced computer and communication technology and systems. ISI develops experimental systems and research papers in the area of informational computation. These include work in software engineering, artificial intelligence systems, systems performance and systems software network protocols, personal teleconferencing, network security and gigabit LANS VLSI, VLSI reliability, low-power circuits, etc.

Publications: An array of technical reports.

Voters Telecomm Watch (VTW) for Internet Education
P.O. Box 7081
New York, NY 10116-7081
(212) 592-3801
shabbir@panix.com
http://www.vtw.org/

The purpose of the VTW is to assure the same liberties and civil rights that are guaranteed in the real world are available in cyberspace as well. It works to educate people about computer networks and how to use them, and it has taken a leadership role in alerting Net users to the threats against free access, privacy issues, copyright, etc.

Web Society
c/o Association for Advancement in Computing in Education/AACE
P.O. Box 2966
Charlottesville, VA 22902
(804) 973-3987
Fax: (804) 978-7449
websoc@websoc.org
http://info.websoc.org/

The Web Society was founded as an international nonprofit group according to Austrian law in February 1995. Its purpose is to "support general, widely accessible and disciplined use of the Net and other wide-area or metropolitan networks." It strongly advocates against the infringement of personal privacy and "is not concerned with the hardware and protocol infrastructure for the Net, but with information, services, tools, and applications of the Net."

World Wide Web Consortium (W3C)
Laboratory for Computer Science
Massachusetts Institute of Technology
545 Technology Square
Cambridge, MA 02139
(617) 253-2613
Fax: (617) 258-5999
http://www.w3.org/hypertext/WWW/Consortium/

The World Wide Web Consortium (W3C), which includes the Laboratory for Computer Science at the Massachusetts Institute of Technology and CERN in Switzerland, exists to develop common standards for the evolution of the World Wide Web. Activities include maintaining a repository of information about the Web for developers and users, and prototyping and sample applications to demonstrate use of new technology.

Selected Print Resources

6

The monographs listed in this chapter have been divided into their general areas of inquiry. Although the subject matter may overlap in many cases, the titles are placed within the group that best describes their emphasis. Cultural Aspects includes a broad array of books that deal with everything from the technicalities of building the National Information Infrastructure (NII) to the issues that are evolving in the world we call cyberspace. Business Aspects include subjects about making money on-line and paying for the infrastructure. Educational Aspects includes many examples of how technology is changing the classroom. And the Internet section lists just a few of the hundreds of new books that have been published recently about how to use the Information Highway. Selected magazine titles are provided at the end of the chapter because of the prominent role they have taken in covering the issues of the Information Revolution.

Books

Cultural Aspects

Anderson, R. H., T. K. Bikson, S. A. Law, B. M. Mitchell, C. R. Kedzie, B. Keltner, C. W. A. Panis, J. Pliskin, P. Srinagesh. **Universal Access to E-Mail: Feasibility and Societal Implications.** Santa Monica, CA: RAND, 1995. 267 pp.

RAND is a consulting organization that conducts studies of important issues that impact society or have the potential to do so. They have made available this report on the possibilities of providing universal access to e-mail in the United States (see Electronic Texts).

Baldwin, Thomas F., D. S. McVoy, and C. Steinfeld, eds. **Convergence: Integrating Media, Information, and Communication.** Thousand Oaks, CA: Sage Publications, 1995. 440 pp.

This book examines the overwhelming pressures that are driving the convergence of the media and communication industries, given the availability of new technologies. It makes some predictions about what this change holds for society in the future.

Blanton, Tom, ed. **Top Secret Computer Messages the Reagan/ Bush White House Tried To Destroy.** New York: The New Press, 1995. 256 pp. (plus 1.44-MB computer disk).

This is a remarkable compilation of electronic mail messages that were archived during the Reagan and Bush administrations. For the first time, the issue of what constitutes a historical document came to the fore as President Bush's staffers fought to exempt these communications from federal law that held they should be preserved. For more information, contact Tom Blanton at nsarchiv@gwis2.circ.gwu.edu.

Brand, Stewart. **The Media Lab.** New York: Penguin Books, 1988. 285 pp.

The author is one of the pioneers of alternative living as publisher of the *Whole Earth Review* and a true founding member of cybercommunities with the establishment of the Whole Earth 'Lectronic Link on-line bulletin board service in 1985. This book is a first look at the Media Lab, the research facility on the campus of the Massachusetts Institute of Technology that was founded by Nicholas Negroponte. Many of the new digital technologies have had their genesis there or have been modified by the people who have gone through its doors.

Broadhurst, Judith. **The Woman's Guide to Online Services.** New York: McGraw-Hill, 1995. 418 pp.

Concerned by the low percentage of women on-line, Broadhurst invites women into the community of on-line users and orients them to the myriad opportunities available. She focuses on a wide range of subjects that affect and interest women, from issues of career, finance, and politics to those of marriage, family, and aging. She is very concerned that if women do not take part in on-line activities, they will miss out on where the decisions will be made.

Brook, James, and Iain A. Boal, eds. **Resisting the Virtual Life: The Culture and Politics of Information.** San Francisco: City Lights, 1995. 278 pp.

A collection of essays that center on the culture being developed on the Internet, this is a new offering with very diverse points of view.

Carroll, Jim, and Rick Broadhead. **The Canadian Internet Handbook, 1995 Edition.** Scarborough, Ont. Prentice Hall Canada, 1995. 911 pp.

The best-seller among Internet-related books in Canada, this is the second edition of the popular overview of Net-related sources and issues that are unique to that country. It includes case studies of how 17 associations, corporations, charities, and individuals make use of the Internet. More information is available at http://lydian.csi.nb.ca/handbook/adv.htm.

Cherny, Lynn, and Elizabeth Reba Weise, eds. **Wired Women: Gender and New Realities in Cyperspace.** Seattle: Seal Press, 1996. 269 pp.

This book is a collection of essays and reflections written by women who have been using and reporting on the Internet for years. It provides some suggestions for women who might be tentative about logging on and exploring the new virtual worlds.

Condat, Jean-Bernard, and Nicolas Pioch. **Internet.** Montreal: J.C.I., 1994. 214 pp.

Written by two of France's Internet experts on the Internet, this French-language book provides basic information about the possibilities for using the Internet. The authors advocate implementation of the Net as soon as possible.

d'Agostino, Peter, and David Tafler, eds. **Transmission: Toward a Post-Television Culture.** Thousand Oaks, CA: Sage Publications, 1995. 336 pp.

The editors have made their inquiry into the converging roles of media and interactive technologies from the point of view of the most dominant media in our culture: television. The book examines what these changes mean for the basic institutions in society.

Drake, William, ed. **The New Information Infrastructure: Strategies for U.S. Policy.** New York: The 20th Century Fund, 1995. 448 pp.

Communications and information analysts address some of the major policy issues involved in the development of the Information Infrastructure on the national, as well as global, level. Issues addressed include corporate influence on the delivery of information, deregulation and the impact on public accessibility, and the international aspect of connecting networks. More information is available at http://communication.ucsd.edu/wdrake/fundbook.html.

Eager, Bill. **The Information Superhighway Illustrated.** Indianapolis, IN: Que, 1994. 184 pp.

Illustrated with many graphic representations, this work provides technical details about the way network hardware and software combine to form the Information Superhighway.

Ford, Andrew. **Spinning the Web: How To Provide Information on the Internet.** New York: Van Nostrand Reinhold, 1995. 227 pp.

A comprehensive primer, written by an English computer expert with over 15 years of experience, this book covers topics ranging from connecting to the Internet to publishing information on the World Wide Web. It is listed here because it also includes discussions of copyright concerns and security consider-ations along with the practical "how-to" information.

Gates, Bill. **The Road Ahead.** New York: Viking, 1995. 304 pp.

The founder and CEO of Microsoft, the world's largest software company, presents his vision of the information future and where the data highway will lead us. This package also includes an interactive CD-ROM that includes the full text of the book, plus many other features, like a view inside his new home. More information is available on the Web at http://www.roadahead. com/.

Gay, Martin, and Kathlyn Gay. **The Information Super-highway.** New York: Twenty-First Century Books, 1996. 112 pp.

The authors have presented this basic information about the development of what will become the broadband interactive information system of the near future. Their book is targeted toward young adults and strives to make the technical aspects and social issues of connectivity simple yet meaningful.

Grossman, Lawrence K. **The Electronic Republic: Reshaping Democracy in the Information Age.** New York: Viking Penguin, 1995. 290 pp.

Grossman offers suggestions in this work on what policy might be implemented to allow Americans to improve the representa-tive system that has functioned for two centuries without suffer-ing from the dangers of public opinion—driven government that the Constitution was written to prevent. He discusses how the new communication technologies could be implemented to increase the sort of grassroots participation that most Americans say is desirable.

Hafner, Katie, and Matthew Lyon. **Where Wizards Stay Up Late: The Origins of the Internet.** New York: Simon & Schuster, 1996. 320 pp.

This book has been well received by most of the Internet veter-ans responsible for the development of the infrastructure from the early 1960s on. It is a thorough look at the personalities, motivations, the genius, and the occasional luck behind what has become the most important technological development of recent times.

Hafner, Katie, and John Markoff. **Cyberpunk—Outlaws and Hackers on the Computer Frontier.** New York: Simon & Schuster, 1991. 368 pp.

This is a compilation of interviews with some of the most famous and infamous teenaged "crackers" who made headlines in the early part of the decade.

Halberstam, David. **The Next Century.** New York: Morrow, 1991. 126 pp.

Halberstam is a renowned historian who applies his knowledge of the past as he predicts the world of the future. This work includes a chapter on the impact of information (and other) technologies on the way people will behave.

Heap, Nick, R., Thomas, G. Einon, R. Mason, and H. MacKay, eds. **Information Technology and Society.** Thousand Oaks, CA: Sage Publications, 1995. 448 pp.

This is a thorough reader on the issues that are being impacted by the Information Revolution: social, political, and technological. The editors focus on work, education, political processes, and future possibilities.

Ho, James K. **Prosperity in the Information Age: Creating Value with Technology—From Mailrooms to Boardrooms.** Wilmette, IL: Infotomics, 1994. 308 pp.

The author argues that people, not hardware and software, drive the advancement of life and work. He suggests a "winning mindset for everyone seeking meaningful work and rewarding life in the Information Age." More information is available on the Web at http://www.uic.edu/~jimho/pia.html.

Jones, Steven G., ed. **CyberSociety: Computer-Mediated Communication and Community.** Thousand Oaks, CA: Sage Publications, 1995. 256 pp.

Jones, an associate professor and chair of the faculty of communication at the University of Tulsa, calls on his considerable experience to examine on-line communities like Usenet news, commercial service providers like America Online, and multi-user dungeons. The collection of papers analyzes computer-mediated communication from the viewpoint of feminism, political science, anthropology, speech communication, literature, and media studies.

Kahin, Brian. **Information Infrastructure Sourcebook.** Boston: JFK School of Government/Harvard University, 1994. 1,700 pp.

The National Information Infrastructure initiative has generated hundreds of documents. Many of them are archived in this large volume. Speeches, vision statements, pending legislation, etc., are archived here.

Kahin, Brian, and James Keller, eds. **Public Access to the Internet.** Cambridge, MA: MIT Press, 1995. 400 pp.

This is a balanced collection of 17 articles that deal with the important issues in enabling widely available access to the Internet at a time of rapid commercialization and growth. Especially helpful for network managers, politicians, and other professionals, the volume is divided into five parts: the Public Access Agenda, the Sociology and Culture of the Internet, Establishing Network Communities, Accommodating New Classes of Users, and Pricing and Service Models.

Kehoe, Brendan. **Zen and the Art of the Internet.** 3rd ed. Englewood Cliffs, NJ: PTR Prentice Hall, 1994. 193 pp.

One of the first books about the use and culture of the Internet, this primer by Kehoe is now legendary. It provides excellent information about what one can do on the Net, as well as the basics of how to accomplish it. An earlier version is available on the Web at http://sundance.cso.uiuc.edu/Publications/Other/Zen/zen-1.0_toc.html.

Kling, Rob. **Computerization and Controversy: Value Conflicts and Social Choices.** 2d ed. San Diego: Academic Press, 1966. 961 pp.

This anthology focuses on the social aspects of computing. Sixty-four articles deal with the controversies in computer and information systems as applied to the productivity of organizations, empowerment of workers, women's work, etc.

Levy, Steven. **Hackers: Heroes of the Computer Revolution.** Garden City, NY: Anchor Press/Doubleday, 1984. 458 pp.

Levy provides a history of the hackers and the culture of home-bred computer inventors who ultimately helped develop the Internet and Usenet.

Lynch, Daniel, and Marshall Rose. **Internet System Handbook.** Reading, MA: Addison-Wesley, 1993. 900 pp.

This large volume of reference material contains essays written by the people responsible for the development of what has become known as the Internet. It includes some historical perspective that will help in interpreting the direction of the National Information Infrastructure. It includes a substantial bibliography.

Malamud, Carl. **Exploring the Internet: A Technical Travelogue.** Englewood Cliffs, NJ: PTR Prentice Hall, 1992. 379 pp.

Malamud's observations on the development of the Internet and the emerging global village is written from the point of view of having visited 56 cities in 21 countries.

Mitchell, William J. **City of Bits: Space, Place, and the Infobahn.** Cambridge, MA: MIT Press, 1995. 225 pp.

This book, by a Massachusetts Institute of Technology professor, is a thorough examination of the world that is coming to be called cyberspace. It is available in Web-based hypertext format (see Electronic Texts) as well as in traditional paperbound form.

Moore, Dinty. **The Emperor's Virtual Clothes: The Naked Truth about Internet Culture.** Chapel Hill, NC: Algonquin Books, 1995. 219 pp.

Moore was an Information Highway novice when he set out to discover what it was all about. His approach is a "walk in the electronic woods" (in the style of Henry David Thoreau's retreat to Walden Pond) to get a sense of what the Internet is about for those who are "technologically innocent." Moore provides a simple overview of the technical aspects of the Net, and he also provides a view into the real-life situations that make this world often scary and always interesting.

Naisbett, J. **Global Paradox: The Bigger the World Economy, the More Powerful Its Smallest Players.** New York: William Morrow, 1994. 304 pp.

Naisbett, who also wrote *Megatrends 2000* (William Morrow, 1991), predicts how the emerging technologies will affect the marketplace and society. He concentrates on the implications of the Information Highway.

Negroponte, Nicholas. **Being Digital.** New York: Alfred A. Knopf, 1995. 243 pp.

Written by one of the founders of the MIT Media Lab, this work is Negroponte's look into the near future. The essay tracks the changes in information technology that have occurred in the last ten years to bring us to the point where he says bits, "the DNA of information," are replacing atoms as the basic commodity of human interaction.

Ogden, Frank. **The Last Book You'll Ever Read.** Toronto: MacFarlane, Walter & Ross, 1993. 212 pp.

The work of one of Canada's favorite futurist speakers, this book (which includes a companion diskette of digital information) is full of predictions about life in the twenty-first century. Ogden, like some other modern seers, sees the eventual replacement of printed text on paper by digital displays.

Otte, Pete. **The Information Superhighway beyond the Internet.** Indianapolis, IN: Que, 1994. 241 pp.

Otte shares his vision of what the communications networks will look like in the future. Unlike many authors who attempt to predict the future of information technology and connectivity, his vision is grounded in an understanding of the basics.

Postman, N. **Technopoly, the Surrender of Culture to Technology.** New York: Vintage Books, 1993. 222 pp.

Postman takes a very negative view of the effect emerging technologies have on our society and culture. He does ask some important questions about how technology is introduced into the society.

Rheingold, Howard. **Virtual Reality.** New York: Simon & Schuster, 1992. 415 pp.

———. **The Virtual Community: Homesteading on the Electronic Frontier.** New York: HarperPerennial, 1994. 335 pp.

This is one of the most often quoted texts on the subject of communities in cyberspace. It is written by one of the true pioneers in the field of reporting on digital communication issues. This book is an excellent starting point on the subject of Net culture. It is also available in an on-line version (see Electronic Texts).

This is a book about the history and implications of the development of "virtual reality." It is a thorough exploration of the subject of cyberreality up to 1991. It is still very useful, especially since it provides insight and explodes some of the myths perpetuated by the media.

Rose, Candi, and Dirk Thomas. **net.sex.** Indianapolis, IN: Sams Publishing, 1995. 250 pp.

Sex in cyberspace is one of the media's favorite topics. Rose and Thomas have taken the time to study the issue, and they have provided a "Discreet Guide to the Adult Side of the Internet," as this volume is subtitled. More information is available on the Web at http://www.mcp.com/sams/books/net.sex/.

Rose, Donald. **Minding Your Cybermanners.** New York: Alpha Books, 1995. 196 pp.

Rose has written a guide to successfully joining the community data stream for the "newbies." The book includes netiquette tips, acronym definitions, how-tos, and a smiley index.

Roszak, Theodore. **The Cult of Information: The Folklore of Computers and the True Art of Thinking.** New York: Pantheon Books, 1986. 238 pp.

Roszak surveys the scene and finds that the "data glut" is jeopardizing humanity's ability to think. This situation, driven by information technology, may even cause us to lose our freedom, he posits.

Sclove, Richard E. **Democracy and Technology.** New York: The Guilford Press, 1995. 338 pp.

Sclove presents his ideas regarding what it will take to make certain that technology is democratized. His basic tenants are these: Citizens ought to be able to participate in the shaping of their society's circumstances; technologies affect and constitute those circumstances; and the design and practice of technology should be democratized.

Shea, Virginia. **Netiquette.** San Francisco: Albion Books, 1994. 154 pp.

Written for the new Internet user, this book may prove to be an invaluable source of information about the culture. It includes basic advice on style for individuals, businesses, etc., and lays out the tenants of Net etiquette. An excerpt is available via e-mail by sending a message to netiquette-request@albion.com with the subject: "archive send core."

Shields, Rob, ed. **Cultures of Internet: Toward a Social Theory of Cyberspaces and Virtual Realities.** Thousand Oaks, CA: Sage Publications, 1995. 240 pp.

Using articles contributed by many authors who live, work, and report on the Internet, this work examines the foundations and history of the development of the infrastructure. It also analyzes the role of government policy in the establishment of what is becoming the on-line world.

Shirky, Clay. **Voices from the Net.** Emeryville, CA: Ziff-Davis Press, 1995. 250 pp.

Shirky, an on-line activist, presents the Internet as a developing community with a culture like no other. The book examines the origins of the Net and then introduces the reader to some of the myriad diverse identities that frequent that cyberworld. More information is available on the Web at http://www.rhythm.com/~bpowell/Atlas/VOICES.htm.

Stoll, Clifford. **Silicon Snake Oil: Second Thoughts on the Information Highway.** New York: Doubleday, 1995. 247 pp.

This book is a critique of the hyperbole surrounding the development of the Information Highway. Stoll is a computer information expert who argues that much of what has been promised will never, or should never, occur.

Strangelove, Michael. **Understanding Internet: The Democratization of Mass Media and the Emerging Paradigm of Cyberspace.** Ottawa, Ont., Canada: SIE, 1994.

This is a new book by an experienced citizen of cyberspace. According to the author's introduction, the work "is an encyclopedia of changes that are occurring and may yet transpire as the result of the emergence of the first democratic form of mass media to appear on this dying planet. It is an attempt to summarize years of exploring the Internet as a new communication medium and as a force for social and personal change." He is making a new chapter of the work available on-line on a semi-regular basis (see Electronic Texts).

Strassmann, Paul A. **Information Payoff: The Transformation of Work in the Electronic Age.** New York: Macmillan, 1985. 298 pp.

Strassmann was a vice president of the Information Products Group at Xerox Corporation when he wrote this prediction of how work would change because of information technology. He analyzes the change from the perspective of individuals, organizations, and society.

Talbott, Stephen L. **The Future Does Not Compute: Transcending the Machines in Our Midst.** Sebastopol, CA: O'Reilly & Associates, 1995. 502 pp.

Talbott argues that although we are mostly enthralled with the possibilities that computers and network technology might provide, we tend to leave unexamined the possibility that this technology represents the internalization of the logic and rationality of the computer into human consciousness. The author knows the subject area well as an editor for O'Reilly & Associates, the publisher of many Internet- and computer-related titles. He focuses on the concepts of on-line communities, computers in education, electronic composition, and detachment from "real life" as he asks his readers to think about their relationship to the "intelligent machine." More information is available at http://www.ora.com/.

Tapscott, D., and A. Caston. **Paradigm Shift: The New Promise of Information Technology.** New York: McGraw-Hill, 1993. 337 pp.

The authors address both the technologies involved and the world context in which they are being applied. The implications are that the world is changing in major ways because of the application and acceptance of information technology.

Taylor, H. Jeanie, Cheris Kramarae, and Maureen Ebben, eds. **Women, Information Technology, and Scholarship.** Urbana, IL: Center for Advanced Study, University of Illinois, 1993. 127 pp.

This book provides an introductory exploration into many of the issues that impact women who are entering the new "electronic frontier" of cyberspace. Women are typically underrepresented on most commercial networks and the Internet, and their presence within the computer-user community has been scarce. This work grew out of the University of Illinois at Urbana-Champaign's Center for Advanced Study interdisciplinary group, whose main goal was to study the new communication technologies and their impact on women within the university environment.

Tennant, Roy, John Ober, and Anne Lipow. **Crossing the Internet Threshold: An Instructional Handbook.** Berkeley, CA: Library Solutions Press, 1994. 168 pp.

The package is designed for librarians teaching Internet basics. While it is definitely a new user's technical guide, it also emphasizes community-building and the use of proper "netiquette." It includes fact sheets for quick reference.

Toffler, Alvin. **Powershift: Knowledge, Wealth, and Violence at the Edge of the 21st Century.** New York: Bantam Books, 1990. 585 pp.

Toffler, one of the world's most respected futurists, paints a relatively dark picture of the coming age. Included is an important chapter on how technology will affect the emergent economy.

————. **The Third Wave.** New York: William Morrow, 1980. 544 pp.

Futurist Toffler presents his Wave Theory of the ages of development. He shows how, in the Third Wave (the information technology era), demands are butting up against the expectations of those people who have been raised to believe in the values of the Second Wave.

Turkle, Sherry. **Life on the Screen: Identity in the Age of the Internet.** New York: Simon & Schuster, 1995. 347 pp.

This book examines how the Internet breaks down the boundaries between humans and technology as people participate in virtual worlds. Turkle is a professor of the sociology of science at MIT, and she is recognized as an authority on the interaction between technology and psychology.

Wood, Lamont. **The Net after Dark.** New York: John Wiley & Sons, 1994. 352 pp.

The subtitle of this work is "The Underground Guide to the Coolest, the Newest, and the Most Bizarre Hangouts on the

Internet, CompuServe, AOL, Delphi, and More." The book is valuable to those readers who are looking for information about accessing the underground resources available through digital networked communications. It can provide some direct contact with the most controversial resources. More information is available on the Web at http://www.texas.net/users/lwood/tnad.html.

Business Aspects

Burrus, D. **Technotrends.** New York: Harper Business, 1993. 376 pp.

The book is an overview of the emerging technologies and the trends that can be inferred from their application. The work concentrates on the effect these new tools will have on the workplace and in the markets.

Cronin, Mary J. **Doing More Business on the Internet.** New York: Van Nostrand Reinhold, 1995. 368 pp.

The subtitle of this work explains its intent: "How the Electronic Highway Is Transforming American Companies." Cronin is a professor of management at the Carroll School of Management, Boston College. Her 20 years of experience in information management and technology are the basis for her advice about what it takes for a business to use the capabilities of the Internet.

————. **Global Advantage on the Internet.** New York: Van Nostrand Reinhold, 1996. 358 pp.

Cronin's follow-up to her basic text on doing business on the Net, this work presents information on how firms can be more competitive in an international marketplace that has been opened via the use of digital information technologies. The book includes case studies and information on infrastructure and laws that apply to 20 different countries.

Eager, William. **The Information Payoff.** Englewood Cliffs, NJ: PTR Prentice Hall, 1995. 246 pp.

This business-oriented publication shows how companies around the world are using electronic communications to improve productivity and increase employee participation. Interviews with managers at Fortune 500 companies are used to show how the latest digital communications applications are changing the way corporations do business.

Ellsworth, Jill H., and Matthew V. Ellsworth. **The Internet Business Book.** New York: John Wiley & Sons, 1994. 376 pp.

The result of extensive research, this book is a primer on how to do business on the Net. There are sections devoted to Internet navigation basics, but the main thrust is on marketing using digital communications. An effort has been made to show how existing business strategies can evolve to include the Internet as a strategy. The book is also available in Japanese, Italian, Portuguese, and Greek. More information is available on the Web at http://www.wiley.com/Compbooks/InternetKit/ibbchap.html.

————. **Marketing on the Internet: Multimedia Strategies for the World Wide Web.** New York: John Wiley & Sons, 1995. 404 pp.

Specifically oriented to establishing a business presence on the World Wide Web, this is a follow-up to the coauthors' primer, *The Internet Business Book* (John Wiley & Sons, 1994). After presenting some basic information about how to get connected, it then focuses on the dos and don'ts of Web page development for commercial success.

Janal, Dan. **Online Marketing Handbook.** New York: Van Nostrand Reinhold, 1995. 370 pp.

Subtitled "How To Sell, Advertise, Publicize, and Promote Your Products and Services on the Internet and Commercial Online Services," this book's intent is obvious. Taking a case history approach, the author provides many examples of what should and should not be done while promoting products and services on the digital communications networks.

Vogelsang, Ingo, and Bridger Mitchell. **Telecommunications Competition: The Last Ten Miles.** Cambridge, MA: MIT Press, 1995. 210 pp.

This book analyzes the factors driving the competition to provide the on-ramp from homes to the Information Highway. The authors argue that because technology has lowered the costs of providing the access, smaller firms will be able to provide these services once the overhaul of the Telecommunications Act is completed. Case studies of similar situations in England are presented.

Educational Aspects

Collins, Mauri, and Zane Berge. **Computer-Mediated Communication and the Online Classroom.** Cresskill, NJ: Hampton Press, 1995. A series of three books.

This series of three books deals with many aspects of computer-mediated communication (CMC) in the educational setting. In volume 1 (Computer-Mediated Communication and the Online Classroom: Overview and Perspectives) the authors show that the term *computer-mediated communication* is used to encompass the merging of computers and telecommunications technologies to support teaching and learning, and they survey the range of educational users of CMC. Volume 2 (Computer-Mediated Communication and the Online Classroom in Higher Education) presents the reports of various educators who have demonstrated the capabilities of CMC in higher education. Volume 3 (Computer-Mediated Communication and the Online Classroom in Distance Learning) provides an overview of emerging techniques for distance educational delivery systems. For more information on these books, send e-mail to Listserv@GUVM. georgetown.edu with the message body "GET intro2.ham."

Ellsworth, Jill H. **Education on the Internet.** Indianapolis, IN: Sams Publishing, 1994. 591 pp.

Ellsworth reveals the broad array of educational resources available via the Internet. Within sections dedicated to K–12, college, and graduate school levels, she presents practical lesson ideas and projects for existing curricula as well as ways to teach about the Internet itself. The author also includes a discussion of distance education.

Finkel, LeRoy. **Technology Tools in the Information Age Classroom.** Wilsonville, OR: Franklin, Beedle & Associates, 1991. 168 pp.

The book is designed as an introductory text in early teacher preparation courses. It provides an overview of the subject and selected articles about educational technology, and then gives a list of activities to try. The author also makes an attempt to predict what the future will hold for teachers trying to use the latest information tools. More information is available at http://www.fbeedle.com/bookinfo/34-5.html.

Frazier, Deneen, with Barbara Kurshan and Sara Armstrong. **Internet for Kids.** Alameda, CA: SYBEX, 1995. 314 pp.

The authors provide a starting point for parents and teachers who want to give children a boost into cyberspace. The book includes many practical tips and directions for "virtual excursions" that are designed to empower children. More information is available at http://www.parentsplace.com/shopping/codys/forkids.cgi?15995.

Harris, Judi. **Way of the Ferret—Finding Educational Resources on the Internet.** Portland, OR: Society for Technology in Education, 1994. 209 pp.

This book has proven to be very popular with teachers trying to incorporate Internet resources into their curriculum. Based on Harris's "Mining the Internet" column in the journal *The Computing Teacher*, this work provides basic information on how to navigate the Net and includes 15 different types of activities that teachers can apply immediately. For more information, send e-mail to iste@oregon.uoregon.edu.

Kearsley, Greg, Mary Furlong, and Beverly Hunter. **We Teach with Technology.** Wilsonville, OR: Franklin, Beedle & Associates, 1992. 176 pp.

This text is an overview of the substantial advances that have taken place in the integration of technology into the curriculum. The presentation here is through the eyes of experienced teachers who have become adept at using the new tools to facilitate teaching. More information is available at http://www.fbeedle.com/bookinfo/37-x.html.

McClure, Charles, et al. **Libraries and the Internet/NREN Perspectives, Issues and Challenges.** Westport, CT: Meckler Corporation, 1994. 500 pp.

This is the report of a study to determine the new role for libraries in the developing national information infrastructure.

Maurer, Hermann, ed. **Educational Multimedia and Hypermedia, 1995.** Charlottesville, VA: AACE, 1995. 840 pp.

This volume is a record of the ED-MEDIA 95 World Conference on Educational Multimedia and Hypermedia. Containing over 100 papers dealing with the latest thinking in educational technology systems, computer-mediated communication, computer-supported cooperative work, distance education, hypermedia, multimedia, virtual reality, and much more, it is a good source for information on trends that will be important in the near term. For further information, send e-mail to AACE@Virginia.edu.

Steen, Douglas R., Mark R. Roddy, Derek Sheffield, and Michael Bryan Stout. **Teaching with the Internet: Putting Teachers before Technology.** Bellevue, WA: Resolution Business Press, 1995. 336 pp.

Teachers wrote this book for their colleagues who are considering using the Internet to supplement teaching tools. It discusses the means of connecting, but it also provides thoughtful advice on when and when not to use the new capabilities. Many real-life examples of Internet use in the classroom are included, as well as a listing of education-related resources. More information is available at http://www.halcyon.com/ResPress/teacher. htm.

Still, Julie, ed. **The Internet Library Case Studies of Library Internet Management and Use.** Westport, CT: Meckler Corporation, 1994. 200 pp.

This volume presents case studies of the ways in which libraries have altered their relationships with their patrons and with information.

Strudwick, Karen, John Spilker, and Jay Arney. **Internet for Parents.** Bellevue, WA: Resolution Business Press, 1995. 384 pp.

Designed to give children a head start in their studies and in their future careers by connecting the family's computer to the Internet, this volume also includes software to facilitate that process. The book provides simple instructions for connecting and provides many pointers to resources that will be of value to families with children. More information is available at http://www.halcyon.com/ResPress/parents.htm.

Wallet, Katherine B., Patrick Golden, and Ronald Vasaturo. **Educator's Guide to the Internet.** Hampton, VA: Virginia Space Grant Consortium, 1994. 170 pp.

The book is the result of research funded by the Eisenhower Math/Science Consortium. It is designed by educators, for educators, to be a user-friendly guide to making the Internet work for them in the classroom. On-line projects, lesson plans, graphics, and software are discussed. The package includes a diskette of helpful ancillary software. For more information, contact vsgc@pen.k12.va.us.

The Internet

Ackermann, Ernest. **Learning To Use the Internet: An Introduction with Examples and Exercises.** Wilsonville, OR: Franklin, Beedle & Associates, 1995. 368 pp.

This detailed book has been designed to serve as a classroom introduction to the Internet. Ackermann provides background information about the network of networks and presents practical ways in which it can be used. Emphasis is on learning the basic Internet tools, including e-mail, gopher, archie, Hytelnet, WAIS, and the WWW browsers. More information is available at http://www.fbeedle.com/bookinfo/92-2.html.

————. **Learning To Use the World Wide Web.** Wilsonville, OR: Franklin, Beedle & Associates, 1996. 405 pp.

This "how-to" work begins with pertinent information about the Internet and the World Wide Web. It then goes on to explain how to use a browser, where to go on the Web, how to write HTML documents, and how to use e-mail and the other TCP/IP protocols. More information is available at http://www.fbeedle.com/wwwlist.html.

Butler, Mark. **How To Use the Internet.** Emeryville, CA: Ziff-Davis Press, 1994. 160 pp.

Mark Butler is an experienced Internet user who has produced a fully illustrated primer for the non–computer user. The reader is led through simple steps with clear text and pertinent illustrations to accomplish specific tasks. More information is available at http://www.mcp.com.

December, John, and Neil Randall. **World Wide Web Unleashed.** 3rd ed. Indianapolis, IN: Sams Publishing, 1994. 1,392 pp.

This large volume is as comprehensive a resource for information about the World Wide Web as anyone would care to access. More information is available at http://www.mcp.com.

Eddings, Joshua. **How the Internet Works.** Emeryville, CA: Ziff-Davis Press, 1994. 240 pp.

From the series *How the Computer Works*, this heavily illustrated text presents the basics of Internetworking in a clear and thorough manner. The technology is well presented, as are the tools and what they can access on the Net. More information is available at http://www.rhythm.com/~bpowell/Atlas/HINTWKS.htm.

Engst, Adam. **Internet Starter Kit for Macintosh.** Indianapolis, IN: Hayden Books, 1994. 640 pp.

The cover says this book is "everything you need to get on the Internet," and it is. Adam Engst is a respected expert on Macintosh-related issues, and this package makes connecting a Mac as simple as one-two-three. A diskette with essential software is included. The book is also available on-line in hypertext format at http://www.mcp.com/hayden/iskm/book.html.

Engst, Adam, Corwin Low, and Michael Simon. **Internet Starter Kit for Windows.** Indianapolis, IN: Hayden Books, 1994. 600 pp.

This Microsoft Windows user guide is an excellent and thorough resource for easy configuration for Internet connectivity. The volume includes Windows software to facilitate setup. The hypertext version is available from Hayden Books at their Web site, http://www.mcp.com/hayden/iskm/book.html.

Estrada, Susan. **Connecting to the Internet.** Sebastopol, CA: O'Reilly & Associates, 1993. 170 pp.

Estrada has included a long list of Internet service providers to choose from, and she helps readers decide on the best type and best-priced connection for their business or personal needs. The book does not cover Net navigation.

Gach, Gary. **A Pocket Guide to the Internet.** New York: Pocket Books, 1996. 347 pp.

Based on frequently asked (and answered) questions from the author's basic Internet literacy classes, this guide is an effort to make the Net accessible to a mass audience. The first half is "how-to," with emphasis on Internet as not only a community of networks but also a network of communities. The second half is an almanac, exploring resources for ten major subject areas: libraries, education, business, science, publishing, arts, entertainment, computers, government, and society. More information is available at gach@uclink3.berkeley.edu.

Gagnon, Eric. **What's on the Web.** Fairfax, VA: Internet Media, 1995. 472 pp.

The book is a comprehensive guide to sites on the World Wide Web. It features reviews of what the authors consider to be the best Web sites, and it includes a 5,821-entry subject index and Web site finder. The book is supplemented by an on-line Web site of its own, Jump City, at http://www.jumpcity.com/ NEWHOME.html. There the reader is prompted to enter a four-digit "jump code" that is found in the printed text describing a particular site. This shortcut is designed for the purpose of facilitating Web navigation.

Glossbrenner, Alfred. **Internet 101: A College Student's Guide.** Blue Ridge Summit, PA: Windcrest, 1995. 350 pp.

This book presents Internet navigation basics specifically directed to the college student. The author provides instruction by creating typical scenarios his reader might deal with on a day-to-day basis. These include roommate problems, finding a summer job, studying abroad, discovering new musical groups, and dealing with love and sex. The bare essentials on how to access newsgroups, gopher sites, and mail lists are included. More information is available at http://www.io.org:80/ ~thought/wwmm.html.

Godin, Seth. **E-Mail Addresses of the Rich and Famous.** Reading, MA: Addison-Wesley, 1994. 130 pp.

Godin has compiled a directory of more than 1,000 e-mail addresses of famous politicians, reporters, and other celebrities.

Hahn, Harley, and Rick Stout. **The Internet Yellow Pages.** 3rd ed. New York: Osborne/McGraw-Hill Publishing, 1996. 447 pp.

In an attempt to provide some semblance of order to the resources available on the Internet, the authors have created this useful subject index. Look for the latest edition for the most up-to-date information.

Held, Gilbert. **Complete Cyberspace Reference and Directory.** Macon, GA: 4-Degree Consulting (Van Nostrand Reinhold), 1995. 765 pp.

A practical reference directory that lists over 15,000 electronic mail addresses from proprietary and public networks, this volume also includes guidance on addressing e-mail, and it has a useful glossary of related terms. There is also a listing of important telephone numbers.

Krol, Ed, and Paula Ferguson. **The Whole Internet for Windows 95.** Sebastopol, CA: O'Reilly & Associates, 1995. 574 pp.

This is the latest in *The Whole Internet* series by Ed Krol, an expert in the tools of Internet navigation. This volume focuses on the special abilities to access the Internet and on-line services built into Microsoft Corporation's new Windows 95 operating system. It also includes an expanded catalog that lists many information resources available to Internet surfers. More information is available at http://www.ora.com/.

LaQuey, Tracy. **The Internet Companion: A Beginner's Guide to Global Networking.** 2d ed. Reading, MA: Addison-Wesley, 1994. 262 pp.

Many consider this work to be the bible of on-line primers. A free, "distributive" full-text HTML version of the second edition is available on-line (see Electronic Texts).

Mathiesen, Michael. **Marketing on the Internet.** Gulf Breeze, FL: Maximum Press, 1995. 400 pp.

Subtitled "A Proven Twelve-Step Plan to Promoting, Selling, and Delivering Your Products and Services to Millions over the Information Superhighway," this is a comprehensive guide to creating an Internet presence for a commercial enterprise. Some especially useful sections are available free of charge on the Net (see Electronic Texts).

Pfaffenberger, Bryan. **Internet in Plain English.** New York: MIS Press, 1994. 463 pp.

Terms, abbreviations, and acronyms that pertain to computer-mediated communication and the Internet are available in this volume, which is organized like a dictionary.

Quarterman, John S., and Carl-Mitchell Smoot. **E-Mail Companion.** Reading, MA: Addison-Wesley, 1994. 318 pp.

The basics of e-mail technique and addressing are the main focus of the book. There is a section on sending e-mail to networks that are not directly linked to the Internet.

Savetz, Kevin M. **Your Internet Consultant—The FAQs of Life Online.** Indianapolis, IN: Sams Publishing, 1994. 550 pp.

Written in the style of FAQs (Frequently Asked Questions), this book answers 361 common questions related to the Internet. For information and the table of contents, e-mail savetz@rahul.net with the words *send YIC* in the subject line.

Scheller, M., K. Boden, A. Geenen, and J. Kampermann. **Internet: Werkzeuge und Dienste—von "Archie" bis "World Wide Web."** Berlin, New York: Springer-Verlag, 1994. 368 pp.

This German-language Internet primer includes historical background material as well as the basics of connecting and navigating. Portions of the work are in HTML format at http://www.ask.uni-karlsruhe.de/books/inetwd.html.

Tamosaitis, Nancy. **net.talk.** Emeryville, CA: Ziff-Davis Press, 1994. 80 pp.

The Internet culture has developed a unique shorthand language that it uses in messages posted as e-mail or in Usenet newsgroups. The smiley (a text-based graphic representation of feelings) and acronyms like IMHO ("in my humble opinion") are favorite devices for digital communicators. This book attempts to codify their use. It also quotes celebrities on how they "talk" on the Net. More information is available at http://www.rhythm.com/~bpowell/Atlas/NETALK.htm.

Magazines

Boardwatch
8500 West Bowles Avenue, Suite 210
Littleton, CO 80123
Monthly; $5.95 per issue

This is a relatively old publication in its genre, being one of the first to document the rise of electronic bulletin board systems. Since 1989 it has kept abreast of the changes that information technology has made possible and reports extensively on issues affecting the Web.

Forbes ASAP
Forbes, Inc.
New York City
Quarterly; sent to subscribers only

This is *Forbes* magazine's quarterly supplement on the people, technologies, and issues that are defining the Information Age. George Gilder is a contributor to most issues, and the periodical (begun in 1992) has become a respected resource for business as it looks to the future of commerce changed by developing information technologies.

Internet World
Mecklermedia Corporation
20 Ketchum Street
Westport, CT 06880
Monthly; $4.95 per issue

This magazine, started in 1992, is Mecklermedia's entry into the expanding world of digital communications reporting. It has timely articles on the basics of Internet navigation, but also includes viewpoints on legislation, community-building, and the other pertinent issues of information technology. For more information, contact info@mecklermedia.com.

The Net
Imagine Publishing, Inc.
1350 Old Bayshore Highway, Suite 210
Burlingame, CA 94010
Monthly; $4.99 per issue

One of the newest entries in the on-line periodical mix, *The Net* has provided an overview of interesting sites, reviewed tools, and provided some editorial opinion about the changing nature of cyberspace since 1995. For more information, contact mfrost@ thenet-usa.com.

NetGuide
CMP Media, Inc.
600 Community Drive
Manhasset, NY 11030
Monthly; $2.95 per issue

Since 1995 *NetGuide* has been a good source for interesting resources available on the World Wide Web. It allocates some pages in each issue to the social implications of the new technologies, but its focus is more technical in nature than some other Internet periodicals. For more information, contact netmail@netguide.cmp.com.

Wired
Wired Ventures Ltd.
520 3rd Street
San Francisco, CA 94107-1815
Monthly; $4.95 per issue

Wired is one of the first periodicals whose editorial content is involved almost exclusively with the world of digital communications and the issues that are evolving from its application. Started in 1993, its style has spawned several imitators; however, this magazine continues to be the best source for reporting on telecommunications events and points of view. For more information, contact info@wired.com.

Selected Nonprint Resources

7

These resources are all available on-line with the exception of the videos that make up the final section of this chapter. In some cases the universal resource locators (URLs) provided for the Net-based listings may be inaccessible or changed. That is the nature of the Net. For this reason the first section below provides the URLs for the most popular Internet search engines. These sites can be used to discover if a particular resource is currently available at another URL or to determine what new related data has been made available on-line.

Immediately following the list of search sites is a guide to freely accessible bibliographies and indexes on the Net that relate to the issues described in chapter 1. These may be good starting points for readers familiar with the Internet. Following that section is a listing for e-texts (digital books), which is divided into sections that generally address cultural, government, and educational concerns relating to the application of the new information technologies. Also included is a short list of some on-line books about the Internet that should prove helpful for novice and intermediate users.

The final section of electronic resources is an eclectic collection of on-line journals and magazines (e-zines, as the latter are called), which will provide the reader ample opportunities to discover and explore the nature of the Information Revolution. Many would argue that in these dynamic publications lie the definitions of the new age.

Net Search Engines

Dejanews	http://www.dejanews.com/
Excite	http://www.excite.com/
Infoseek	http://www.infoseek.com/
Lycos	http://www.lycos.com/
Magellan	http://www.magellan.com/
Open Text	http://www.opentext.com/
WhoWhere?	http://www.whowhere.com/
Yahoo	http://www.yahoo.com/

Bibliographies and Indexes

Included in this section are some of the Net listings of resources dealing with telecommunications; communications studies, including computer-mediated communication; information technologies; and related topics. The researcher seeking facts, opinions, and the most current thinking on issues related to the changes brought about by the digital revolution would be well advised to begin looking among these Internet sites. Note that the commercial on-line services—America Online, CompuServe, Prodigy, Dia-Log, etc.—also provide ready access to many electronic texts related to this inquiry, but have not been included here because of the costs involved. Virtually all of the resources listed here are available for no charge.

On-Line Bibliographies

Annenberg Publications Online. Evanston, IL: Annenberg Washington Program in Communications Policy Studies of Northwestern University, 1996.
http://www.annenberg.nwu.edu/pubs/

This is the on-line repository for many of Annenberg's 145 publications related to emerging issues in communications. These free, full-text documents are categorized by subject and are available for downloading.

ARL 5th Edition of Directory of Electronic Publications.
Washington, DC: Association of Research Libraries, 1996.
gopher://arl.cni.org:70/11/scomm/edir/edir95

This hard-copy standard reference work for serials on the Internet now lists nearly 2,500 scholarly lists and 675 electronic journals, newsletters, and related titles. The directory provides instructions for electronic access to each publication. A gopher server has been established to provide free electronic access to much of the data provided in the traditional print publication.

Benton Foundation's Communications Policy Publications.
Washington, DC: The Benton Foundation, 1995.
http://cdinet.com/cgi-bin/lite/Benton/Catalog/catalog.html

The Benton Foundation "promotes public interest values and noncommercial services for the National Information Infrastructure." This site lists their on-line papers analyzing pertinent public issues of the NII.

Bibliography of Internetworking Information. Internet
Engineering Task Force. Ann Arbor, MI: Merit Network,
August 1990.
ftp://nic.merit.edu/documents/fyi/fyi3.txt

This bibliography of TCP/IP Internetworking is one of the Request for Comments prepared by the User Services Working Group of the Internet Engineering Task Force. It includes a listing of technical resources that pertain to the TCP/IP protocol. "The intent of this bibliography is to offer a representative collection of resources of information that will help the reader become familiar with the concepts of Internetworking. It is meant to be a starting place for further research. There are references to other sources of information for those users wishing to pursue, in greater depth, the issues and complexities of the current networking environment."

Bibliography of Organizational Computer-Mediated
Communication. Cambridge, UK: Ian A. Rudy, 1995.
http://shum.huji.ac.il/jcmc/rudybib.html

The owner of this Web page notes that "this bibliography is currently oriented towards electronic mail in organizations. The following areas are not covered in depth, though some references of relevance are given: the Internet, and tools to navigate it; computer-mediated communication in teaching; computer-supported cooperative work; group decision support systems; video conferencing; electronic data interchange (EDI); communication standards (e.g., ISDN). This bibliography may be used for educational, noncommercial purposes provided that the copyright and permission notices are retained in all copies."

Business Researcher's Interests. Pittsburgh, PA: Yogesh Malhotra, 1995, 1996.
http://www.pitt.edu/~malhotra/interest.html

According to his home page, "Yogesh Malhotra is currently pursuing a Ph.D. in business administration with a major in MIS on a fellowship awarded by Katz Graduate School of Business, University of Pittsburgh. His research interests lie in studying how information systems and information processes influence, and are influenced by, the phenomena generally known as "emergent organizational forms." He has made his research work available in a searchable format on the Web.

Business Use of the Internet, Print Sources. Houston, TX: Tenagra Corporation, 1995.
http://arganet.tenagra.com/Tenagra/books.html

This Web site is a valued-added resource on print material that deals with business and the Internet. It is provided free of charge by the Tenagra Corporation. Links attached to the book or periodical name will take the user to a new file with pertinent information on that resource. Some books are further linked to home pages, etc.

Byte Magazine Archives. New York: McGraw-Hill, 1996.
http://www.byte.com/

This computer magazine's home page includes a search engine that will allow retrieval of articles and features from the archives. A search of the phrase "information technology" returned dozens of hyperlinked titles. Access is free.

CIOS/Comserve. Rotterdam Junction, NY: Communication Institute for Online Scholarship, 1996.
http://cios.llc.rpi.edu/

The Communication Institute for Online Scholarship (CIOS) operates Comserve, an on-line service for scholars interested in human communication research. Comserve includes a resource library, white pages, and journal indexes. Full access is reserved for those individuals who log in from a machine that is associated with an organization that supports the CIOS institutional affiliates program. A fee is required.

CMC Bibliography. Troy, NY: Computer-Mediated Communication Studies Center, John December, 1996.
http://www.december.com/cmc/info

John December's listing of resources related to computer-mediated communication is one of the most nearly complete and up-to-date in the world. This particular site contains listings for some books and articles of interest to researchers in digital communications studies, but its best feature is the hyperlinks to other on-line bibliographies. This listing has evolved since 1992.

CMC/December Bibliography. Troy, NY: John December, October 1993.
http://www.december.com/john/papers/cmcbib93.txt

John December has made his "Selected Readings in Computer-Mediated Communication, Communication Theory, Computer Networks, and the Internet" listing available to anyone who cares to use it for noncommercial, educational purposes. It was the qualifying exam reading list for his doctorate in communication and rhetoric.

Communications Archive. West Chester, PA: Meta-info-labs, David Barberi, 1996.
http://sunsite.unc.edu/dbarberi/papers/

This archive of communications-related papers (especially in the subject areas of virtual communities, chats, IRC, MUDs, and MOOs) is maintained by SunSite at the Chapel Hill campus of the University of North Carolina. Full-text versions of papers are available for downloading at no charge.

Computer and Communication Entry Page. Berkeley, CA: Webstart Communications, 1996.
http://www.cmpcmm.com/cc/

James Donnelley has created a searchable Web site with links to a great deal of relevant data on computers and communication, including companies, conference listing, media, organizations, programs and projects, standards, Usenet groups, and FAQs.

Computers, Freedom, and Privacy Video Library. Topanga, CA: Sweet Pea Communications, 1995.
http://websites.earthlink.net/~cfpvideo/

"Educational videos and resources about human liberties and freedoms in the information age." Provided by Sweet Pea Communications, this Web page has links to information on videos that deal with such subjects as privacy, access to government information, computing ethics, cryptography and encryption, civil liberties, censorship, law enforcement, hackers, computer crime, constitutional law, and caller ID. Descriptions of the videos available from this source will be found in the final section of this chapter.

CPSR Publications. Palo Alto, CA: Computer Professionals for Social Responsibility, 1995.
http://www.cpsr.org/dox/publications/publications.html

This Web page is the Computer Professionals for Social Responsibility's bibliography of the organization's papers and articles available in their *CPSR Newsletter*, with a listing of articles dating back to 1983. Divided into subjects, the bibliography includes citations in the following areas: global/national/community information infrastructure, directions and implications of advanced computing, education, computers and the environment, ethics, computers in the workplace, privacy and civil liberties, voting and elections, reliability and risk, women and computing, etc.

Current Cites. Berkeley, CA: Information Systems Instruction & Support (ISIS), monthly publication (ISSN: 1060-2356).
ftp://ftp.lib.berkeley.edu/pub/Current.Cites/

The Library, University of California, Berkeley, produces this publication monthly. Contributors, including Teri Rinne, David Rez, Nathan Meyer, Richard Rinehart, and Roy Tennant, scan 30-plus journals in library and information technology for selected articles on disc technologies, networks and networking, electronic publishing, hypermedia, and multimedia. Annotations are included.

Archived issues can be found at the URL listed above. *Current Cites* is sent free, automatically, to all subscribers with an Internet mail address. To subscribe, send the message "sub cites [your name]" to listserv@library.berkeley.edu.

EPIC Resources. Washington, DC: Electronic Privacy
Information Center, 1996.
http://epic.org/

A repository for on-line documents of the Electronic Privacy
Information Center, this Web site has links to papers on the clipper chip, the digital telephony proposal, national ID cards, medical record privacy, credit records, and the sale of consumer
data. Access is free.

Free On-Line Dictionary of Computing. Imperial College,
London: Denis Howe, 1993–1996.
http://wombat.doc.ic.ac.uk/

According to the dictionary's author, "FOLDOC is a searchable
dictionary of acronyms, jargon, programming languages, tools,
architecture, operating systems, networking, theory, conven-
tions, standards, mathematics, telecomms, electronics, institutions, companies, projects, products, history, in fact anything to
do with computing." It contains more than 8,600 entries.

FS-1037C: Glossary of Telecommunication Terms. Washington,
DC: Institute for Telecommunication (ITS), 1995.
http://www.its.bldrdoc.gov/projects/1037c/1037.html

The Institute for Telecommunication (ITS) is the research and
engineering branch of the National Telecommunications and
Information Administration, a part of the U.S. Department of
Commerce. They have provided this on-line *Glossary of Telecommunications Terms* (FS-1037C) as directed by federal guidelines. Normal updates occur every five years.

ICLU: Your Rights in Cyberspace. Yolanda Jones and Will
Sadler. Bloomington, IN: Indiana University School of Law,
December 1994.
http://www.law.indiana.edu/law/iclu.html

This page contains pointers to various resources on the Internet
that deal with ownership of public materials, Internet basics,
cryptography and privacy, free speech, censorship, defamation,
criminal law issues, sex in cyberspace, and organizations protecting cyber-rights, as well as miscellaneous and general
guides.

Information Society Journal Articles. Information Society.
London: Taylor and Francis, 1995.
http://www.ics.uci.edu/~kling/tisbib.html

Information Society, published since 1981, is a forum for analysis of the impacts, policies, concepts, methodologies, and cultural change related to trends in the advance of information technology. A bibliography of all articles published since 1981 is available on the Web.

Information Sources: The Internet and Computer-Mediated Communication. Troy, NY: John December, 1995.
http://www.december.com/cmc/info

Arguably the best starting point for anyone who has Net access and wishes to access on-line resources related to the broad topic of computer-mediated communication. December allows educational, personal, or nonprofit use of his work and provides it "without expressed or implied warranty." This is an excellent Web site.

Media History Project. Kristina Ross. Boulder, CO: The Media History Project, 1995–1996.
http://www.mediahistory.com

The introductory material accessible at this Web site explains it best: "From petroglyphs to pixels, this site offers access to media history–related archives, syllabi, lectures, essays, and additional educational material, including specialty Web pages incorporating text, images, and audio clips." Access is free.

National Information Infrastructure Virtual Library Home Page. Washington, DC: Information Infrastructure Task Force (IITF) and the Council on Competitiveness, 1996.
http://nii.nist.gov/pubs.html

Established by the Commerce Department as part of the IITF, this Web library provides a comprehensive collection of resources on national information infrastructure topics. Full-text copies of the books, documents, and reports are available for free downloading.

Network Bibliography. Berlin, Germany: Henning Schulzrinne, December 1995.
http://rockmaster.fokus.gmd.de/netbib/

This bibliography is very extensive and searchable. It includes conference papers and some technical reports dating as far back as 1926. Currently, the bibliography contains 29,000 entries with 3,000 links to on-line papers. This is highly technical information.

SJCPL's List of Public Libraries with Internet Services.
Southbend, IN: St. Joseph County Public Library, 1996.
http://sjcpl.lib.in.us/homepage/PublicLibraries/PublicLibrary
Servers.html

Don Napoli, head librarian at SJCPL and the man responsible
for making his library the first on the Internet with a Web page,
maintains this comprehensive hyperlinked list of international
libraries that are on the Net.

Sunergy. Mountain View, CA: Sun Microsystems, 1996.
http://www.sun.com/sunergy/

Sun Microsystems, a business that specializes in hardware and
software for Internet and digital connectivity applications, sponsors Sunergy, a program that produces satellite television broadcasts dealing with the latest technologies in the computer
industry. It also maintains a library of white papers, reading
lists, transcripts, and videos of previous satellite transmissions.
Access is free.

TechSearch. Manhasset, NY: CMP Media, 1994–1996.
http://techweb.cmp.com/techweb/programs/registered/
search/cmp-wais-index.html

This is the searchable retrieval site for the complete content of all
of CMP's publications dating back to 1 January 1994. Magazines
related to digital communications include *Communications Week,
Communications Week International, Electronic Engineering Times,
HomePC, Informatiques Magazine, InformationWeek, Interactive Age,
Max, CD-ROM, NetGuide, Network Computing, OEM,* and *Windows
Magazine.* Access is free.

Telecom Information Resources on the Internet. Ann Arbor, MI:
Jeffrey MacKie-Mason, 1994–1996.
http://www.spp.umich.edu/telecom-info.html

Included in this searchable index of over 2,000 communications-
related resource links maintained at the University of Michigan
are "references to information sources relating to the technical,
economic, public policy, and social aspects of telecommunications. All forms of telecommunication, including, voice, data,
video, wired, wireless, cable TV, and satellite, are included."

Unofficial Internet Book List. Blue Lake, CA: Kevin Savetz
Publishing, 1994–1995.
http://www.northcoast.com/savetz/booklist/

Subtitled "The Most Extensive Bibliography of Books about the Internet," this bibliography is updated approximately four times per year. As of this writing, the most current version is 2.0, dated 2 August 1996. This version includes 543 books, most of which are annotated. Access is free. The list is available at the URL listed above, or one can receive it via e-mail by sending the following message: (To:) booklist-request@northcoast.com; (Subject:) archive; (Body:) send booklist. An autoresponder will send the list in return e-mail very shortly after receipt of the request. It is now available on America Online.

WWW Virtual Library: Communications &
Telecommunications. Geneva, Switzerland: Analysys Limited, 1995.
http://www.analysys.co.uk/commslib.htm

According to information provided by the company that provides this hyperlinked directory, "Analysys is the largest independent consultancy in Europe specializing solely in the telecommunications field." They have provided a starting point for on-line research in computer-mediated communications subjects, including broadband, broadcasting, economics education, Internet working and LANS, journals and other electronic media, policy and regulation, social issues, teleworking and telemedicine, standards, testing and protocols, and U.S. government sources. Access is free.

ZDNet Search. Emoryville, CA: Ziff-Davis Press, 1994–1995.
http://www.zdnet.com/cgi-bin/taos_mf.pl?unix

This Web page allows the visitor to search for text strings in any of the archived Ziff-Davis magazines, including *Computer Life, Computer Life UK, FamilyPC, Computer Gaming World, Inter@ctive Week, MacUser, MacWeek, PC Computing, PC Direct UK, PC Magazine, PC Magazine UK*, and more. Access is free.

Electronic Texts

Cultural Aspects

Anderson, R. H., T. K. Bikson, S. A. Law, B. M. Mitchell, C. R. Kedzie, B. Keltner, C. W. A. Panis, J. Pliskin, P. Srinagesh. **Universal Access to E-Mail: Feasibility and Societal Implications**. Santa Monica, CA: RAND, 1995.
http://www.rand.org/hot/

RAND has made this report on the possibilities of providing universal access to e-mail in the United States available in PDF or HTML format. It is free for downloading.

Beamish, Anne. **Communities Online: A Study of Community-Based Computer Networks**. Master's thesis. Cambridge, MA: Massachusetts Institute of Technology, 1995.
http://alberti.mit.edu/arch/4.207/anneb/thesis/toc.html

This on-line, hyperlinked version of Beamish's master's thesis provides a broad view of the new communities that are developing via digital links. It includes an excellent bibliography.

Belson, David. **The Network Nation Revisited**. Thesis. Hoboken, NJ: Stevens Institute of Technology, 1994.
http://www.stevens-tech.edu/~dbelson/thesis/thesis.html

Belson's thesis analyzes 14 predictions presented in *The Network Nation* (Hiltz and Turoff, Addison-Wesley, 1978), the seminal text on computer-mediated communication. Among those predictions: By the mid-1980s computerized conferencing will be a prominent form of communications in most organizations and will be widely used in the greater society by the 1990s, and networks will offer opportunities to disadvantaged groups to acquire skills and facilitate working at home for a large percentage of the workforce.

Electronic Frontier Foundation. **EFF Quotes Collection**. San Francisco, CA: Electronic Frontier Foundation, 1996.
http://www.eff.org/pub/EFF/quotes.eff

On the quotes collections home page is this description of the work: "A collection of the wittiest and stupidest, most sublime and most inane comments ever said or written about free speech, cryptography, privacy, civil liberties, networking, government, communication, society, human nature, reason, optimism and pessimism, progress, and more." The file is updated frequently and is free for downloading.

Gilder, George. **Telecosm Articles**. Philadelphia, PA: Portman Communciation Service, 1995.
http://www.seas.upenn.edu/~gaj1/ggindex.html

This series of articles by George Gilder provides background that may help readers understand the concepts and technologies related to the deployment of an Information Superhighway. The articles first appeared in *Forbes ASAP* and have been compiled in a book, *Telecosm*, published in 1996.

Hughes, Kevin. **From Webspace to Cyberspace**. Palo Alto, CA: Enterprise Integration Technologies, 1995.
http://www.eit.com/~kevinh/cspace/

This work, available in PDF or PostScript format, is the sequel to *Entering the World Wide Web: A Guide to Cyberspace*. The author provides an excellent survey of the history and development of the World Wide Web, as well as creating a context for the implementation of new information technologies within the larger picture of societal change. He also analyzes where cyberspace might be in the short term.

Mitchell, William J. **City of Bits: Space, Place, and the Infobahn**. Cambridge, MA: MIT Press, 1995.
http://www-mitpress.mit.edu/City_of_Bits/

This examination of the world that is coming to be called cyberspace is available in Web-based hypertext format as well as in traditional paperbound form (see Selected Print Resources).

Progress & Freedom Foundation. **Cyberspace and the American Dream: A Magna Carta for the Knowledge Age (Release 1.2)**. Washington, DC: Progress & Freedom Foundation, 1994.
http://www.glocom.ac.jp/WhatsNew/MagnacartaPFF.html
http://www.pff.org/pff/position.html

Represented as the cumulative ideas of dozens of thinkers, the main text is closely aligned with the philosophies of Esther Dyson, George Gilder, George Keyworth, and Alvin Toffler. This work is an attempt to explain the nature of the changes that are occurring because of the adaptation of new information technologies and the rise of cyberspace.

Rheingold, Howard. **The Virtual Community: Homesteading on the Electronic Frontier**. San Francisco: Howard Rheingold, 1993.
http://www.well.com/user/hlr/vcbook/

Rheingold is the former editor of *The Whole Earth Review*, and he has reported extensively on the issues of information technology and the digital future. This book, which looks at the phenomenon of on-line community-building, is free for downloading. The author asks, should you enjoy it, that you please find the hard-copy version, too (see Selected Print Resources).

Scheer, Léo. **La Démocratie Virtuelle**. Flammarion, 1994.
http://www.quelm.fr/CSphere/N1/ExclusifU.html

This French-language text considers the way information technology will be able to facilitate a "virtual democracy" movement. It is written by one of the experts in telecommunications in France.

Sterling, Bruce. **The Hacker Crackdown: Law and Disorder on the Electronic Frontier**. Texinfo, ed. 1.2. San Francisco, CA: Bruce Sterling, 1994.
http://www.eff.org/papers/hacker_crackdown/crack.html

Sterling, a reporter and science fiction writer, was one of the first to use the term *cyberpunk*. This book reveals the real story behind the Legion of Doom and Operation Sundevil, the federal government's initiative to arrest computer hackers they felt were responsible for compromising government intelligence and the telecommunications infrastructure in 1990. The incident led to the founding of the Electronic Frontier Foundation.

Strangelove, Michael. **Understanding Internet: The Democratization of Mass Media and the Emerging Paradigm of Cyberspace**. Otta200
wa, Canada: Strangelove Internet Enterprises, 1994.
http://www.strangelove.com/publish/paradigm

Strangelove makes a new chapter of this work available on-line on a semiregular basis.

Government Aspects

Allen, Kenneth C., et al. **Survey of Rural Information Infrastructure Technologies**. Boulder, CO: Institute for Telecommunication Sciences, 1995.
http://www.its.bldrdoc.gov/its/spectrum/rural/ruralrep.html

The National Telecommunications and Information Administration of the U.S. Department of Commerce has made this Special Publication (95-33) available in HTML, ASCII, or PDF format. According to the abstract, "This report defines a set of distinct voice, computer, and video telecommunication services; describes several rural information applications that make use of these services; and surveys various wireline and wireless systems and technologies that are being used or might be used to deliver these services to rural areas."

Cross-Industry Working Team. **Copyright Act of 1976, as Amended (1994), Including the Semiconductor Chip Protection Act of 1984 and the Audio Home Recording Act of 1992**. Lawyers Cooperative Publishing, 1994.
http://www.law.cornell.edu/usc/17/overview.html

The HTML-formatted version of this federal statute is presented here as a searchable electronic document. As the parameters of copyright begin to change because of the way publishing and retrieving information is being redefined in the Information Age, the document will undergo some intense scrutiny in the next few years.

High Performance Computing and Communications. **High Performance Computing and Communications: Foundation for America's Information Future**. Washington, DC: HPCC, 1995.
http://www.hpcc.gov/blue96/index.html
This is the HPCC annual report for fiscal year 1996. It reports on the latest applications affecting change on the Internet and related digital networks.

High Performance Computing and Communications. **High Performance Computing and Communications: Technology for the National Information Infrastructure**. Washington, DC: HPCC, 1995.
http://www.hpcc.gov/blue95/index.html
This is the HPCC's fiscal year 1995 annual report of progress. It focuses on the technical side of the NII architecture.

High Performance Computing and Communications. **High Performance Computing and Communications: Toward a National Information Infrastructure**. Washington, DC: HPCC, 1994.
http://www.hpcc.gov/blue94/index.html
The fiscal year 1994 blue book annual report of the HPCC lays out the charge and expected activities of the HPCC as it relates to digital networking.

Information Infrastructure Task Force. **NII Progress Report: September 1993–1994**. Washington, DC: U.S. Department of Commerce, 1994.
http://www.csto.arpa.mil//NII_Report_94.html
This report from the Information Infrastructure Task Force provides information on the development of the national information infrastructure through 1994. It focuses on several areas of progress, including small businesses providing new services made possible by the emerging information technologies,

telecommuting, distance education, telemedicine, citizens' interaction with government officials, and disabled Americans' use of networks to communicate.

Magid, Jonathan, and Darlene Fladager. **The National Information Infrastructure: Agenda for Action**. Washington, DC: U.S. Department of Commerce, 1994.
http://sunsite.unc.edu/nii/toc.html

This document is the hypertext version of the Clinton administration's vision for the NII, or the Information Superhighway. It delineates the key elements of the infrastructure, as well as the partnerships that will have to be defined if the NII is to enhance democratic institutions as well as the commercial viability of the Net for the citizens of the United States.

National Research Council. **Realizing the Information Future: The Internet and Beyond**. Washington, DC: National Academy Press, 1994.
http://xerxes.nas.edu:70/1/nap/online/rtif/

Members of the National Research Council, drawn from the councils of the National Academy of Sciences, the National Academy of Engineering, and the Institute of Medicine, wrote this examination of architectural and deployment issues relating to the national information infrastructure.

U.S. Department of Commerce. **Common Ground: First Report of the National Information Infrastructure Advisory Council**. Washington, DC: U.S. Department of Commerce, 1995.
http://www.uark.edu/~niiac/toc.html

This is the progress report of the first year's activity of the NIIAC, the citizens' advisory council of the U.S. Department of Commerce's effort to coordinate the deployment of the National Information Infrastructure.

Educational Aspects

McKenzie, Jamie. **Net Profit**. Bellingham, WA: Jamie McKenzie, 1995.
http://www.pacificrim.net/~mckenzie/netprofit.html

The subject of the work is the use of cyberspace in educational settings. This book is available from the author in hard copy, and the hyperlinked version is available for a fee.

Paulsen, Morten Flate. **The Online Report on Pedagogical Techniques for Computer-Mediated Communication**. Oslo, Norway: Morten Flate Paulsen, 1994.
http://valhall.nki.no:80/~morten/#t

This 55-page report was written by one of the experts in the field of distance education. Paulsen is an assistant professor at the NKI Department of Distance Education in Oslo, Norway. His credits include the design of the EKKO computer conferencing system and the establishment of the NKI Electronic College. He has made the report available as shareware in either Microsoft Word or HTML formats.

Stone-Martin, Martha, and Laura Breeden, eds. **FARNet Stories Project: 51 Reasons To Build the National Information Infrastructure**.Washington, DC: FARNet, 1994.
gopher://gopher.cni.org:70/h0/cniftp/miscdocs/farnet/www/catindex

The Federation of American Research Networks (FARNet), issued a call for tales to be included in their Network Stories Project in February 1993. This is the summary of the results of that project, including stories from the 50 states and the District of Columbia on how the Net is being utilized for education, research, economic development, health care, and opportunities for people with disabilities.

The Internet

de Presno, Odd. **The Online World**. Arendal, Norway: Odd de Presno, 1995.
http://login.eunet.no/~presno/index.html

This is one of the oldest and most respected resource handbooks dealing with the practical side of using the global on-line information network as seen from an international perspective. This version has hypertext links to sites mentioned in the text, but an ASCII version is also available. If you register with the author, you can sign up to have both the ASCII and the hypertext versions sent regularly on diskette, and *The Online World Monitor* newsletter will also be sent free of charge.

EARN Association. **The Guide to Network Resource Tools**. Amsterdam: EARN Association (TERENA), 1993–1994.
http://www.earn.net/gnrt/notice.html

The EARN Association (1984–1994) was responsible for coordinating important networking services in Europe, the Middle

East, and Africa. This document, an explanation of useful tools for retrieving digital network data, was one of the services that the association provided to end users. The book is available free of charge.

Engst, Adam C. **Internet Starter Kit**. Indianapolis, IN: Hayden Books, 1995.
http://www.mcp.com/hayden/iskm/book.html
Adam Engst is a well-known expert on Macintosh-related computer issues. His hard-copy version of this work (see Selected Print Resources) is the most often used text for Mac users connecting their machines to the Net. At this site, Engst has created a hyperlinked and expanded version of the Mac and Windows starter kits.

Gaffin, Adam. **EFF's (Extended) Guide to the Internet, Texinfo Ed**. San Francisco: Electronic Frontier Foundation, 1994.
http://www.eff.org/papers/eegtti/
Formerly known as *Big Dummy's Guide to the Internet*, this book was written by Gaffin for a joint project of Apple Computer, Inc. and the Electronic Frontier Foundation. Now in HTML format as a Web-based publication, this primer on accessing the Internet is also available for ASCII downloading in Hungarian, Italian, Japanese, Polish, and Russian. The Web text is fully searchable.

Hughes, Kevin. **Entering the World Wide Web: A Guide to Cyberspace**. Palo Alto, CA: Enterprise Integration Technologies, 1994.
http://www.eit.com:80/web/www.guide/
Written when Hughes was a student, this hypertext book is one of the best introductions available anywhere to the world of the Internet and Web-based information resources. Hughes's expertise has taken him to a designing position with Enterprise Integration Technologies.

Kehoe, Brendan P. **Zen and the Art of the Internet: A Beginner's Guide to the Internet**. Urbana, IL: University of Illinois, Brendan Kehoe, 1992.
http://sundance.cso.uiuc.edu/Publications/Other/Zen/zen-1.0_toc.html
Slightly dated but packed full of very useful information on the protocols and tools related to navigating on the Internet, the first edition of this e-text primer—a master's thesis—is available free

of charge in HTML format. More recent editions of the work are in print (see Selected Print Resources).

LaQuey, Tracy. **The Internet Companion: A Beginner's Guide to Global Networking**. Rockport, MA: Online BookStore, 1994. http://www.obs-us.com/obs/english/books/editinc/obsxxx.htm

The is the Online BookStore's free, "distributive" full-text HTML version of the second edition of LaQuey's best-selling book (see Selected Print Resources).

Mathiesen, Michael. **Marketing on the Internet**. Santa Cruz, CA: Maximum Press, 1995. http://netcenter.com/yellows/cover.html

The author has excerpted some especially useful sections of this comprehensive guide to creating an Internet presence for a commercial enterprise and made them available free of charge on the Net.

Partl, Hubert. **HTML-Einführung: die Sprache des World Wide Web**. Hubert Partl, Universität für Bodenkultur in Wien, 1995. http://www.boku.ac.at/htmleinf/

This German-language book on hypertext markup language (HTML) is written in HTML.

Pesce, Mark. **VRML Browsing and Building Cyberspace**. Indianapolis, IN: Macmillan Computer Publishing, New Riders, 1995. http://www.mcp.com/general/news7/vrml2.html

Written by one of the pioneers of the new virtual reality markup language, a language that will eventually add a third dimension to the World Wide Web, this book is the first to discuss the subject. Some sample chapters are available on-line.

Powell, Bob, and Karen Wickre. **Atlas to the World Wide Web**. Emeryville, CA: Ziff-Davis Press, 1995. http://www.rhythm.com/~bpowell/Atlas/toc.htm

As its name implies, this "mapping" of cyberspace is designed to guide the newcomer and experienced traveler around the digital world known as the Web. The publishers have made this book available on-line in HTML format and included many links to resources and information on the development of the Net.

Wolf, Gary, and Michael Stein. **Aether Madness, an Offbeat Guide to the Online World**. Berkeley, CA: Peachpit Press, 1994.
http://www.aether.com/Aether/
This on-line book is a full-text version of the authors' tour of some of the most bizarre sites and personalities in cyberspace.

Electronic Journals and Magazines

access online. Urbana-Champaign: National Center for Supercomputing Applications at the University of Illinois at Urbana-Champaign (UIUC), 1995–1996.
http://www.ncsa.uiuc.edu/Pubs/access/accessDir.html
This is the electronic archive of the print version of this technical journal that publishes articles related to research in digital issues. Information on subscribing to the print version is available here.

ALAWON. Washington, DC: American Library Association, Washington Office, 1995–1996.
http://www.lib.ncsu.edu/stacks/alawon-index.html
This e-mail publication of the American Library Association provides updates and alerts to its subscribers on issues that relate to government action on libraries and education. The free newsletter is available only in electronic form. Back issues and other documents are available. To subscribe, send the message "subscribe alawo [your name]" to listserv@uicvm.uic.edu.

Canadian Journal of Communication. Waterloo, Ontario: Wilfrid Laurier University Press, 1995–1996.
http://edie.cprost.sfu.ca/cjc/cjc-info.html
This peer-reviewed quarterly in the field of communications studies and journalism education has been created as an experiment in the electronic delivery of a refereed academic journal. Many articles here address the subject of computer-mediated communication.

Caught in the 'Net. Williams Lake, BC, Canada: Todd Sullivan, *Williams Lake Advocate*, 1995–1996.
http://www.awinc.com/imagehouse/caught/
This Web site houses the current and archived columns of writer Todd Sullivan of British Columbia, Canada. His wanderings

around the Net are reported in the *Williams Lake Advocate* every week.

CDT Policy Posts. Washington, DC: Center for Democracy and Technology, 1995–1996.
http://www.cdt.org/publications/pubs.html

This is the regular news publication of the Center for Democracy and Technology, which is, according to the CDT, "the authoritative source for accurate, up-to-date information and detailed analysis of public policy issues affecting civil liberties on-line." Information on subscribing via e-mail is available at the Web site.

CLiCK Interactive Magazine. Ultimo, NSW, Austrlia: Radiant Productions, 1996.
http://www.click.com.au

A new free magazine on the Web, this publication focuses on the people, ideas, and products that are driving interactive multimedia on CD-ROM, the Internet, the World Wide Web, and other evolving broadband services. The publishers produce a companion CD-based magazine that interfaces with this material but is not necessary for access.

CMC Magazine. Troy, NY: December Communications, 1996.
http://www. december.com/cmc/mag/current/toc.html

The free newsletter produced by computer-mediated communication expert John December "reports on people, events, technology, and issues; opinions and perspectives about the state and direction of CMC studies; research description, speculation, reports, and results." For serious students of the field, this is an excellent resource.

c|net online. San Francisco: c|net, inc. 1996.
http://www.cnet.com/

This is a commercial multimedia company's on-line magazine, replete with advertisements, but also full of useful information technology articles and interviews with those people creating cyberspace.

Computer Underground Digest (Cu-Digest or CuD). DeKalb, IL: Jim Thomas, Department of Sociology, NIU, 1996.
http://www.soci.niu.edu:80/~cudigest/

According to the editor's description, this free weekly electronic newsletter "is an open forum dedicated to sharing information among computerists and to the presentation and debate of diverse views." Issues generally addressed are those that involve privacy and freedom of speech on the Net. CuD is available as a Usenet newsgroup: comp.society.cu-digest, or via e-mail subscription. Visit the Web site for details.

Critical Mass. Burnaby, BC, Canada: Simon Fraser University, 1996.
http://hoshi,cic.sfu.ca/~cm
Begun as an experimental project by six communications students at Simon Fraser University in the summer of 1995, this e-zine offers a Canadian perspective on mass communication issues while also serving as a forum for discussion of these issues.

Current Cites. Berkeley, CA: Information Systems Instruction & Support (ISIS), 1990–1996.
http://sunsite.berkeley.edu/CurrentCites
The monthly publication of the Library at the University of California, Berkeley, surveys over 30 journals in library and information technology for selected articles on optical disc technologies, computer networks and networking, electronic publishing, and hypermedia and multimedia. The citations are given with brief annotations of the contents. Access and subscription information for this free newsletter is available at the Web site.

Cyber Business Journal. Albuquerque, NM: Computer Coach/ Virtual Presence, 1995–1996
http://swcp.com/~coach/CBJ/
This free commercial on-line magazine promises to help the businessperson "take full advantage of what the Global Communications & Information Revolution is bringing....We will focus on the concepts of business communications and information handling."

Cyber Culture. Arlington, TX: Creativision Publishing Corporation, 1996.
http://www.cvp.com/cyber/
"Dedicated to the new digital world and anything and anyone involved. We provide free access to all readers who have a Web browser. Topics are eclectic and will stay that way!" This is a new electronic magazine that deals in broad issues related to anything on the Net.

Cybersphere. Paris: Quelm, 1996.
http://www.quelm.fr/CybersphereU.html
Cybersphere is the first French-language on-line magazine dealing with the Information Age and its implications for society. An English translation of some sections is also available.

d.Comm. London: The Economist Newspaper Ltd., 1995–1996.
http://www.d-comm.com/
This free commercial Web-based magazine does not have a print counterpart. The intent is to cover all types of information technology issues, networking issues, communications, etc. It also includes a search utility to facilitate the recovery of archived data.

DEOSNEWS. Oslo, Norway: Morten Flate Paulsen, NKI, Department of Distance Education, 1996.
This is an electronic journal that deals with the developments in distance education. Free e-mail subscriptions can be obtained by sending the following message to listserv@psuvm.psu.edu: Subscribe DEOSNEWS Your Full Name.

Digital Future Digest. Hart Publishing, 1996.
mailto:majordomo@lists.csn.net
This free e-mail newsletter claims to provide the latest-breaking news on developments affecting the "Internet, on-line services, FCC, telecommunications, software, and much more." To subscribe, send an e-mail message to majordomo@lists.csn.net with the message: subscribe digital_future youremailaddress in the body. The subject is ignored.

Edupage. Washington, DC: Educom, 1996.
http://www.educom.edu/web/edupage.html
Edupage is one of the most respected and most often quoted electronic newsletters available on the Net. Its goal is to provide a summary of news items that relate to information technology three times each week as a service of Educom (see Directory of Organizations). The free issues are available at the URL above and via e-mail subscription in several languages.

EFFector Online Newsletter. San Francisco, CA: Electronic Frontier Foundation (EFF), 1996.
http://www.eff.org/pub/EFF/Newsletters/EFFector/
The EFF makes this newsletter, which reports on their organizational activities and calls for action, available on-line free of

charge. The EFF is concerned about privacy and freedom of speech and access issues as these are redefined by the emerging technologies.

Electronic School. Alexandria, VA: National School Boards Association, 1995.
http://www.access.digex.net/~nsbamags/e-school.html

This e-journal is a supplement to *The Executive Educator* and *The American School Board Journal*, traditional print magazines. The editors' goal is to provide information and direction for educators and school leaders who are attempting to incorporate information technologies into the educational process. Full-text articles deal with many subjects related to digital communications in the school setting.

Elektra. Boston: Digitas, Harvard University, 1994–1996.
http://www.digitas.org/

Harvard's first on-line publication, *Elektra* is a project of Digitas, a student organization focusing on technologies such as multimedia, virtual reality, wireless communication, personal digital assistants, the Information Superhighway, and interactive television.

FaulknerWeb. Pennsauken, NJ: Faulkner Information Services, 1995–1996.
http://www.faulkner.com/

This is a free electronic magazine published by a commercial service provider and available only on the World Wide Web. The information here focuses on the computer and communications industries, with a heavy emphasis on the latest information technologies and trends.

From Now On: The Educational Technology Journal.
Bellingham, WA: Jamie McKenzie, 1996.
http://www.pacificrim.net/~mckenzie/

This electronic newsletter is available via e-mail or on the World Wide Web. It deals with the issues of applying new information technologies to education in general and the K–12 classroom in particular. Information regarding free subscriptions is available at the Web site.

GLOSAS NEWS. Flushing, NY: Global Systems Analysis and Simulation Association, 1996.
http://solar.rtd.utk.edu/friends/education/educ.html

This is the electronic bulletin of the Global Systems Analysis and Simulation Association. The publication is free to e-mail subscribers, and archived editions are available at the URL above. It is a superior source of information on the trends that are driving the development of the Net.

HotWired. San Francisco: HotWired Ventures LLC, 1996.
http://www.hotwired.com/

Arguably the definitive on-line magazine site, *HotWired* is the electronic version of *Wired* magazine, the print monthly that has done more to define the emerging character of cyberspace than any other publication to date. Access to articles is free.

IAT Briefings. Durham, NC: Institute for Academic Technology (IAT), 1996.
http://www.iat.unnc.edu

The URL above is the site for the archive of the information technology journal produced by IAT (see Directory of Organizations) in electronic format.

INFOBITS. Durham, NC: Institute for Academic Technology (IAT), 1996.
http://www.iat.unc.edu/infobits/infobits.html

Infobits is described as an e-mail service of the Institute for Academic Technology's Information Resources Group. The service delivers a newsletter each month that covers news from a number of information technology and instruction technology sources. Free subscription information is available at the Web site.

Information Technology and Disabilities. Washington, DC: Equal Access to Software and Information, 1996.
http://www.rit.edu/~easi

This is a refereed journal devoted to the issues of development and effective use of new and emerging technologies by computer users with disabilities. The journal is free and available via several sources on the Net. Information is available at the Web site.

INFOSYS: The Electronic Newsletter for Information Systems. Washington, DC: Boyd and Fraser Publishing, 1995.
mailto:listserv@american.edu

This is a free biweekly e-mail newsletter for "faculty, students, and practitioners in the field of Information Systems." The publication updates its readers on the news, conferences, meetings, papers, and other publications that involve information technology. To subscribe to *INFOSYS*, send the following one-line e-mail message to listserv@american.edu: subscribe infosys your first name your last name [e.g., subscribe infosys John Smith]. Back issues are archived at http://www.lib.ncsu.edu/stacks/ infosys-index.html.

Innovation. NewsScan, Inc., 1995.
Innovation-request@newsscan.com

The masthead of this fee-based weekly e-mail newsletter says, "Because time and information are your most valuable assets, Innovation offers a weekly summary of trends, strategies, and innovations in business and technology, giving you an executive briefing on ideas for the future." It tends to do a very credible job of reporting on these issues, and a trial subscription is available.

Interesting Times. Theodor Holm Nelson. Sausalito, CA: Mindful Press, 1994.
http://www.picosof.com/849

This is the occasional newsletter site of one of the visionary pioneers who helped to develop what has come to be considered cyberspace. Nelson coined the terms "hypertext" and "hypermedia."

InterFace Magazine. Victoria, BC, Canada: InterFace, 1996.
http://vvv.com/interface/

The publisher describes the intent of this e-zine on the opening screen: "The premise of this publication is to help bridge the invisible gap between the user on that side of the screen, and the computer/tool on this side.... By showcasing the changing face of technological advance, we provide insightful and fascinating subject areas interrelated to the evolution of the human creative spirit."

Internet Monthly Reports. Ann Arbor, MI: Internet Research Group, 1994–1996.
gopher://nic.merit.edu:7043/11/internet/newsletters/internet.monthly.rep ort

This gopher-based resource reports the monthly communications to the Internet Research Group on the accomplishments, milestones, and problems encountered by the participating organizations. This is normally technical information.

Interpersonal Computing and Technology: An Electronic Journal for the 21st Century. College Park, MD: Department of Education, University of Maryland, 1995.
mailto: LISTSERV@LISTSERV.GEORGETOWN.EDU: INDEX IPCT-J

This e-journal continues to be a well-respected resource for discussion of the issues surrounding computer-mediated communication. It was originated by the renowned professor and expert in computer-mediated communication issues, Gerald M. Phillips, who recently died in 1996. To obtain a list of all available files, including back issues, send the following message to LISTSERV@LISTSERV.GEORGETOWN.EDU: INDEX IPCT-J. The name of each issue's table of contents file begins with the word *CONTENTS*.

Jim Upchurch ONLINE. Montgomery, AL: Jim Upchurch and *The Montgomery Advertiser,* 1995.
http://www.mont.mindspring.com/~jtu3/online.html

The author of a column on information technology issues and the on-line environment posts the text of articles that "appear more or less every other Monday in the 'Business Monday' section of *The Montgomery* (Alabama) *Advertiser.*"

The Journal of Computer-Mediated Communication. Los Angeles: Annenberg School for Communication (USC) and the School of Business Administration, Hebrew University of Jerusalem, 1996.
http://cwis.usc.edu/dept/annenberg/announce.html

This e-journal is a scholarly undertaking that reports on the trends and research affecting computer-mediated communications. The HTML-formatted publication is available free of charge.

LIBRES: Library and Information Science Research Electronic Journal. Kent, OH: Kent State University, 1994.
gopher://vega.lib.ncsu.edu:70/11/library/stacks/libres;
gopher://refmac.kent.edu:70/1D-1%3a3450%3aLIBRES

LIBRES is a communication medium for students and professionals in the discipline of information science. The main focus is on ideas and projects pertaining to how the new digital technologies will affect libraries and research. For information on access, check the URLs above.

MEME. New York: David S. Bennahum, 1996.
http://www.reach.com/matrix/

"Your Filter to CyberSpace" is the description provided by the publisher of this excellent free newsletter that can be accessed on the Web or via e-mail subscription. The focus of this biweekly is the changing nature of society as we push further into the Information Age. "Meme" is a contagious idea that replicates like a virus.

National School Network Testbed Newsletter. Cambridge, MA: BBN Corporation, 1996.
http://copernicus.bbn.com/testbed2/TBdocs/Documents.html

BBN is administering a grant from the federal government to develop an educational network test bed to demonstrate the advantages and problems school districts are having as they begin to utilize the resources of the cyberworld. Free copies of the newsletter, which reports on the progress of this project, are available at the Web site.

Net-Happenings. InterNIC Directory & Database Services, Gleason Sackman, 1994–1996.
http://www.mid.net:80/NET/

Gleason Sackman has distributed this electronic "newsletter" listing of the newest and most recently updated Internet-based resources since 1994. He often must wade through hundreds of announcements of sites that people want him to publicize to his subscribers. There is now a Web site that archives the past and most recent postings. It includes a search engine to help retrieve listings in a particular category. Information on subscribing to the mail list is available at the URL above.

The Network Observer. San Diego: Phil Agre, Department of Communication, University of California, San Diego, 1996.
http://communication.ucsd.edu/pagre/tno.html

Normally published as an automatic e-mail newsletter every month, this publication is the work of Phil Agre and often includes his writings on the subject of computer-mediated communication and community-building on the Net. Agre also includes updates, alerts, and articles written by others who have important contributions to make in this emerging field. Information on subscribing is available at the Web site.

Online. Steve Kelley, Kennebunk, ME: *York County Coast Star*, 1996.
http://www.cybertours.com/yccs/online.htm

Online is a weekly column written by Steve Kelley for the *York County Coast Star* newspaper in Kennebunk, Maine. The paper makes the column, which centers on events and trends in cyberspace, available free of charge via e-mail. Information is at the Web site.

Online Business Today. Ft. Lauderdale, FL: Home Page Press, 1996
mailto: obt.text@hpp.com

Online Business Today is a free electronic newsletter that covers the world of business applications and opportunities on the Net. To subscribe, send e-mail to the URL cited above.

Online Chronicle of Distance Education and Communication.
Ft. Lauderdale, FL: Nova Southeastern University, 1995.
mailto: listproc@pulsar.acast.nova.edu
http://www.fcae.nova.edu/disted/disted.htm

The masthead of this e-journal says, "In the Industrial Age, we went to school. In the Communication Age, schools can come to us. This is the message implicit in the evolution of distance education." The issues addressed here deal with information technology and distance education. To subscribe, send a message to the URL cited above, and in the first line type: SUB DISTED your_full_name.

Road and Hack. New Haven, CT: PC Lube and Tune, Howard Gilbert, 1996.
http://pclt.cis.yale.edu/pclt/roadhack.html

This publication is a private project of Howard Gilbert, a senior research programmer at Yale University. He provides updated insights into the world of the Net, especially as it relates to the more technical aspects of protocols and developing software.

The Scout Report. Madison, WI: Net Scout Services, 1996.
http://rs.internic.net/scout_report-index.htm

Provided via e-mail and on the Web by the InterNIC administrative service of the Internet, this free newsletter reports on the new and interesting resources that have come on-line or been modified in the past week. Directions for subscribing to the e-mail delivery service are available at the Web site.

Seidman's Online Insider. Manhasset, NY: Robert Seidman & CMP Media Inc., 1996.
http://techweb.cmp.com/net/online/current/columns/seidman/online_insider

Subtitled "A Weekly Summary of Events in the Consumer On-line Services Industry," this e-mail and Web-based newsletter always contains the most up-to-date information on the changes that occur in and around the on-line commercial services like America Online, CompuServe, and the Microsoft Network. The weekly newsletter is available at the Web site or via a free e-mail delivery.

Syllabus Magazine. Sunnyvale, CA: Syllabus Press, 1995–1996.
http://www.syllabus.com/syllmag.html

Archives of the print magazine are available at this site for downloading. The publication deals with the latest information on educational technologies, including software and use of the Net for communications and information retrieval.

Telecom Post. Palo Alto, CA: Free Speech Media LLC, Coralee Whitcomb, 1995–1996.
mailto: listserv@cpsr.org
http:// snyside.sunnyside.com/dox/telecom-post/

Whitcomb's reasons for starting this newsletter are best said in her words: "This spring and early summer will witness the design and passage of legislation that will shape our communication infrastructure for many years to come. In an effort to keep the Internet community abreast of legislative events...this alert will cover the issues and concerns of the public interest community and point to actions that can be taken on behalf of these issues." This free electronic newsletter is distributed on several mail lists. To subscribe, e-mail the URL above with the message: SUBSCRIBE TELECOM-POST YOUR NAME.

TidBITS. Seattle, WA: Adam and Tonya Engst, 1995–1996.
http://www.dartmouth.edu/pages/TidBITS/TidBITS.html

This e-mail newsletter is a free weekly electronic publication that reports on interesting products and events in the computer industry, currently with an emphasis on the world of the Macintosh. It has timely articles on the development of the Net. For information on how to subscribe, where to find back issues, etc., send e-mail to info@tidbits.com.

Web Informant Newsletter. Port Washington, NY: David Strom, 1995–1996.
http://www.strom.com/
This publication is an HTML-formatted occasional newsletter from a writer who also does work for respected communications periodicals and books. This site covers high-tech marketing, communications, and computer trade publishing issues.

Web Review. Sebastopol, CA: Songline Studios, 1996.
http://webreview.com
This World Wide Web magazine takes a look at "important developments that are arriving from every direction, as people use the Web as a business tool, a community-builder, and an expressive medium." The magazine is free to readers who want to learn more about the developers, businesspeople, and new applications that are driving the Web.

Web Watch. San Diego, CA: Tom Munnecke, SAIC, 1995.
http://tom.itl.saic.com/webwatch/index.htm
The author of this free weekly column discusses some of the general capabilities of the Web and its implications for our future.

The Weekly Bookmark. DeKalb, IL: Matt Alberts, 1995.
http://www.webcom.com/weekly/thisweek.html
Alberts publishes this free newsletter every week to apprise subscribers of new sites that appear to be interesting on the World Wide Web. Information on how to receive the free ASCII version by e-mail is at the Web site.

Videotapes

An extensive collection of educational videos about human liberties and freedoms in the Information Age has been made available by the CFP Video Library Project, P.O. Box 912, Topanga, CA 90290, URL: http://www.forests.com/cfpvideo/. These VHS videos are tapes of speeches and panel discussions presented at the Computers, Freedom & Privacy conferences (1991–1996) that were organized by the Computer Professionals for Social Responsibility. A free catalog and discount pricing information are available at cfpvideo@earthlink.net or (800) 235-4922.

Access to Government Information (CFP-113)
Length: 89 min.
Date: 1991
Cost: $55.00

Individual and corporate access to federal, state, and local information about communities, corporations, legislation, administration, the courts, etc., is the topic for the panel made up of David
Burnham, Transactional Records Access Clearinghouse; Harry
Hammitt, publisher, Access Reports; Katherine Mawdsley, associate librarian, University of California, Davis; and Robert Veeder, Office of Management & Budget. They discuss the thorny
problem of allowing access while protecting privacy.

Censorship and Content Control on the Internet (CFP-609)
Length: 80 min.
Date: 1996
Cost: $55.00

As the Internet becomes global and national boundaries start to
blur, countries are considering censoring material controversial
to their respective societies: Germany may extend its strict laws
against neo-Nazi hate speech to the World Wide Web; newly
emerging democracies in Eastern Europe and Asia are weighing
approaches to free expression online; Britain and the U.S.
Congress are attempting to censor sexually explicit material.

   Featuring: Daniel Weitzner, Center for Democracy & Tech-
nology; Herbert Burkert, European Commission; Gara LaMarche,
Human Rights Watch; Kate Martin, Center for National Security
Studies.

The Communications Decency Act of 1996 (CFP-605)
Length: 102 min.
Date: 1996
Cost: $55.00

The CDA, part of the 1996 Telecommunications Reform Act,
made it a criminal offense (punishable by two years in prison
and a fine) to transfer by interactive computer service in a way
that could be viewed by people under age 18, any words or pictures that might be considered "indecent." The American Civil
Liberties Union and 60,000 Internet users promptly filed suit to
challenge the constitutionality of the measure. This panel, taped
while the trial was under way, includes speakers on both sides
of the issue explaining their viewpoints.

Featuring: Daniel Weitzner, Center for Democracy & Technology; Jill Lesser, People for the American Way; Barry Steinhardt, ACLU; Bruce Taylor, National Law Center for Families and Children.

Computer Surveillance in the Workplace (CFP-209)
Length: 97 min.
Date: 1993
Cost: $55.00

Gary Marx, Massachusetts Institute of Technology; Willis Ware, RAND Corporation; and Kristina Zahorik, U.S. Senate Labor Committee, debate the issue of new technologies that provide opportunities for employee surveillance, as well as communication. What right to privacy should workers expect in the workplace? What are the employer's concerns, and how should these interests be weighed?

Computer-Based Surveillance of Individuals (CFP-110)
Length: 90 min.
Date: 1991
Cost: $55.00

David Flaherty, professor, University of Western Ontario; Judith Krug, American Library Association; Gary Marx, professor, Massachusetts Institute of Technology; and Karen Nussbaum, National Association of Working Women, discuss why privacy matters. The panel looks at the role of privacy in a democracy and examines the erosion of privacy standards on-line.

The Constitution in the Information Age (CFP-101)
Length: 75 min.
Date: 1991
Cost: $55.00

This is the keynote address of the Computers, Freedom & Privacy Conference by Harvard law professor and constitutional law expert Laurence Tribe, who proposes a Twenty-Seventh Amendment extending Bill of Rights protections to the on-line world.

Copyright and Freedom of Expression on the Internet (CFP-606)
Length: 108 min.
Date: 1996
Cost: $55.00

Is copyright obsolete in the digital age? Are the economics of digitally producing and distributing information products so fundamentally different that copyright becomes a barrier to free speech? Or, in the global networked world, will there inevitably be only one law of copyright and free expression? What will it be?

Featuring: Pamela Samuelson, professor of law, Cornell University; David Post, Cyberspace Law Institute; Brent Hugenholtz, Information Law Institute, Amsterdam; Chris Barlas, Author's Licensing & Collecting Society in London.

Cryptography, Privacy, and National Security (CFP-210)
Length: 77 min.
Date: 1993
Cost: $55.00

The panel on this tape discusses the topic of public encryption. Should the FBI or some other federal agency be allowed to hold the key to private individuals' secretly encoded information? Participants include experts in the field: Jim Bidzos, RSA Data Security; David Bellin, Pratt Institute; John Perry Barlow, Electronic Frontier Foundation; John Gilmore, Cygnus Support; Whitfield Diffie, Sunsoft, Inc.; and Dorothy Denning, Georgetown University.

DNA Testing and Genetic Data Banks (CFP-206)
Length: 70 min.
Date: 1993
Cost: $55.00

John Hicks, FBI Laboratory; Tom Marr, Cold Spring Harbor Laboratory; Paul Mendelsohn, Neurofibromatosis, Inc.; Peter Neufeld; and Madison Powers, Kennedy Center for Ethics, debate the issues of medical information privacy in regard to on-line genetic data banks.

Electronic Money (CFP-608)
Length: 94 min.
Date: 1996
Cost: $55.00

This timely panel defines the ground rules for international discussion of digital money, considering payment systems based on cards and the Internet; examines law enforcement concerns about digital money laundering versus privacy concerns in Net transactions; and explains the role of companies like Netscape, Microsoft, VISA, and America Online in developing competing standards.

Featuring: David Chaum, DigiCash, inventor of secure digital transactions; Stan Morris, U.S. Financial Crimes Enforcement

Network; Kawika Daguio, American Bankers Association; Rafael Hirschfeld, Center for Mathematics and Computer Science, Amsterdam.

Electronic Speech, Press, and Assembly (CFP-112)
Length: 91 min.
Date: 1991
Cost: $55.00

Eric Lieberman; John McMullen, *Newsbytes*; George Perry, vice president and general counsel, Prodigy Services Company; Jack Rickard, editor, *Boardwatch* magazine; Lance Rose; and David Hughes, Old Colorado City Communications, are the panel in this videotaped discussion of electronics rights to freedom of assembly and publishing on the Internet.

Ethics and Education (CFP-114)
Length: 83 min.
Date: 1991
Cost: $55.00

Sally Bowman, Computer Learning Foundation; Jonathan Budd, National Institute of Justice; Dorothy Denning, professor, Georgetown University; John Gilmore, Cygnus Support; Richard Hollinger, associate professor, University of Florida; and Donn Parker, SRI International, present ethical principles for copying of data and software and the distribution of confidential information.

Ethics, Morality, and Criminality (CFP-203)
Length: 89 min.
Date: 1993
Cost: $55.00

A panel of experts discusses law enforcement issues like wiretapping and the prevention of electronic break-ins on the Net. Guests include Scott Charney, U.S. Department of Justice; James Settle and J. Michael Gibbons, Federal Bureau of Investigation; Mike Godwin, Electronic Frontier Foundation; Emory Hackman, Capitol Area Sysops Association; and Don Delaney, New York State Police.

For Sale: Government Information (CFP-204)
Length: 82 min.
Date: 1993
Cost: $55.00

The issue is who owns the data that is being collected by the government regarding the activities and characteristics of the nation's citizens. Panelists are Dwight Morris, *Los Angeles Times* Washington Bureau; Ken Allen, Information Industry Association; Maurice Freedman, American Library Association; Evan Hendricks, *Privacy Times*; Fred Weingarten, Computing Research Association; Franklin S. Reeder, U.S. Office of Management and Budget; Costas Toregas, Public Technology, Inc.; Robert R. Belair, Kirkpatrick & Lockhart; and George Trubow, John Marshall Law School.

Free Speech and the Public Telephone Network (CFP-205)
Length: 81 min.
Date: 1993
Cost: $55.00

A panel discusses the prospect of telephone companies operating as information providers rather than common carriers. Does this scenario present a promise or a threat for access, diversity, and fair market competition? Henry Geller, Markel Foundation; Eli Noam, Columbia University; John Podesta, Podesta Associates; and Jerry Berman, American Civil Liberties Union Information Technology Project, are the participants.

Freedom and Privacy in the Information Society: A European Perspective
Length: 61 min.
Date: 1996
Cost: $55.00

An insider's look into the European Union's developing policy toward harmonization of international laws related to electronic cash, electronic banking, protection of personal privacy rights in collection and use of databases, and international copyright laws.

Featuring: George Metakides, Director of the European Union's Program for Research and Development in Information Technologies.

Freedom in Cyberspace (CFP-201)
Length: 50 min.
Date: 1993
Cost: $55.00

Allen Neuharth, founder of *USA Today*, presents a keynote address on the differing regulatory constraints on publishers of newspapers, owners of television stations, and the telephone services. He argues for applying the freedom of press rights that have been enjoyed for 200 years by newspapers equally to evolving telecommunications-based information services.

International Developments in Cryptography (CFP-602)
Length: 93 min.
Date: 1996
Cost: $55.00

The world's most experienced data security experts explain what is needed to achieve secure worldwide electronic commerce without tumbling into cryptographic chaos, and explore how to resolve tensions between countries, governments, industries, and citizens' rights to privacy.

Featuring: Dorothy Denning, security specialist, professor of computer science, Georgetown University; Nick Mansfield, cryptography expert, information security advisor for Shell International Petroleum operating in over 100 countries; Michael Nelson, White House Office of Science and Technology, advisor on encryption and telecommunications policy.

International Perspectives and Impacts (CFP-103)
Length: 75 min.
Date: 1991
Cost: $55.00

This is a panel discussion by Robert Veeder, U.S. Office of Management and Budget; Tom Riley, Canadian specialist, international computer privacy issues; David Flaherty, professor, University of Western Ontario, Canada; and Ronald Plesser, general counsel, U.S. Privacy Protection Study Commission. The experts discuss how other countries protect personal information and models for securing private communications.

Law Enforcement and Civil Liberties (CFP-108)
Length: 83 min.
Date: 1991
Cost: $55.00

The panel deals with the issue of new technologies that have derailed law enforcement's ability to define proper procedures against unwarranted search and seizure. Sheldon Zenner, attorney, Katten, Muchin & Zavis; Kenneth Rosenblatt, deputy district attorney, Santa Clara County, California; Mitchell Kapor, president, Electronic Frontier Foundation; Mike Gibbons, supervisory special agent, Federal Bureau of Investigation; Cliff Figallo, executive director, The WELL; Sharon Beckman, attorney, Silverglate & Good; and Mark Rasch, attorney, U.S. Department of Justice, look at the legal standards that should apply in cyberspace.

Law Enforcement Practices and Problems (CFP-107)
Length: 90 min.
Date: 1991
Cost: $55.00

This panel discussion features investigators and prosecutors who are on the front lines of computer crime investigation. They discuss the unique problems of enforcing the law in cyberspace, and they urge computer users to work with law enforcement officers to train them in the uses of the technology. Panelists include Robert Snyder, Public Safety Department, Division of Police, Columbus, Ohio; Donald Delaney, senior investigator, New York State Police; Dale Boll, U.S. Secret Service, Washington, D.C.; and Don Ingraham, assistant district attorney, Alameda County, California.

Legislation and Regulation (CFP-109)
Length: 82 min.
Date: 1991
Cost: $55.00

This is a panel discussion on the role legislatures should play in protecting privacy and ensuring access to public information, legal problems posed by computing and computer networks, approaches to improving government processes, and caution about limits to legislative solutions. Participants are Jerry Berman, American Civil Liberties Union Information Technology Project; Paul Bernstein, attorney, LawMUG BBS and Electronic Bar Association; Bill Julian, committee chief counsel, California State Assembly; Steve McLellan, Washington Utilities & Transportation Commission; Elliot Maxwell, Pacific Telesis; and Craig Schiffries, Senate Judiciary Committee.

Mass Communication vs. Mass Media (CFP-604)
Length: 99 min.
Date: 1996
Cost: $55.00

Traditional print and broadcast media are based on a one-to-many model that implies a concentration of power—a single voice speaking to many passive listeners. Computers linked together into a network of networks introduce a new many-to-many mass communication model in which any individual has the power to be heard based on what they have to say and how they say it.

Featuring: Sander Vanocur, veteran network TV reporter; John Schwartz, *Washington Post*; Bill Kovach, Nieman Foundation, Harvard University; Mike Godwin, Electronic Frontier Foundation; *Wired* magazine; Donna Hoffman, Vanderbilt University; John Seigenthaler, Freedom Forum First Amendment Center.

Network Environments of the Future (CFP-106)
Length: 41 min.
Date: 1991
Cost: $55.00

Professor Eli Noam of Columbia University speaks on the overwhelming amount of information that is barraging people today. He argues for common carriage "rights of way" to prevent the slowdowns that can occur on networks.

Personal Information and Privacy—I (CFP-104)
Length: 75 min.
Date: 1991
Cost: $55.00

This video presents a debate between Janlori Goldman, director, Project on Privacy and Technology, American Civil Liberties Union; and John Baker, senior vice president, consumer and government affairs, Equifax, Inc. The question is, "Who does your personal information belong to? And should government and private companies routinely collect, collate, and market data about private citizens?" A second question, "Should individuals have absolute control over secondary use of their personal information?" is debated by Alan Westin, professor, Columbia University; and Marc Rotenberg, director, Computer Professionals for Social Responsibility.

Personal Information and Privacy—II (CFP-105)
Length: 75 min.
Date: 1991
Cost: $55.00

Simon Davies, University of New South Wales, Australia; Evan Hendricks, editor/publisher, *Privacy Times*; Tom Mandel, SRI

International; and Willis Ware, RAND Corporation, participate in a panel discussion of the ethics behind the reselling of personal data to corporations and marketers.

Privacy and Intellectual Freedom in the Digital Library (CFP-208)
Length: 86 min.
Date: 1993
Cost: $55.00

How can current library practices to protect intellectual freedom be applied to emerging information networks? This and other intellectual property and electronic library issues are discussed by panel members Marc Rotenberg, Computer Professionals for Social Responsibility; Robert A. Walton, CLSI, Inc.; Steve Cisler, Apple Computer, Inc.; and Jean Armour Polly, Liverpool (New York) Public Library.

Privacy and the Global Information Infrastructure (CFP-611)
Length: 96 min.
Date: 1996
Cost: $55.00

Privacy concerns go global as the World Wide Web pits transnational commerce against differing governmental policies. A panel of international policymakers exchange perspectives on urgent questions regarding digital security standards, including the responsibilities of the Internet service provider and encryption and privacy regulations.

Featuring: Marc Rotenberg, Electronic Privacy Information Center; Colin Bennett, author; Paul A. Comeau, Quebec Information & Access Commission; Peter Hustinx, Netherlands data protection office; Christine Varney, U.S. Federal Trade Commission.

Private Collection of Personal Information (CFP-207)
Length: 92 min.
Date: 1993
Cost: $55.00

Panelists play roles consistent with their real-life activities to analyze how legislation may balance personal privacy concerns against information industry practices. Participants include Janlori Goldman, Privacy and Technology Project, ACLU; John Baker, Equifax, Inc.; James D. McQuaid, Metromail; James Rule, State University of New York, Stony Brook; Mary Culnan,

Georgetown University; Patrick D. Hadley, Citicorp; and Ronald Plesser, Piper & Marbury.

Public Policy for the Twenty-First Century (CFP-211)
Length: 78 min.
Date: 1993
Cost: $55.00

Mara Liasson of National Public Radio interviews visionaries Peter Denning, George Mason University; Mitchell Kapor, Electronic Frontier Foundation; Simon Davies, Privacy International; Roland Homet, Executives, Inc.; and Esther Dyson, EDventure Holdings. With the advent of the new information technologies that will alter work, wealth, values, institutions, and political boundaries, what kind of society do we want to create? What public policies now exist that may work against your vision?

Security Capabilities, Privacy, and Integrity (CFP-111)
Length: 69 min.
Date: 1991
Cost: $55.00

William Bayse, FBI assistant director of technical services, explains the FBI's National Crime Information Center (NCIC) system with its 64,000 terminals across the country, including many mobile units in police cars.

Trends in Computers and Networks (CFP-102)
Length: 90 min.
Date: 1991
Cost: $55.00

This is a panel discussion by six scientists, who explain the technical aspects of network technology and cryptography. The focus is on the impact this has on privacy, business security, and equitable access issues. Panel members are Peter Denning, Research Institute for Advanced Computer Science; John Quarterman, Texas Internet Consulting; Peter Neumann, SRI International; Martin Hellman, professor, Stanford University; David Chaum, professor, Amsterdam; and David Farber, professor, University of Pennsylvania.

Where Do We Go from Here? (CFP-115)
Length: 82 min.
Date: 1991
Cost: $55.00

This tape includes the recommendations of many of the confer-
ence's participants on how best to protect privacy rights on the
Net in the future. Featured on this video are Mary Culnan, David
Hughes, Donald Ingraham, Mitch Kapor, Eric Lieberman, Paul
Bernstein, Donn Parker, Craig Schiffires, and Robert Veeder.

Who Logs On? (CFP-202)
Length: 82 min.
Date: 1991
Cost: $55.00

A debate between Linda Garcia, U.S. Office of Technology
Assessment; Alfred Koeppe, New Jersey Bell; and Brian Kahin,
Kennedy School of Government, Harvard University, concern-
ing who will pay for the deployment of high-speed educational
and rural networks.

Glossary

analog A way to measure an event that continuously samples the changes occurring in the observable phenomenon. The measuring device is so constructed as to act in some manner analogous to the original event.

applet A small computer application that will allow specific functions to be run on the Internet or a local-area network (LAN) without the need to own or load the software on the client machine. This type of software was made famous by Sun Microsystems' Java.

archie An Internet protocol that allows for the searching of particular file names (or parts of names) that can be retrieved through file transfer protocol (FTP).

ASCII The American Standard Code for Information Interchange, which in most cases refers to simple, unformatted text information.

asynchronous A type of communication that does not rely on real-time response to a query or a command. E-mail correspondence is an example of asynchronous interaction.

backbone The primary lines of the Internet, where most of the data traffic moves.

bandwidth The speed at which information can be transmitted through a network. It is helpful to visualize this as the diameter of the pipe.

BASIC Beginner's All-purpose Symbolic Instruction Code. BASIC is the computer programming language that got Bill Gates started.

bit The binary digit. It is represented by either a one or a zero, which signify an "on" or "off" state. It is the basic unit of digital measurement.

browse To navigate through the various pages of information on the World Wide Web. *Cruise* and *surf* refer to the same function.

browser Client software that allows a user to access information, or cruise, the World Wide Web.

byte Eight bits of information and the amount of data it takes to define one alphanumeric character.

CERN European Laboratory for Particle Physics, located in Switzerland. This was the place where the World Wide Web was developed.

client Software that resides on a computer (or the machine itself) that is connected to a network of other computers. This software is designed to ask for information from server software residing somewhere on that network. This client-server model of interactivity is the basis for the functions taking place on the Internet.

computer-mediated communication (CMC) The process that uses networked telecommunications systems to allow people to create and exchange digitized media.

cruise See *browse*.

cyberspace The most overused term of the 1990s, *cyberspace* has come to mean anything associated with the Internet, virtual reality, and the potential that digital information brings for creating a new world. Its genesis is a 1984 work by science fiction author William Gibson, who described it as more like a parallel universe and a realm of pure information. The prefix *cyber*, from the Greek meaning to steer or govern, was first introduced into the common parlance by Norbert Wiener in the 1940s, when he was creating the field of cybernetics.

digital A way to measure an event, picture, text, sound, internal organ, etc., that relies on fixed-interval sampling, as opposed to continuous "analog" measurement. Then, using a binary system that is the language of computers and their networks, that data is encoded using only ones and zeroes.

domain name The alphabetic translation of the Internet protocol address that identifies a server on the Net.

dumb terminal A type of digital device that consists of a keyboard and a display screen that can be used to enter and transmit data to, and display data from, a computer to which it is connected on a network. It has no processing capacity or storage capability.

e-mail Electronic mail. This is one of the most often used protocols available to users of the Net. It typically utilizes the least bandwidth and the most minimal of resources of all Internet services.

file transfer protocol (FTP)   An Internet protocol that allows for the transfer of binary or pure text files from a file server to a client computer on a network.

flame   An especially nasty attack on the ideas or character of another Netizen posted to a mail list or newsgroup.

frequently asked questions (FAQs)   The FAQ was developed as an organizational tool and a historical archive of the "rules" operant in Usenet newsgroups. New members of a group could be referred to the FAQ as a shorthand method to answer a common question.

gopher   A hierarchical information system developed at the University of Minnesota in order to make the navigation through the maze of Internet-based data less complicated. It is another of the TCP/IP protocols.

hotlink   See *hyperlink*.

http   See *hypertext transfer protocol*.

hyperlink   Any of the various objects (text, pictures, etc.) that have been programmed on a World Wide Web page to call up for display a subsequent Web page, graphic, movie, sound, or new application.

hypertext   The fundamental concept of the linking that creates the matrix of pages and other media on the World Wide Web. It presents information in a nonlinear form and in many different formats.

hypertext markup language (HTML)   The coding that turns ASCII text into readable Web pages. A document in HTML format can be read with a browser.

hypertext transport protocol (HTTP)   The protocol that allows the World Wide Web to function on the Internet.

Integrated Services Digital Network (ISDN)   The system that allows for the transmission of digital data on phone lines.

Internet Explorer   A Web browser developed by the Microsoft Corporation.

Internet protocol (IP)   See *transmission control protocol/Internet protocol*.

Internet relay chat (IRC)   An Internet protocol that allows two or more connected computer users to "chat" in real-time mode. Participants use client software to type messages that all other participants can see.

Internet service provider (ISP)   A private company that sells access to the Internet. Typically, ISPs will maintain a minimum of T1 connectivity to an even larger provider.

InterNIC   The Internet Network Information Center, which controls domain names within the United States.

kilobit   100 bits, used when referring to the bandwidth capabilities of a medium.

kilobyte (KB)   1,024 bytes.

link   See *hyperlink*.

local-area network (LAN)   The rudimentary unit of computer networking. It takes two connected computers to establish a LAN.

mail bomb   The act of sending hundreds or thousands of electronic mail messages to a user's e-mail account in the hopes that the recipient's system will shut down.

mail list   There are thousands of Internet mail lists organized to exchange information on a particular subject. Almost all are automated and run under listserv, listproc, or majordomo software, but they can be manual and highly controlled. Typically, one would subscribe to a list by sending an e-mail message to the list maintainer. Once a member of the list, sending one message to the server computer gets it distributed to every other member.

megabits   A thousand bits, used when referring to the bandwidth capabilities of a medium.

modem   Modulator-demodulator, a device that enables the transmission of digital signals over analog lines. A modem is necessary for most people to gain access to the Net.

Mosaic   This Web browser was the first graphical interface client made available to the general public for cruising the World Wide Web. It was developed at the National Center for Supercomputing Applications at the University of Illinois. It was called the "killer app" of its day because it was the software application that seemed to have the most potential for changing the nature of how people used the computer.

multimedia   This term seems to be redefined constantly. In general, it refers to the computer's capabilities to seamlessly blend text, graphics, sound, and full-motion video in a single platform. The World Wide Web is emerging as the prototype of a full multimedia Information Superhighway.

multiuser domain or multiuser dungeon (MUD)   A very popular, text-based game that allows multiple players to interact in real-time as self-defined characters in a fantasy environment.

Net   The Internet and the succeeding phases of its deployment and evolution.

Netizen   One who regularly uses the services of the Internet.

Netscape   A company and a browser. The Netscape Communications Corporation began distributing its highly evolved version of a Web browser to Internet users for free in 1995. Within a year, it is estimated that Netscape software was used by at least 75 percent of the market, making it the de facto standard of the newest and most popular Internet protocol.

news   See *Usenet*.

newsgroup   An on-line forum for discussions on at least 7,500 different topics. Usenet manages and provides access to most publicly accessible newsgroups, though there are forums created for and accessible only to customers of the commercial on-line services.

page   A document on the World Wide Web that may contain text, pictures, movies, sounds, and embedded hyperlinks to other pages, text, graphics, etc. It is referred to as a "home page" when it is the first document in an array of related pages. Normally a URL will refer to an individual's or company's home page.

pipe   The medium (wire or cable) through which information is transmitted.

portable document format (pdf)   A standard created by Adobe Systems with its Acrobat software. Authors of formatted documents are able to convert their work into pdf before distributing it across the Net. People who want to view or purchase the work are required to obtain the free Acrobat Reader software in order to make sense of the file.

protocol   The accepted rules by which a system will be set up to communicate data and exchange information. Software that creates such an environment is usually referred to as a *language*.

provider   See *Internet service provider*.

real time   Communication that occurs in the same time frame at all ends of the connection. This is synchronous dialogue; like what takes place in a typical phone conversation.

router   A network computer that is specially configured to receive packets of data for resending to the appropriate address.

server   A computer (and the software that supports it) connected to a network that is configured to "serve up" or present information when queried by client software from another network-connected computer. On the Internet, a dedicated machine can provide FTP, gopher, e-mail, and HTTP services, among others.

site   Usually refers to a particular server on the Internet. For example, the Web site for the White House is http://www.whitehouse.gov/.

spam   The act of sending a commercial message to hundreds, or all, of the newsgroups and many of the mail lists accessible on the Net.

spectrum   In terms of wireless communications, wavelengths that vibrate at different rates are said to occupy different parts of the spectrum.

surf   See *browse*.

T1   A type of telephone connection that is capable of moving 1.5 megabits of data per second.

T3   A type of telephone connection that is capable of moving 45 megabits of data per second.

telecommunications   Any process that uses electronic transmission as a means to move text, sound, pictures, video, data, etc.

telephony   The new term being used for the old telephone service providers. It is believed that with the passage of the Telecommunications Reform Act of 1996 and the merging of technologies and digital services between once-distinct industries, a new name is appropriate.

transmission control protocol/Internet protocol (TCP/IP)   The underlying language of the Internet upon which all other protocols rely.

universal resource locator (URL)   The "address" needed to activate a Web browser. It is written in the minimal form http://www. olympus.net/ if it refers to a Web-based (HTTP) document or page.

Unix   A computer operating system that allows for multiple processes to be handled simultaneously. There are many different versions of the operating system, which in itself was written in C programming language. It is the predominant operating system used on the Web, although Windows NT is making a play for some of the market.

Usenet   A computer network that uses the UUCP protocol, part of the Unix operating system. It serves as the home of thousands of publicly accessible discussion forums known as newsgroups, or simply "news." While not actually part of the Internet (it does not speak TCP/IP), many gateways are maintained so that Internet users have the chance to read and post messages to groups that they find to be of interest.

veronica   A program that searches gopher databases for specified text strings.

virtual   Close after *cyber-*, one of the most overworked terms used when referencing on-line activity and artificial existence. It is derived from the term *virtual reality*, which is coming to be understood as any different interpretation of information that might account for an individual's perception of life. This interpretation may be aided (manipulated) by a computer-generated image in portable eye-gear, for example, or through the reproduction of the sounds of a symphony orchestra in a pair of earphones.

wide-area network (WAN)   A computer network that is extensive in geographic terms. The Internet is the ultimate WAN.

World Wide Web (WWW)   Known more commonly as the Web, this is the portion of the Internet carrying packets of data in support of the HTTP protocol. That is, it appears to the user as a graphic representation of information in various forms that are all linked. The user may choose to navigate from one Web site to another by clicking the computer's mouse point on a hyperlinked element of the Web page. That activates a command in the TCP/IP language to display a new page of binary data in the form of text, pictures, movies, etc., that corresponds to the hyperlink URL code.

Index

Marty Gay is currently a freelance writer concentrating in the area of educational and communication technologies. He also works as a consultant for various educational initiatives, including several with the Washington State Office of the Superintendent of Public Instruction, the Washington State University Extention Learning Center, the Evergreen Tech Team, Community Computer Communications (COM3™), and Group Exploring the National Information Infrastructure (GENII). After graduating from the University of Notre Dame and doing post graduate work at California Lutheran University, he had the opportunity to work in a wide range of fields. He has been a special education teacher, a community skills instructor, and a producer/ director for television. More recently, Mr. Gay has owned and operated his own businesses including two successful restaurants and a catering business in Southern California.

He moved to Port Townsend, Washington, in 1993 with his wife, Michelle and their five-year-old son, Dakota. A grown daughter, Nissa, lives in California. His collaboration with his mother, the accomplished Kathlyn Gay, has resulted in a dozen books for the young adult market in the past three years. Since Ms. Gay is located 2,500 miles away, that work has been facilitated by e-mail and Internet connectivity.

Mr. Gay answers his e-mail at martini@ olympus.net.

He also maintains a web site that continually updates much of the information that is found on the new Information Revolution. Readers of the book are invited to visit periodically to learn the latest about changes taking place because of advances in information technologies. The URL for his page is http://www. olympus.net/personal/martini/InfoRev.html.